The
Modern Witch's
Complete
Sourcebook

D1456667

Also by Gerina Dunwich

Candlelight Spells
Circle of Shadows
The Concise Lexicon of the Occult
Everyday Wicca
Magick Potions
Priestess and Pentacle
Wicca A to Z
The Wicca Book of Days
Wicca Candle Magick
Wicca Craft
The Wicca Garden
Wicca Love Spells
The Wicca Spellbook
A Wiccan's Guide to Prophecy and Divination
Your Magickal Cat
The Pagan Book of Halloween
Exploring Spellcraft

The
Modern Witch's
Complete
Sourcebook

THIRD EDITION

Gerina Dunwich

CITADEL PRESS
KENSINGTON PUBLISHING CORP.
www.kensingtonbooks.com

CITADEL PRESS books are published by

Kensington Publishing Corp.
850 Third Avenue
New York, NY 10022

All Kensington titles, imprints, and distributed lines are available at special quantity discounts for bulk purchases for sales promotions, premiums, fund raising, educational, or institutional use. Special book excerpts or customized printings can also be created to fit specific needs. For details, write or phone the office of the Kensington special sales manager: Kensington Publishing Corp., 850 Third Avenue, New York, NY 10022, attn: Special Sales Department, phone 1-800-221-2647.

Citadel Press and the Citadel logo are trademarks of Kensington Publishing Corp.

First printing: September 2001

10   9   8   7   6   5   4   3   2

Printed in the United States of America

Library of Congress Control Number: 2001091785

ISBN 0-8065-2293-3

With love do I dedicate this book to Al Jackter and my mother.

Special thanks and bright blessings to Kathleen Kmen for her contributions to the Recommended Reading Section, and all else who participated in this project in one way or another. Thank you from the heart for helping to make this possible!

Contents

Introduction

Wicca, which is an Old English word meaning "wise," is a positive, Earth-oriented, nature religion with ancient roots that are pre-Christian. It gloriously celebrates the life force, encourages spiritual growth, and includes seasonal rites to attune oneself to the beauty, magick, and love of Mother Nature and Goddess Earth.

Like the New Age spirituality movement, which has steadily been gaining momentum throughout the past ten years or so, Wicca is also growing, changing, and expanding. As more people become educated and enlightened to the ways of Wicca, the negative stereotypes and misconceptions associated with modern Witches and Pagans are gradually being shed.

Wicca is not a passing fad. It is a strong religion of light and love, both ancient and contemporary, that is here to stay.

This resource book was painstakingly put together for the purpose of connecting Wiccans, Pagans, and New Age spiritualists from around the world, and to help promote Wicca (the Craft of the Wise), Earth-Goddess religions, and all positive spiritual paths. All efforts have been made to produce a thorough and up-to-date compilation of listings to serve the entire Wiccan, Pagan, and New Age community as an invaluable resource directory. If I have accidentally left anyone out, or if any of the listings change or become discontinued by the time this book is published, I sincerely apologize and will do my best to correct any incomplete or incorrect information in future editions.

This revised and expanded edition is composed of sixteen important sections: organizations and covens, Wiccan and Pagan churches, schools, books and publishers, periodicals, astrology, herbs, metaphysical shops, mail order companies, psychic and paranormal, resources for gay and lesbian Pagans, festivals, gatherings and workshops, the left-hand path, Pagan potpourri, a Who's Who of the Wiccan community (which features some of the most talented, well-known, accomplished, and respected members of the Wiccan community worldwide), and a recommended reading list. Many organizations and businesses are listed in more than one section.

Whether you are searching for special occult supplies, a Pagan parenting group, the nearest Wiccan church, a Witchcraft correspondence course, a networking organization for gay and lesbian Witches, dream-catchers, mandrake roots, or astrological computer software, you are guaranteed to find it within the pages of this book!

If you are not presently listed in this book and wish to be considered for future editions, please write to me at the address below for a free application form. (To be listed there is no charge whatsoever.) If you are already listed, please keep me updated as to any changes regarding your listing(s). You may write to me in care of the publisher, or directly: Gerina Dunwich, P.O. Box 4263, Chatsworth, California 91313. (Please include a self-addressed stamped envelope.)

May the Goddess and the God in all of Their mysterious ways bless you with an abundance of Light, Love, Mirth, and Magick!

Blessed Be

The
Modern Witch's
Complete
Sourcebook

1

Organizations
and Covens

In this section you will find the listings of many different organizations serving the needs of the Wiccan and Pagan communities around the world. Included are networking, contact, and support groups, Witches' covens, and various organizations that sponsor Pagan gatherings, provide education to the public, and protect the civil and religious rights of Wiccans, Pagans, and other "nonmainstream" religious groups.

This section also contains the listings of a number of Wiccan and Pagan churches. They are included here (instead of in the next chapter, which is devoted to legally recognized churches) because either they are not yet legally recognized or their legal status was unknown at the time of this writing.

Alabama

Forest Glen Coven of Wicca
P.O. Box 130106
Birmingham, Alabama 35213

Wiccan Student Circle

E-mail: janel@hydro.geo.ua.edu

A student group at the University of Alabama in Tuscaloosa.

Arizona

Church of All Worlds—Crossroads ProtoNest

P.O. Box 857

Tempe, Arizona 85280

Contact: Rebeccalyn Jenson

Publishes a nest newsletter called *Tri-Bia*. Send $1.00 for a sample copy.

Desert Henge Coven

P.O. Box 40451

Tucson, Arizona 85717

Formed in 1982, this is one of the oldest covens in the state of Arizona. Following the Gardnerian tradition, it is divided into an Inner Court Coven and an Outer Court training group. Sponsors Arizona's oldest public class on Wicca and emphasizes the social interactions of coven as family. The current High Priest and High Priestess are Rik Johnson and Dianna Armentrout.

The Divine Circle of the Sacred Grove

16845 N. Twenty-Ninth Avenue, no. 1346

Phoenix, Arizona 85023

(602) 433-7951

E-mail: scribe@grove.org

An international referral network for solitary practitioners and groups of various Wiccan traditions. Sponsors the annual High Desert Mid-Summer Spirit Gathering. To have your name added to their mailing list, write, call, or e-mail them.

Mooncircle Pagan Network

P.O. Box 12104

Tuscon, Arizona 85732

(602) 881-1186

Pagan Arizona Network
P.O. Box 17933
Phoenix, Arizona 85011
(602) 230-5354

Networking for Pagan groups and solitary practitioners throughout the state of Arizona.

Tucson Area Wiccan Network
P.O. Box 482
Tucson, Arizona 85702

A local referral network for Wiccans, Pagans, and all followers of the Wiccan Rede. Provides "social, spiritual, and educational interactions."

Arkansas

Ozark Pagan Council
P.O. Box 605
Springdale, Arkansas 72764

Student Pagan Association
Fayetteville, Arkansas
E-mail: pagan@comp.uark.edu

California

American Druidic Church
c/o Jay and Patricia Tibbles
P.O. Box 2642
Fontana, California 92334

Ancient Religions Society
2265 Westwood Boulevard
Los Angeles, California 90064
(213) 506-8670

Local and regional referrals for groups and individuals who follow the Old Ways.

Ancient Religions Society

1157½ W. Thirtieth Street, Box B-3
Los Angeles, California 90007
(213) 856-2824

A religious organization run by students at UCLA that provides education, information, networking, and social contacts for Wiccans, Pagans, and other individuals belonging to nonmainstream religions.

Bay Area Pagan Assemblies

P.O. Box 4159
Mountain View, California 94040
(408) 559-GAIA

A local referral network and nonprofit organization servicing the San Francisco area's Pagan community. Publishes *Pagan Muse and World Report.* Sample copy: $3.95.

Branching

414 E. Cedar, no. 9
Burbank, California 91501

P.O. Box 3155
East Hampton, New York 11937

"A support group for solitary Wiccans and Pagans, Branching is a group of people on a positive path who network by mail. Membership directory is offered. Survey done by members tells us what our members' interests are. We share ceremonial themes, rituals, lunar workings, long-distance magick, healing." Publishes an occasional newsletter.

Church of All Worlds Central

P.O. Box 1542
Ukiah, California 95482
(707) 463-1432

The oldest Neo-Pagan church in the United States, founded in 1962, and legally incorporated in 1968. Inspired by the science fiction novel *Stranger in a Strange Land,* by Robert Heinlein. The first Pagan church to be legally incorporated in Australia. Over fifty "nests" worldwide. Holds monthly meetings and owns festival lands in California and Kentucky. Write for additional information.

Church of All Worlds—Delta Dragon Nest
P.O. Box 77741
Stockton, California 95267
Contact: David Hall

Church of All Worlds—Hwysddyrnysdd ProtoNest
P.O. Box 488
Laytonville, California 95454
Contact: Maerian Morris

Church of All Worlds—Live the Dream
6454 Van Nuys Boulevard, no. 150
Van Nuys, California 91401
Contact: Terry Gibbons

Church of All Worlds—Star City Sanctuary
P.O. Box 5001
Chatsworth, California 91313

Publishes a Nest Newsletter called *Stardate*. Send $1.00 to receive a sample copy.

Covenant of the Goddess
P.O. Box 1226
Berkeley, California 94701

An international council network and the largest federation of covens and solitary elders from different Wiccan traditions. Sponsors a newsletter and a festival, and also issues ministerial credentials.

Earth Religions Integrative Network
P.O. Box 482
Mount Shasta, California 96067

This is a local referral network that sponsors classes and rituals for the Sabbats.

The Educational Society for Pagans
115 W. California Boulevard, no. 161
Pasadena, California 91105
(818) 583-9353 (recorded information)
Formerly the Pallas Society. Provides educational resources and networking. Promotes public outreach work for Southern California Wiccans and Pagans.

Elderflower
P.O. Box 31627
San Francisco, California 94131
(916) 558-0607
Organizes the annual Womenspirit Festivals. Write or call for more information and current registration fees.

Faery-Faith Network
P.O. Box 15222
Newport Beach, California 92659
Contact: Kisma K. Stepanich
"The Network offers membership to the Faery-Faith Tradition and a seasonal newsletter packed full of information on the Tradition, such as other world journeys, book and music reviews, a calendar of related events, and some very special merchandise. Members also receive a network listing of other members, which includes street and E-mail addresses, twice a year."

The Foundation for Shamanic Studies
Dr. Michael Harner, Director
P.O. Box 1939
Mill Valley, California 94942
(415) 380-8282; fax: (415) 380-8416

The Index
P.O. Box 1646
Santa Cruz, California 95061
(408) 427-5347
A local referral network for the Pagan community of Santa Cruz and the central California coast. For additional information, please send a self-addressed stamped envelope.

Moon Lodge Network
204½ E. Broadway
Costa Mesa, California 92627
(714) 548-0551

An international referral network and council for women interested in spiritual visioning and healing. It also provides workshops and annual ceremonies, and publishes a biannual journal.

Neo-African Network
c/o Technicians of the Sacred
1317 N. San Fernando Boulevard, Suite 310
Burbank, California 91504

An "informal" international network for followers of Voudoun, Santeria, Macumba, Thelemic Voudoun, and the Family Traditions. No membership fees are required.

New Wiccan Church (International Office)
N.W.C.
P.O. Box 162046
Sacramento, California 95816

An international federation of Elders of certain British Wiccan traditions (Alexandrian, Gardnerian, Kingstone, Majestic, Mohsian, Silver Crescent, etc.) dedicated to preserving initiatory Craft in an ethical manner. Founded in 1973. Publishes *Red Garters, International*. Send self-addressed stamped envelope with two first-class stamps for information on membership, networking, or contact referrals to traditional groups.

Pagan Broadcasting System
P.O. Box 16025
North Hollywood, California 91615

A computer bulletin board.

Pagan/Occult/Witchcraft Special Interest Group of Mensa
P.O. Box 9336
San Jose, California 95157

Support Abused Wiccans
201 W. Moneta
Bakersfield, California 93308

The Susan B. Anthony Coven
P.O. Box 11363
Piedmont, California 94611

Women's Spiritual Network and Database of Central California and Beyond
P.O. Box 3903
Salinas, California 93912

Women's Spirituality Forum
P.O. Box 11363
Piedmont, California 94611
(510) 444-7724
Contact: ZsuZsanna Budapest

A nonprofit, Goddess-oriented organization providing a lecture series, classes, cable television shows, spiral dances, and retreats.

United We Circle
3208 Cahuenga Boulevard
West Hollywood, California 90068
(213) 876-4032

A local Witchcraft organization made up of members of the Los Angeles Wiccan Religious Community. Organizes letter-writing campaigns and press conferences.

Colorado

Earth Spirit Pagans
P.O. Box 1965
Colorado Springs, Colorado 80901
(800) 731-2650

An organization dedicated to the preservation and continued vitality of Pagan religions and cultures. Provides a caring and nurturing environment for practitioners of Pagan paths, including regular rituals, classes, workshops, handfastings, Wiccanings, and memoriams. Donations are tax deductible.

The Web
P.O. Box 1871
Boulder, Colorado 80306
(303) 939-8832

A local referral network for Pagans and Witches seeking Craft-related activities, education, support, and "Pagan-friendly" professionals.

World Pagan Network (WPN)
c/o Chris West
721 N. Hancock Avenue
Colorado Springs, Colorado 80903

A networking and contact resource for the seeking Pagan. WPN is staffed by volunteers from around the world. If you are looking for Pagans in your community or are moving around the world, WPN can help you. Request for information should include the following: name, address, country, and area where you are looking for contacts. There is no fee for this service. If you would like to volunteer as a contact, please write for details.

Connecticut

The Connecticut Wiccan and Pagan Network
P.O. Box 1175
New Milford, Connecticut 06776

This organization is dedicated to meeting the needs of the greater Wiccan and Pagan community in Connecticut and surrounding areas. Sponsors discussion groups, open Sabbat circles, a coven/study group referral service, classes, and various social events. Also publishes a quarterly newsletter, *The Wiccan Read,* and a cross-quarterly Connecticut Pagan Calendar, which accepts submissions of articles, art, poetry, etc. All Wiccan and Pagan-related events are listed without charge.

Craft Wise
P.O. Box 2277
Milford, Connecticut 06460
(203) 374-6475
E-mail: www.craftwise.com
Sponsors Pagan gatherings across the United States and Canada. The object of the gatherings is to bring quality instruction and rituals to communities across the country, sharing knowledge and skills with those who are isolated or simply not in touch with trained teachers. The group's purpose is fundamentally that of an open teaching community clustered in the alternative religions and the occult community.

New Wiccan Church of Connecticut
N.W.C.
c/o Lady of the Brook
P.O. Box 11
Plainfield, Connecticut 06374

Witches Information Network
415 Campbell Avenue
West Haven, Connecticut 06516
(203) 932-1193
A local referral council established to educate the public about Witches. Also provides coven and group referrals.

Florida

Alachua Pagan Alliance
P.O. Box 12625
Gainesville, Florida 32604
An organization that provides referrals for various Earth-centered and Goddess traditions, as well as public education on the practice of Paganism.

Azure of Eternity / Azure's Gateway
P.O. Box 450161
Sunrise, Florida 33345
E-mail: azure003@aol.com
A Gardnerian-based eclectic grove currently accepting new seekers.

Church of All Worlds—Holy Oak Nest
P.O. Box 12625
Gainesville, Florida 32604
Contact: Paul MoonOak, coordinator

Church of the Ancient Sacred Mother
4700 A-8 Babcock Street N.E.
Palm Bay, Florida 32905
Contact: Jacque Zaleski

Circle by the Sea
c/o Unitarian Universalist Fellowship
2601 St. Andrews Boulevard
Boca Raton, Florida 33434

Circle Moonhenge
B. J. Walker
4211 S.W. Fiftieth Street
Gainesville, Florida 32608

Covenant of Unitarian Universalist Pagans (CUUPS)
c/o U.U. Church of Fort Myers
13211 Shire Lane
Fort Myers, Florida 33912

Crone's Cradle Conserve
P.O. Box 1207
Citra, Florida 32113

Danae's Sun
P.O. Box 47384
Jacksonville, Florida 32247
Contact: Dana Solis

An international mail network for teens and young adults from all positive, nature-honoring spiritual paths. $5.00 membership fee includes letter exchange and quarterly magazine.

First Coast CUUPS
c/o U.U. Church of Jacksonville
7405 Arlington Expressway
Jacksonville, Florida 32211
Contact: Joyce Johnson
E-mail: adj@gate.net

Gainesville CUUPS
c/o Gainesville U.U. Fellowship
2814 N.W. Forty-Third Street
Gainesville, Florida 32606

Life Spring
2190 Traymore Road
Jacksonville, Florida 32207

An organization that provides local networking for Pagans in the state of Florida. Write or call for additional information.

Moonpath
c/o Unitarian Universalist Church of Ft. Lauderdale
3970 N.W. Twenty-First Avenue
Oakland Park, Florida 33309

Pagan Allied Network International, Inc.
Write to: PAN
P.O. Box 290864
Temple Terrace, Florida 33687
(904) 521-3647

An international council that sponsors Sabbat celebrations open to all Pagans. Provides international networking for groups and individuals.

Pagan Pathways
J. Kay
2835 Teton Trail
Tallahassee, Florida 32303
E-mail: voltaire@nettally.com

For more information about this Pagan study group, write or contact by E-mail.

Southeast Florida Pagan Coalition
P.O. Box 848896
Hollywood, Florida 33084
(305) 923-4192

Pagan networking and community ritual. All groups and covens are welcome.

Spiraling Heart Coven
P.O. Box 15872
Tallahassee, Florida 32317
E-mail: tardren@mailer.fsu.edu

Wiccan Religious Cooperative of Florida, Inc.
3936 S. Semoran Boulevard, Suite 116
Orlando, Florida 32822
(407) 657-2182; (407) 725-4316
Provides discussion groups, educational classes, seminars, worship circles, work groups, cultural and social activities, and networking opportunities for the Wiccan community.

Georgia

Church of All Worlds—Newt's Egg
P.O. Box 965145
Marietta, Georgia 30066
(404) 565-0946

Church of All Worlds—ProtoNest of the Phoenix
3058 Azlee Place N.W.
Atlanta, Georgia 30328
E-mail: CatDeville@aol.com

Church of All Worlds—Sunrise Coast ProtoNest
7082 Hodgson Memorial Drive, no. 3
Savannah, Georgia 31406
(912) 356-9524

The Sisterhood of Avalon
Contact: Jhenah Afaloak
Marietta, Georgia
E-mail: YnisAvalon@aol.com

Women's empowerment through the exploration of the Avalonian Mysteries.

Idaho

Earth Tribe—Pagan Division
P.O. Box 92
Burley, Idaho 83318

An eclectic Wiccan and human rights organization emphasizing Pagan religious freedom. Legally incorporated in the state of Idaho in

1993 and serving as the Idaho chapter of Witches Against Religious Discrimination.

Illinois

Circle of Danu
1310 W. Lunt Avenue, no. 507
Chicago, Illinois 60626

Eleusis
P.O. Box 257996
Chicago, Illinois 60625

Midwest Pagan Council
P.O. Box 160
Western Springs, Illinois 60558

A regional and national council of Midwest Pagan groups. Sponsors the Pan Pagan Festival and other events and publishes a newsletter.

Pagan Interfaith Embassy
3257 West Eastwood
Chicago, Illinois 60625

Temple of the Sacred Lady of Avalon
P.O. Box 247
Normal, Illinois 61761
(309) 829-8898

Winter Wren, High Priestess, and Brann Myrria Du Loch, Priest. Eclectic group with a Celtic/Native American base. Meets for training, feasts, and moons.

Universal Spirituality
c/o Tara Nelsen
602 N. Michaels
Carbondale, Illinois 62501
(618) 529-5029

A networking/discussion group dedicated to the sharing of information, experiences, and New Age/Pagan spiritual beliefs and practices. Provides networking and presentations on a weekly basis.

Witches Against Religious Discrimination (WARD)
c/o Winter Wren
P.O. Box 247
Normal, Illinois 61761

Indiana

Indiana Witches Against Religious Discrimination
WARD
c/o Diana Barnett
7317 W. One Hundred Thirty-Fourth Court
Cedar Lake, Indiana 46303
(219) 374-7245

A statewide Witchcraft and Wiccan antidefamation network, founded in 1993.

Elf Lore Family (ELF)
Box 1082
Bloomington, Indiana 47402

A nonprofit organization providing Pagan networking, craftworking, survival skills, forest care, and woodland folklore. It maintains a nature sanctuary, survival education center, and a woodland meeting ground known as Lothlorien.

The Inkwell Circle
P.O. Box 4193
Anderson, Indiana 46013

A national mail network for Wiccans, Pagans, and others of a positive spiritual path.

Pagan Educational Network (PEN)
P.O. Box 1364
Bloomington, Indiana 47402

A nonprofit Pagan organization providing national networking, volunteering, education, and letter writing. PEN publishes a regular newsletter, *Water*, with resources and educational information. One-year membership: $12.00. Send a self-addressed stamped envelope for a membership form or to receive additional information.

Ring of Troth
P.O. Box 212
Sheridan, Indiana 46069

Wyrd House
P.O. Box 1824
Indianapolis, Indiana 46206

A Pagan and Wiccan meeting place which draws individuals from the central Indiana area as well as from the states of Illinois, Ohio, Kentucky, and Michigan. Members network monthly and share workshops, conversation, music, and information. They believe all persons are connected by the "Web of Wyrd" and welcome interactions with all who share similar interests.

Iowa

Iowa Pagan Access Network
IPAN
P.O. Box 861
Iowa City, Iowa 52244

"For people from Goddess-centered and/or Earth-based spiritual traditions." Network listings, newsletter, resources, and educational projects for Iowa and surrounding states. Listings are free. Newsletter subscriptions: $20.00–$40.00 (sliding scale); sample copy: $3.00 with self-addressed stamped envelope.

Iowa Wiccan-Pagan Network
c/o Lady Isadora
P.O. Box 2483
Des Moines, Iowa 50311

Provides referrals to covens and solitary practitioners of the Craft in Des Moines and central Iowa. Holds monthly potluck meetings, discussions, and occasional Sabbat rituals.

Network of Pagan Midwives
2000 N. Court, no. 13-G
Fairfield, Iowa 52556
(515) 472-0751

Provides networking, support, education, outreach, and references for Pagan individuals seeking a midwife or an apprenticeship. Write or call for free information.

Kansas

Heartland Spiritual Alliance
P.O. Box 3407
Kansas City, Kansas 66103
(816) 561-6111

Founded in 1986, this Pagan organization provides a monthly Spirit Circle for networking and educational purposes. They also sponsor the annual Heartland Spirit Festival for Pagans of all spiritual paths.

Church of All Worlds—Triple Spiral
P.O. Box 44-2394
Lawrence, Kansas 66046
Contact: Teri Chambers

Publishes a Nest Newsletter called *Baranduin*. Send $1.00 to receive a sample copy.

Kentucky

Church of All Worlds—Eggs, Eggs Everywhere
P.O. Box 21955
Lexington, Kentucky 40522
Contact: Moira Mineweaser

Kindred Shadows
3176 Richmond Road, Suite 305
Lexington, Kentucky 40509
Fax: (606) 299-0696

A religious order, dedicated to following a positive Pagan Path. "Our teachings are designed to aid our members in developing their own philosophy of life and finding inner peace from understanding the Old Ways and Laws of the Universe."

The Rosemoon Guild
P.O. Box 23675
Lexington, Kentucky 40523
E-mail: rosemoon@webcom.com
Contact: Elizabeth Rowan

Provides networking, workshops, and social activities for Pagans of various spiritual paths. Write for additional information and a membership application.

Maine

The Upper Group
RR#2, Box 2574A
Harrison, Maine 04040
Contact: M. J. Bryan

Founded in 1991, this organization provides referrals and support to solitaries as well as to groups that follow the Wiccan and Pagan paths. In addition, they investigate all types of paranormal phenomena.

Maryland

Coalition for Pagan Religious Rights
c/o The Turning Wheel Bookstore
8039-A Ritchie Highway
Pasadena, Maryland 21122

A newly-formed group of Witches, Druids, Mystic Christians, Shamans, and other Pagans from the Washington and Baltimore area. Write for more information.

Ecumenicon
P.O. Box 302
11160 Viers Mills Road
Wheaton, Maryland 20902

Free Spirit Alliance
P.O. Box 25242
Baltimore, Maryland 21229
(301) 604-6049

A regional network for Pantheistic groups from different paths in the mid-Atlantic area. Sponsors the Free Spirit Festival and publishes *Free Spirit Rising*. For more information and a list of area groups, send a self-addressed stamped envelope.

Military Pagan Network
John Machate, coordinator
P.O. Box 1268
Forestville, Maryland 20747

Womanspirit Web
P.O. Box 513
Kensington, Maryland 20895
(301) 589-4635

A local and regional network promoting the practices and goals of women's spirituality and planetary healing. Write or call for additional information.

Massachusetts

Boston South Shore and Plymouth Area Pagan Network
P.O. Box 335
Boston University Station
Boston, Massachusetts 02215
Contact: Arachne

A networking group for local Wiccans, Pagans, and other magickal folks.

Church of All Worlds—Circle of Liberty
P.O. Box 1233
Pepperell, Massachusetts 01463
Contact: Inanna Arthen

Church of All Worlds—Polyamethyst Nest
P.O. Box 552
Shutsbury, Massachusetts 01072

Covenant of Unitarian Universalist Pagans (CUUPS)
P.O. Box 640
Cambridge, Massachusetts 02140
(617) 547-6465

An international network of Unitarian Universalists and others who follow the positive paths of Neopaganism and Earth-centered spirituality. Publisher of *Pagan Nuus* and other resource materials.

The EarthSpirit Community

P.O. Box 723
Williamsburg, Massachusetts 01096
(413) 238-4240

A nonprofit organization providing services to a nationwide network of Pagans and others following an Earth-centered spiritual path. Some of EarthSpirit's current projects include participation in several interfaith clergy organizations, sponsorship of a variety of networking and support groups, and participation in the Parliament of the World's Religions. The group also organizes gatherings and seasonal circles, performs legal handfastings (weddings) and other rites of passage, and produces publications, tapes, classes, and workshops. Write or call for membership information.

Full Circle CSCD

37 Clark Road
Cummington, Massachusetts 01026
(413) 634-0262

Provides four Pagan gatherings annually, a quarterly newsletter with a calendar of regional events, public and private ceremonies and instruction, a networking service, workshops, a women's moon lodge, and various other personalized services. Call or write for more information.

MIT Pagan Students Association

c/o Association of Student Activities
MIT
77 Massachusetts Avenue
Cambridge, Massachusetts 02139

The Pathway of the Rose

P.O. Box 698
Ayer, Massachusetts 01432

An international referral network and "phone tree" for Pagans of various traditions.

The Thomas Morton Alliance
51 Plover Road
Quincy, Massachusetts 02169
A Pagan political organization. Write for more information.

University of Massachusetts Pagan Students Association
P.O. Box 117
Student Union Building
University of Massachusetts
Amherst, Massachusetts 01003

Western Massachusetts Pagan Alliance
1500 Main Street
P.O. Box 15083
Springfield, Massachusetts 01115
(413) 746-1432
A regional network for Pagans of different backgrounds and traditions. Provides workshops, lectures, concerts, and open circles.

The Witches League for Public Awareness (WLPA)
P.O. Box 8736
Salem, Massachusetts 01971
A nonprofit organization and "proactive educational network dedicated to correcting information about Witches." Publishes a biannual newsletter.

Michigan

Ancient Altars
2420 Faunce Student Services
Western Michigan University, Box 2
Kalamazoo, Michigan 49008
A spiritual registered student organization on the Western Michigan University campus. Provides networking, education, and support to the Pagan community.

Great Lakes Pagan Council
P.O. Box 8281
Roseville, Michigan 48066
(313) 871-9252
Contact: Oberon

Provides information on Pagan events and activities, promotes community and networking, and works to educate the public about Pagan ways.

Magical Education Center of Ann Arbor
P.O. Box 7727
Ann Arbor, Michigan 48107

Pegasus
3767 W. Michigan Avenue
Battle Creek, Michigan 49017
(616) 963-4353

A regional referral council and "phone tree" for Witches belonging to different traditions.

Sanctuary of the Silver Moon
P.O. Box 6052
Grand Rapids, Michigan 49516
Contact: Storm

Networks with solitary Pagan practitioners as well as incarcerated Pagans.

Web-KORE
4217 Highland Road, Box 213
Waterford, Michigan 48328

An eclectic Neopagan and Wiccan group founded in 1989. It provides monthly meetings and sponsors four large annual rituals.

Minnesota

The Henge of Keltria
P.O. Box 48369
Minneapolis, Minnesota 55448
E-mail: Keltria@aol.com

A nonprofit religious corporation to foster and practice the spiritual and cultural teachings of Celtic Earth-based religions, particularly Keltrian Druidism. They have member groves in both the United States and Canada, and are the publishers of *Keltria: Journal of Druidism and Celtic Magick* and other Neopagan Druid resources. For additional information, send a self-addressed stamped envelope or e-mail.

Omphalos Pagan Community Center
P.O. Box 26752
St. Louis Park, Minnesota 55426
(612) 458-7815

A local network serving the Pagan community in the Twin Cities metropolitan area.

Our Lady of the Lakes
P.O. Box 14872
Minneapolis, Minnesota 55414

Wiccan Church of Minnesota
P.O. Box 6715
Minnehaha Station
Minneapolis, Minnesota 55406

Mississippi

Rainbow Link
P.O. Box 1218
Greenville, Mississippi 38702

Spirit's Forge
Contact: Andrea Hewitt
E-mail: ahewitt@ocean.st.usm.edu

A Pagan group located in Hattiesburg, Mississippi.

Missouri

Amer
P.O. Box 16551
Clayton, Missouri 63105

An organization for individuals experiencing religious discrimination and those wanting information on the occult.

Nevada

Twisted Rose Branches
5545 Mission Road
Fallon, Nevada 89406
Contact: Lady Bronwyn
A regional referral network for like-minded Pagans.

New Hampshire

Aura Pro Nobis
P.O. Box 178
Stratham, New Hampshire 03885

A national networking and support group for Pagans. Provides police and religious harassment contacts and occasionally puts out a newsletter.

Ordo Mysterium Baphe-Metis, Inc.
P.O. Box 156
West Nottingham, New Hampshire 03291
(603) 942-7474

A religious, philosophical, and educational organization for the Thelemic and occult communities.

New Jersey

Jersey Shore Pagan Way
P.O. Box 4212
Long Branch, New Jersey 07740

This organization (founded circa 1974) is run by Gardnerians for the purpose of teaching. It requires no money, just active participation (although it asks for donations for candles and supplies). Periodically sponsors a free grove.

The Living Wicca Foundation
P.O. Box 4186
Dunellen, New Jersey 08812
(908) 575-9807

A legally recognized Wiccan church and nonprofit community service organization serving Central New Jersey. Sponsors various events and publishes a quarterly magazine *Calling the Quarters.*

Polyhymnia (N.J.)
   c/o Andrea Helms
   P.O. Box 43
   Boonton, New Jersey 07005

A traditional Gardnerian coven that does not discriminate with regard to race, gender, or sexual orientation. Member of the Covenant of the Goddess.

Tradition of the Endless Dance
   189 Berdan Avenue, Suite 217
   Wayne, New Jersey 07470

An eclectic Neopagan tradition dedicated to knowledge, and founded on the three drumbeats of truth, trust, and love. Offers classes, study programs, meditations, and rituals.

New York

Church of All Worlds—Purple Pomegranate ProtoNest
   365 Westminster, no. 6E
   Brooklyn, New York 11218
   (718) 469-3846
   Contact: Manawyddan or Mevrian

Gotham COG
   P.O. Box 6208
   Long Island City, New York 11106
   E-mail: RWANDEL@usa.pipeline.com

A local council of the national Witches' organization Covenant of the Goddess.

Hermes' Council
   P.O. Box 803
   Pearl River, New York 10965

A men's group based in the Rockland County area devoted to the study of spiritual and magickal techniques for personal improvement.

This is not a religious tradition, but rather a supplement to one's present spiritual practices, and thus has no religious, political, or sexual agenda.

Holly Oak Village Project
(718) 263-8763

This organization envisions an intentional Pagan community living in shared space. Publishes the *Pagan Place* newsletter and meets on alternate Saturdays at 1:00 P.M. in either Brooklyn or Pawling, New York.

Kathexis Coven
c/o Michael Thorn
P.O. Box 408
Shirley, New York 11967

A traditional coven focusing on contact with nature, devotion to the Goddess and the God, and learning. Member of the Covenant of the Goddess. For more information, send a self-addressed stamped envelope.

Lake Circle
c/o Robert Martens
P.O. Box 83
Colonie, New York 12207
(518) 452-9774

This nondenominational Pagan group hosts weekend campouts in upstate New York in addition to open circles in New York City. Write to be added to the mailing list.

Marymount College Wiccan Grove
c/o Roselyn Fulton
P.O. Box D-30
1395 Lexington Avenue
New York, New York 10126

This organization works both in the school and with the community to make the young Pagan voice heard. It is interested in networking with other student organizations.

Meridian Research
3979 Ockler Avenue
Hamburg, New York 14075
E-mail: meridian@pce.net
Researcher/owner: David Ledwin

Specializes in literary, occult, and metaphysical research on a wide variety of areas and subjects. Fees are negotiable based upon each job and detail of information required.

The New Avalon Centre for Women's Mysteries
P.O. Box 723
Lindenhurst, New York 11757
(516) 226-7967
Contact: Elizabeth J. Nahum

New Moon, New York
P.O. Box 1471
Madison Square Station
New York, New York 10159
(212) 388-8288

A local, nonprofit Pagan organization providing monthly workshops, public rituals, and various networking and social activities for members of the New York Pagan community. Publisher of the monthly community periodical called *Our Pagan Times.*

Our Lady of the Seashore
E-mail: seashore@control.com

This Gardnerian coven (located in Shirley, Suffolk County, Long Island) is accepting students for study directed towards initiation. It is a member of the Covenant of the Goddess, and seeks networking with other covens in the area.

Pagan Resource Guide
c/o John Coughlin
837 Midland Avenue, Box 113
Yonkers, New York 10704
E-mail: jcoughlin@ccm.agtnet.com

Polyhymnia
c/o R. Wandel
P.O. Box 6208
Long Island City, New York 11106

A traditional Gardnerian coven that does not discriminate against race, gender, or sexual orientation.

POWER
SUNY—Stony Brook
E-mail: jgriffin@ccvm.sunysb.edu

POWER stands for Pagan Organization of World Eclectic Religions. It is an organization of students at SUNY—Stony Brook who are interested in Paganism, archaic religion, and other nonmainstream spiritualism. All who are seriously interested are welcome.

Reginleif Felagidh
c/o L. W. Hasten
P.O. Box 290-158
Brooklyn, New York 11229

An Asatru Religious Fellowship dedicated to the worship of the Goddesses and Gods of the North. Affiliated with the Irminsul Aettir, it holds several open meetings and Eddic study groups throughout the year. Write for a copy of the brochure *Is Asatru Right for You?*—a brief introduction to the major concepts of Asatru.

Temple of the Eternal Light
928 E. Fifth Street
Brooklyn, New York 11230

932 McDonald Avenue, Suite 200
Brooklyn, New York 11218

An "omnidenominational" fellowship and Brooklyn's oldest Caballistic Wicca Temple. Offers monthly rituals, classes in Wicca and Ceremonial Magick, and a home study course called *Thirteen Tools Toward Enlightenment.*

Thistledown Coven
P.O. Box 1153
Carmel, New York 10512

An established group in the Windblown tradition with eclectic, Celtic focus. Member of the Covenant of the Goddess.

Triple Star
> 51 McDougal Street, no. 52
> New York, New York 10012

Welsh Rite Traditionalist covens in Manhattan and Queens with a strong focus on ritual, myth, and magick. Outer Courts as well.

U.S. Collective
> E-mail: oyapomba@idt.net

A magickal group that welcomes all spiritual paths and is open to services of Egyptian origin, as well as Voodoo, Shamanistic, Aboriginal, Wiccan, Celtic, Santerian, Shinto, Buddhist, and all other services. Holds circles twice a month and on special occasions.

Wise Woman Center
> P.O. Box 64
> Woodstock, New York 12498
> Contact: Susun Weed

North Carolina

Celebrate the Circle
> c/o Eno River Unitarian Universalist Fellowship
> P.O. Box 2837
> Durham, North Carolina 27715
> Contact: Lance Brown

Charlotte Chapter of the Young Pagans Organization
> P.O. Box 62
> Queens College
> Charlotte, North Carolina 28274

Church of All Worlds—Ancient Totem
> P.O. Box 24731
> Winston-Salem, North Carolina 27114
> (910) 723-8024

Crystal Moon Coven
> P.O. Box 713
> Leicester, North Carolina 28748

MoonDance
P.O. Box 515
Cary, North Carolina 27512

New Earth Church
P.O. Box 5461
New Bern, North Carolina 28561

Pagan Awareness League—North Carolina Chapter
Website: members.aol.com/Palweb/nc.htm

SerpentStone
E-mail: www.geocities.com/RainForest/7263

An eclectic teaching tradition located in Asheville, North Carolina.

Shadow Grove
c/o Tom Pullen, NFCS
P.O. Box 9108
Fayetteville, North Carolina 28311
E-mail: tpullen@coastalnet.com

A comparative religion discussion group. All disciplines and traditions are welcome.

Ohio

Association of Earth Religion Churches
Columbus, Ohio
(614) 263-7611

At the Gate (ATG)
P.O. Box 09506
Columbus, Ohio 43209

ATG links singles nationwide interested in New Age philosophies, spirituality, ecology, peace, animal rights, and personal growth. Write for free information.

Church of Mother Earth
c/o Union of Pagans
P.O. Box 609277
Cleveland, Ohio 44109
(216) 398-5224

CUUPS, Inc.
8190-A Beechmont Avenue, no. 335
Cincinnati, Ohio 45255
(817) 557-3949

Lady of the Sacred Grove and Stone Circle
P.O. Box 5558
Lima, Ohio 45802

Mudfire Windspirit Grove ADF
P.O. Box 16412
Columbus, Ohio 43216
(614) 628-9056

Pagan Community Council of Ohio
P.O. Box 82089
Columbus, Ohio 43202
(614) 261-1022
E-mail: pcco@netwalk.com

This organization sponsors activities for the Pagan residents of Ohio. Educational workshops, ecumenical services, and social events are scheduled throughout the year. Events include: Summerfest (Labor Day weekend), Shadowmas (mid-October), Winterfire (mid-December), Brigid's Fire (late January and early February), Spring Bourne (mid-March), and the Greening (mid-May).

Sacred Earth Alliance
c/o Larry Cornett
890 Alhambra Rd.
Cleveland, Ohio 44110
(216) 692-2124
E-mail: lcorncalen@aol.com

Spirit Weavers
P.O. Box 2867
Toledo, Ohio 43606

What's Brewing Network
P.O. Box 24067
Cincinnati, Ohio 45224
Contact: Logan and Brigid

A national correspondence network for the magickal and Pagan community. Provides an information exchange and networking. It is sponsored by the programmers of *The Witching Hour* radio broadcast, which airs on station WAIF (88.3 FM).

Oklahoma

The Center for Pagan Studies
P.O. Box 4803
Tulsa, Oklahoma 74159

A nonprofit corporation dedicated to public education about Earth-based religions and associated subjects.

Oregon

Church of All Worlds—Cascadia Nest
P.O. Box 40972
Eugene, Oregon 97404
Contact: Danae Denby-Spencer

The Nine Houses of Gaia, Inc.
P.O. Box 14415
Portland, Oregon 97214

A nonprofit organization and regional referral network that sponsors the Northwest Fall Equinox Festival. It also operates the Pagan Information Line and publishes a Pagan newsletter, *Open Ways*.

Veterans for Religious Freedom
National Headquarters
P.O. Box 2272
Portland, Oregon 97208

A national referral council and veterans service organization listed with the Department of Veterans Affairs in Washington, D.C. Pagan veterans who have been the victims of religious discrimination should contact this organization.

Pennsylvania

Children of the Ancient Way
P.O. Box 71313
Pittsburgh, Pennsylvania 15213

An organization dedicated to the preservation and protection of the Earth and all her creatures, and to providing a voice for those Pagans and Pagan friends who wish to work together to create positive changes in the natural, spiritual, and political environments through open participation in activities that promote social and individual growth. Membership is open to all Pagans and Pagan friends who are willing to make a commitment and take a stand in their local areas to improve conditions for all the children of the Earth Mother. Dues are $5.00/year to cover the cost of a bimonthly newsletter. For more information, send a long, self-addressed double-stamped envelope.

Church of All Worlds—Philadelphia ProtoNest
115 Arch Street
Philadelphia, Pennsylvania 19106
(215) 925-2838
Contacts: Conrad Bishop or Elizabeth Fuller

International Society for Celtic Awareness (ISCA)
P.O. Box 141
Willow Grove, Pennsylvania 19090
Contact: Gofannon Moondragon

An international network providing educational, spiritual, and referral services to those who follow a Celtic or Druidic path. It is affiliated with Kindred Spirit, which provides educational and spiritual workshops, open Sabbats, and drumming circles. Also offers a resource guide and directory to its members for various networking contacts.

Kindred Spirit
P.O. Box 141
Willow Grove, Pennsylvania 19090

An open Pagan networking organization hosting workshops, drumming circles, discussions, and Sabbat celebrations. For more information, send a self-addressed stamped envelope.

Mother Spirit
Nan Conner, coordinator
P.O. Box 1360
Exton, Pennsylvania 19341

Pittsburgh Pagan Alliance
P.O. Box 624
Monroeville, Pennsylvania 15146

Created in 1986, its goal is to "unify the diverse occult paths in the Pittsburgh area for mutual exchanges, learning, and fellowship." It is also "a clearinghouse for news, information, and exchanges of scholarly, practical, and experimental knowledge." Membership is open to all who follow a positive occult path, including the Old Religion, Wicca, Asatru, Shamanism, Druidism, Thelema, Ceremonial Magick, and Neopaganism. Write for more information.

The Society of Mystics Network (SOM)
P.O. Box 294
Dallastown, Pennsylvania 17313
Contact: Iscara

An international network providing contacts and referrals to like-minded individuals and groups.

Wiccan/Pagan Press Alliance (WPPA)
P.O. Box 1392
Mechanicsburg, Pennsylvania 17055
Contact: Silver RavenWolf, Director

A well-established organization dedicated to international networking and Pagan publishing. Publishes a newsletter called *Of Writers and Witches*.

Witches Today
P.O. Box 221
Levittown, Pennsylvania 19059
Contact: Tammie Jesberger

Provides networking and services for Wiccans who have experienced discrimination and those who seek more information about the Craft.

Rhode Island

Magi
 c/o Metagion
 184 Angell Street
 Providence, Rhode Island 02906
 Magickally associated group and information exchange.

South Carolina

Cat's Lair Covenant
 P.O. Box 7055
 Sumter, South Carolina 29150

Hazel Thorne Circle
 E-mail: selenem@pobox.com
 Contact: Selene Morgana
 A Pagan discussion group located in upstate South Carolina.

Life Temple Seminary
 P.O. Box 295
 Whitmire, South Carolina 29178

South Dakota

Church of All Worlds—Standing Stones
 P.O. Box 8381
 Rapid City, South Dakota 57709
 Contact: Maureen Moss
 Publishes a nest newsletter called *Stone Soup*. Sample copy: $1.00.

Tennessee

Church of All Worlds—Double Helix Nest
 P.O. Box 121793
 Nashville, Tennessee 37212
 Contact: Star Scoggin

Church of All Worlds—Morningstar ProtoNest
676 Germantown Parkway, no. 404
Cordova, Tennessee 38018
Contact: Scott Johnson

Publishes a nest newsletter called *Southern Oracle*. Sample copy: $1.00.

Omphalos
U.T. Box 16220
Knoxville, Tennessee 87996

A free networking service for Neopagans following the Greek or Roman traditions. Group and individual contacts, festival information, access to rituals, and other reference material.

ShadowMoon Coven
E-mail: morgan@preferred.com
Web sites: www.witches-brew.com/journal
            www.witchhaven.com
            www.witchcraft.net

Tangled Moon Coven
P.O. Box 2773
Clarksville, Tennessee 37042
E-mail: blakek@usit.net

Witches of the Woods
Nashville, Tennessee
(615) 256-5700
E-mail: coa@nashville.net

An eclectic Wiccan circle open to both women and men regardless of sexual orientation.

Texas

Ancient Arts Association
P.O. Box 6051
Fort Hood, Texas 76544

A local referral network created especially for Pagans who serve in the military.

Beaumont Covenant of Unitarian Universalist Pagans
c/o Spindletop Unitarian Church
P.O. Box 6136
Beaumont, Texas 77705
Contact: Richard Jones

Church of All Worlds—Enchanted Egg
P.O. Box 1086
McQueeney, Texas 78123
Contact: Sheleen Williamson

Church of All Worlds—Mother Dragon's ProtoNest
P.O. Box 1586
Sherman, Texas 75091
Contact: Linda Lookingland

Church of All Worlds—U.R. ProtoNest
3031 South Freeway
Fort Worth, Texas 76104
Contact: Bob Reid

Council of the Magickal Arts / Our Lady of the Sacred Flame
P.O. Box 33274
Austin, Texas 78764
A regional (Texas and Oklahoma) council of Pagans and Witches that organizes gatherings and publishes a journal devoted to the arts of magick. One-year membership: $15.00.

Eclectic Association of Tree Huggers (EARTH)
CUUPS: The Earth Chapter
5200 Fannin Street
Houston, Texas 77004

Fort Worth CUUPS
c/o First Jefferson U.U. Church
1959 Sandy Lane
Fort Worth, Texas 76112

Nexus International
P.O. Box 532256
Dallas, Texas 75053
Networking for Pagans, Wiccans, and magickal folks.

Pagan Alliance of Central Texas (PACT)
P.O. Box 12041
Austin, Texas 78711

A regional referral network that provides education to the public and sponsors eight potlucks or informal workshops each year.

The Rune Gild
P.O. Box 7622
Austin, Texas 78713

Utah

Cache Valley Pagan Alliance
155 N. Two Hundred West, no. 2
Logan, Utah 84321
(801) 752-2615

A Pagan community organization serving northern Utah. Holds regular meetings on the full moons, solstices, equinoxes, and cross-quarter days.

The Eagle's Kindred
P.O. Box 521737
Salt Lake City, Utah 84152
Contact: Jerry the Gothi

An Ogden-based organization devoted to Asatru. Holds free and open public rituals and boasts the only Pagan-sponsored Boy Scout troop in the world!

Goddess Circle Worship Service
Sponsored by the Order of Our Lady of Salt, this Dianic Wiccan circle meets at 7:30 P.M. on the second Monday of every month and is open to both women and men. A different Goddess is the focus each month. Currently meets at the Central Community Civic Center, 600 S. Three Hundred East, Room 35-36, Salt Lake City, Utah.

MoonRise, Inc.
2274 S. Thirteen Hundred East, Suite G8-159
Salt Lake City, Utah 84106

This organization publishes a community newsletter for each of the eight Sabbats, with articles that celebrate religious and cultural diversity.

Pagan Student Spirit Alliance

This Pagan group, based at the University of Utah, holds weekly meetings on Tuesdays at 7:00 P.M. in Room OSH-138.

Vermont

Great Mother's Love Network
P.O. Box 8456
Burlington, Vermont 05402
(802) 862-8246

An international referral service and "phone tree" created for the purpose of providing Pagan connections.

Virginia

Church of All Worlds—POD of Dolphins
Route 1, Box 240-B
Check, Virginia 24072
Contact: Lady Damorea

Church of All Worlds—Rowan and Oak
1229 Sixth Street
Roanoke, Virginia 24013
(540) 343-7926

Church of All Worlds—Triskelion Nest
P.O. Box 3434
Merryfield, Virginia 22116

Publishes a nest newsletter called *Crownings On*. Send $1.00 to receive a sample copy.

Coven Fertile Earth
P.O. Box 174
Mechanicsville, Virginia 23111

Coven Hallowsdale
P.O. Box 4671
Richmond, Virginia 23220

Coven Labrys
324 Yanceyville Road
Louisa, Virginia 23093
Contacts: Keyear and Lady Fern

Earth Rising Covenant of Unitarian Universalist Pagans
U.U. Fellowship of the Peninsula
P.O. Box 2597
Newport News, Virginia 23602

Earth Walk
6313 Davis Ford Road
Manassas, Virginia 22111

Fellowship of the Sacred Grove
E-mail: laura@cais.com

A Neowiccan study group located in northern Virginia.

James River CUUPS
First Unitarian Church
1000 Blanton Avenue
Richmond, Virginia 23221

Rising Tide CUUPS
c/o Unitarian Church of Norfolk
739 Yarmouth Street
Norfolk, Virginia 23510

Washington

Aquarian Tabernacle Church
P.O. Box 409
Index, Washington 98256
(360) 793-1945; fax: (360) 793-3537

Founded in 1979, this group holds monthly meetings, sponsors festivals, and provides various services to the Pagan and Wiccan community.

Dionysia
P.O. Box 30511
Seattle, Washington 98103
(206) 322-8572

Moon Circles
9594 First Avenue N.E., no. 413
Seattle, Washington 98115
Contact: Nan Hawthorne

Formerly Circles of Exchange. An introduction service that introduces members to each other and to the "wheel" system of correspondence exchange in one or more general topic wheels, and then encourages them to create their own additional connections. To further this goal of self-established connections, Moon Circles offers a membership directory for those interested in finding others with like interests to start special Wheels or other correspondence. These are published every Candlemas and Lammas. For more information, send a self-addressed stamped envelope.

Mother Rest Sacred Grove
P.O. Box 3713
Blaine, Washington 98231

West Virginia

Broken Gourd Circle
(304) 296-3008
E-mail: mv4020@access.mountain.net

An eclectic Earth and Goddess-based group located in Morgantown, West Virginia.

Earth Dance
P.O. Box 4059
Huntington, West Virginia 25729
E-mail: mayfair@access.eve.net

A multitraditional, Earth-based spirituality circle.

Witches Against Religious Discrimination
c/o Patsy Price
P.O. Box 541
Huntington, West Virginia 25710

Wisconsin

Church of All Worlds—Dragon Family Nest
P.O. Box 13132
Wauwatosa, Wisconsin 53213
Contact: Larry Andersen

Publishes a nest newsletter called *Dragon Droppings*. Send $1.00 to receive a sample copy.

Church of All Worlds—Well of the Phoenix
P.O. Box 77
Dane, Wisconsin 53529
Contact: Jack Ingersoll

Publishes a nest newsletter called *Well of the Phoenix News*. Send $1.00 to receive a sample copy.

Circle Sanctuary
P.O. Box 219
Mount Horeb, Wisconsin 53572
(608) 924-2216

A legally recognized Shamanic Wiccan Church and nonprofit multicultural Nature and spirituality resource center, founded in 1974. It provides international networking, workshops, training programs, and ministerial services, and publishes *Circle Network News*, *Circle Guide to Pagan Groups*, *Pagan Spirit Alliance Newsletter and Directory*, *Sanctuary Circles*, and *Circle Network Bulletin*. Circle also sponsors the annual Pagan Spirit Gathering and a variety of other festivals, retreats, and events. For more information, write or call weekdays between 1 P.M. and 4 P.M. (CST).

The Earth Conclave
P.O. Box 14377
Madison, Wisconsin 53714
Phone and fax: (608) 244-9443
E-mail: conclave@danenet.wicip.org

"A nonprofit educational organization dedicated to the environment and combining the personal and political with the spiritual." Holds conferences, workshops, and family gatherings, and is "interested in establishing a sense of community between all people of Earth-spirit regardless of age, race, tradition/religion, or sexual orientation.

Earth Religions Alliance
P.O. Box 1891
Wausau, Wisconsin 54402

Lady Liberty League
c/o Circle
P.O. Box 219
Mount Horeb, Wisconsin 53572
(608) 924-2216; Fax: (608) 924-5961

A referral network of volunteers affiliated with Circle Network and dedicated to assisting Wiccans, Pagans, and Nature Spiritualists with religious freedom cases. Contact if you have news to report or if you are interested in being a part of the league.

Occulterian Life Church of Wicca
P.O. Box K
Athens, Wisconsin 54411
(715) 257-7195

Founded in 1993 by Apophis Valkyrie, this tradition advocates communing with nature with little emphasis on deity identities, but perceives the Divine Union as a whole. Other branch organizations incorporated with this church are the Solitary Pagan Alliance and the Alternative Religions Alliance. Its ministry is a diverse group that includes Wiccans, Pagans, and others on the polytheistic level. Future projects include *Webweaver*, an international Pagan and Wiccan newsletter.

Of a Like Mind Network (OALM)
P.O. Box 6677
Madison, Wisconsin 53716

An international referral network providing its members with a networking services guide, access to a support hotline, local contacts for spiritual women, and free announcements and ads in its newspaper. To become a member, a subscription to *Of a Like Mind* and a $5.00 fee are required.

Pagan Spirit Alliance (PSA)
c/o Circle
P.O. Box 219
Mount Horeb, Wisconsin 53572
This is "a special Pagan friendship network within Circle Network." It is made up of Pagan individuals who are attuned to positive (helping and healing) magickal ways. One-year membership is a donation of $25.00 or more (U.S. and Canada, $30.00 elsewhere). Members receive a listing in and copy of the PSA membership directory, a subscription to the quarterly PSA newsletter, discounts on certain seminars, workshops, and the festival registration fee for the International Pagan Spirit Gathering (held each summer), and admission to PSA members' meetings.

Reformed Congregation of the Goddess
P.O. Box 6677
Madison, Wisconsin 53716
(608) 244-0072
A Dianic Wiccan organization founded in 1983 and dedicated to those who wish to explore a positive path of spiritual development. Sponsors monthly worship services, workshops, and conferences for feminist women, and offers a training program that ordains Priestesses of the Congregation. Also publishes a newspaper that focuses on women's spirituality and a monthly newsletter called *The Crescent*, which helps members keep in touch with the activities of the RCG.

Canada

CERES
Site L, Box 21
RR 1, Kispiox Road
Hazelton, British Columbia V0J 1Y0

Pagans for Peace Network
P.O. Box 2205
Clearbrook, British Columbia V2T 3X8
Contact: Samuel Wagar
An international referral network providing a newsletter and contacts for politically active left-wing Pagans and Wiccans.

The Wiccan Church of Canada
  109 Vaughan Road
  Toronto, Ontario M6C 2L9

The Wiccan Information Network
  P.O. Box 2422
  Main Post Office
  Vancouver, British Columbia V6B 3W7

United Kingdom

The Association of Hedgewytches
  Lynwood Cottage
  2 Jesu Street
  Ottery St. Mary, Devon, EX11 1EU
  England
A contact and social network for Witches who work independently (whether alone or in couples). It is nonsectarian and no initiation is required. Membership fees (per year): Single adult, £10; couples, £15; student/unemployed, £7.50.

British Druid Order
  P.O. Box 29
  St. Leonards-on-Sea
  East Sussex TN37 7YP
  England
Founded in 1979, this is a Neopagan oriented Druid group whose teachings are based on the *Mabinogion* and other early British and Celtic texts.

Findhorn Community
  The Park
  Findhorn Bay
  Forres IV36 0TZ
  Scotland

House of the Goddess
  33 Oldridge Road
  London SW12 8PN
  England
  Contact: Shan

Founded in the mid-1980s, this "modern Pagan clan and temple" offers healing, counseling, ceremonial services (such as Pagan weddings, divorces, baby-welcomings, and funerals), and Circlework courses to those interested in learning about Neopaganism.

Isle of Avalon Foundation
The Courtyard
2–4 High Street
Glastonbury
Somerset BA6 9DU
England

"A spiritual education center whose main purpose is to make available to visitors and residents the transformative energies of Avalon and the experience of people who live in Glastonbury and elsewhere on the planet." Offers lectures and courses on various subjects, including dowsing, healing, numerology, runes, shamanism, and the teachings of the late Dion Fortune.

London Druid Group
Gordon Gentry
74 Riversmeet
Hertford SG14 1LE
England

Loyal Arthurian Warband
c/o 10 Sine Close
Farnborough
Hants GU14 8HG
England
Contact: King Arthur Pendragon

A politically active group of modern-day Druids.

The Matriarchy Research and Reclaim Network
Wesley House
London Women's Centre
4 Wild Court
London WC2B 5AU
England

A countrywide (Great Britain) network of women who share a love of the Goddess, an interest in our matriarchal past, and a vision of women's spirituality in the present and the future. Publishes the *MRRN Newsletter.*

Odinic Rite
BM Edda
London WC1N 3XX
England

An organization devoted to the Northern Tradition.

Odinshof
BCM Tercel
London WC1N 3XX
England

The Order of Bards, Ovates, and Druids
P.O. Box 1333
Lewes, East Sussex BN7 1DX
England
Contact: Philip Carr-Gomm

Founded in 1717, this group (Druid Tradition) holds monthly meetings, has over one thousand members around the world, and provides a "postal experience-based training program."

Ordo Anno Mundi
BCM Box 6485
London, WC1N 3XX
England

A magickal society offering full training in the Ophidian (serpent-venerating) tradition of the Craft.

Pagans Against Nukes (PAN)
Blaenberem, Mynyddcerrig
Llanelli, Dyfed County
Wales SA15 5BL
United Kingdom

The Pagan Federation
Box BM 7097
London WC1N 3XX
England

Founded in 1971, this is one of Europe's oldest Pagan organizations. It works to educate the public, media, and authorities about Pagan values, beliefs, and practices, and to defend Paganism against misrepresentation. It promotes interaction between Pagans through its contact and pen pal networks and its quarterly magazine, *Pagan Dawn.*

PaganLink
BM Web
London WC1N 3XX
England

A Pagan networking organization established in 1986 "to promote links between the various paths" and "to share energies towards our common aim of manifesting our spiritual and magickal nature in harmony with the Earth."

Pagan ME & Chronic Illness Network (PMECIN)
PMECIN
2 Fairview Cottages
Mill Road
Wingham Well
Canterbury, CT3 INP
England

A special organization devoted to aiding Pagans with myalgic encephalomyelitis (ME), chronic fatigue syndrome (CFS), and other chronic illnesses.

Ring of Troth and Rune Gild
BM Aswynn
London WC1N 3XX
England

"A religious organization dedicated to the promotion and practice of the native heathen folk religion of northern Europe."

Subculture Alternatives Freedom Foundation
Sorcerer's Apprentice
6–8 Burley Lodge Road
Leeds LS6 1QP
England

Australia

Church of All Worlds
P.O. Box 408, Woden, ACT
Australia 2606
Phone: 06-299-2432; fax: 06-299-4100

Order of the Silver Star
P.O. Box 570
Parkes, New South Wales
Australia 2870
A religious organization involved with Hermetic magick.

France

Wicca International Witchcraft
6 rue Danton
94270 Kremlin-Bicetre

Germany

B. Norris Perry, MHR
6412-B Hurtgen Drive
Anderson Barracks
D-55278 Dexheim
Phone: 049-6133-60323

Solitary Wiccan (member no. P5149792 of the American Counseling Association) offers free counseling services to depressed or troubled sisters and brothers in the Pagan community. Confidential therapy. Also a member of the Association for Specialists in Group Work and the International Association for Addictions and Offender Counselors.

Isis of the Silver Star
Ostergasse 9
71706 Markgroningen
Phone: 07-145-3450
Contact: Ulrich Glaser

Ireland
Church of All Worlds—Foggy Bog
Herne's Cottage
Ethelstown Kells
County Meath
Contacts: Janet Farrar, Stewart Farrar, Gavin Bone

Druid Clan of Dana
Clonegal Castle
Enniscorthy, Eire (Ireland)

This well-organized and rapidly expanding Neopagan Druid organization is affiliated with the Fellowship of Isis. It publishes a magazine called *Aisling.*

Japan
Japanese Pagan Network
Ikari Segawa
7-22-4 Minamisyowa-Cho
Tokushima City 770

Switzerland
Ordo Arcanae Lucis Deae
Sunnehaldenstrasse 7
CH-8311 Brutten
Phone: 41-52-347-1002
Contact: Dio Wier

Prison Study Groups
Agents of Ariadne Study Group
Scott Sandlin, no. 201712
CCO, 216 Gebdron Road
Iron River, Michigan 49935

Beto-1 Freedom Group
Charles Tolan, no. 612454
Beto-1 Unit, Box 128
Tennessee Colony, Texas 75880

Brotherhood of Ancient Ways Study Group
Falcon Flamestar, no. 173033
ACI Box 1151
Fairfax, South Carolina 29827

Brotherhood of the Goddess Study Group
Dave Anderson
P.O. Box 760
Campbellford, Ontario K0L 1L0
Canada

Cerridwen's Cauldron Study Group
Michael Lee Hood, no. 206728
MPCF, Highway 218 South
1200 East Washington
Mount Pleasant, Iowa 52641

Circle of the Rising Spirit-1 Study Group
Steve Lewis, no. 98984
ASPC Winslow Apache, no. 123
P.O. Box 3240
Saint Johns, Arizona 85936

Circle of the Rising Spirit-2 Study Group
Richard Bable, no. 80218
ASPC Winslow Apache, no. 123
P.O. Box C/5C19
Yuma, Arizona 85366

Clements Units Pagan Study Group
Robert Meek II, no. 629253
TDCJ, 9601 Northeast Twenty-Fourth Avenue
Amarillo, Texas 79107

Earth's Embrace Study Group
John B. Burroughs
P.O. Box 57
Marion, Ohio 43301

Falcon's Lair / Flight of the Phoenix Study Group
Ronald Blackwell, no. 663116
TDCJ-ID Beto Unit, Box 128
Tennessee Colony, Texas 75880

Green Life Fellowship Study Group
Bradley Cox, no. 726905
PACK-1, TDCJ-ID, Route 3, Box 300
Navasota, Texas 77869

Left Hand Path Study Group
Ronald Vroman, no. 235815
KCF
Kincheloe, Michigan 49788

Right Hand Path Study Group
Guy Scott, no. 185553
KCF
Kincheloe, Michigan 49788

Stone Circle Pagans Study Group
William Snodgrass, no. 303563
Grafton Correctional Institution
2500 S. Avon-Belden Road
Grafton, Ohio 44044

Stone Temple Pilots Study Group
Duane Ballard, no. 228951
Box 5500
Chillicothe, Ohio 45601

Templars of the Lost City Study Group
Robert Phillips II, no. 905668
WCC Box 473
Westville, Indiana 4639

2

Pagan and Wiccan Churches

In this section you will find a state-by-state directory of legally recognized Wiccan and Pagan churches and related organizations throughout the United States (and two in Canada). Other churches, covens, and spiritual groups can be found in the first chapter, "Organizations."

Arizona

The Divine Circle of the Sacred Grove   16845 N. Twenty-Ninth Avenue, no. 1346, Phoenix, Arizona 85023; (602) 230-4186

New Age Community Church   6418 S. Thirty-Ninth Avenue, Phoenix, Arizona 85041; (602) 237-3213

Ring of Troth, Inc.   P.O. Box 25637, Tempe, Arizona 85285

California

Ancient Keltic Church   P.O. Box 663, Tujunga, California, 91043

Celtic Witan Church   21000 Lull Street, Canoga Park, California 91304

Church of All Worlds   P.O. Box 1542, Ukiah, California 95483; (510) 549-7777

Covenant of the Goddess   P.O. Box 1226, Berkeley, California 94701

Fellowship of the Spiral Path   P.O. Box 5521, Berkeley, California 94705

Reclaiming Collective   P.O. Box 14404, San Francisco, California 94114; (510) 236-4645

Connecticut

Fanscifiaroan   106 Center Street, Southington, Connecticut 06489

Moonshadow Institute of the Old Religion   P.O. Box 119, Oneco, Connecticut 06373; (401) 397-8857

Pagan Community Church   2333 North Avenue, Bridgeport, Connecticut 06606

Florida

The Church of Iron Oak   P.O. Box 060672, Palm Bay, Florida 32906

Labyrinth Temple of the Goddess   615 W. Virginia, Tampa, Florida 33603

Wiccan Religious Cooperative of Florida, Inc.   3936 S. Semoran Boulevard, Suite 116, Orlando, Florida 32822; (407) 657-2182; (407) 725-4316

Georgia

Keltic Orthodox Order of the Royal Oak   P.O. Box 6006, Athens, Georgia 30604; (706) 369-6813

Illinois

Circle of Danu   c/o B. Dering, 1310 W. Lunt Avenue, Apt. 507, Chicago, Illinois 60640

First Temple of the Craft of WICA   P.O. Box 59, Western Springs, Illinois 60558

Panthea Unitarian Universalist Pagan Fellowship   P.O. Box 608031, Chicago, Illinois 60660

Louisiana

Covenant of the Pentacle Wiccan Church-ATC P.O. Box 23033, New Orleans, Louisiana 70183; (504) 828-7169

Maryland

Free Spirit Alliance P.O. Box 25242, Baltimore, Maryland 21229; (301) 604-6049

Free Spirit Alliance P.O. Box 5358, Laurel, Maryland 20726; (301) 604-6049

Massachusetts

Earthspirit P.O. Box 365, Medford, Massachusetts 02155; (617) 395-1023; Fax: (617) 396-5066

The Iseum of Venus Healing (The Church of Isis Rising) P.O. Box 698, Ayer, Massachusetts 01432

Michigan

The Religious Order of the Sons of Heimdallr P.O. Box 814, Douglas, Michigan 49406; (616) 857-4463

Sanctuary of the Silver Moon P.O. Box 6052, Grand Rapids, Michigan 49516

Missouri

Greenleaf Coven P.O. Box 924, Springfield, Missouri 65802; (417) 865-5903

Sanctuary of Formative Spirituality P.O. Box 159, Salem, Missouri 65560; (314) 689-2400

New Hampshire

Our Lady of Enchantment 39 Amherst Street, Nashua, New Hampshire 03060; (603) 880-7237

New Jersey

The Living Wicca Foundation P.O. Box 4186, Dunellen, New Jersey 08812; (908) 575-9807

New Mexico

The Church of Our Lady of the Woods, Inc. P.O. Box 1107, Los Alamos, New Mexico 87544; (505) 662-5333

Our Lady of the Shining Staar P.O. Box 520, Church Rock, New Mexico 87311; (505) 488-5364

New York

Ar nDraiocht Fein: A Druid Fellowship, Inc. P.O. Box 516, East Syracuse, New York 13057; (800) DRUIDRY

Hawthorn Grove, Inc. P.O. Box 706, Monticello, New York 12701

Temple of Eternal Light 928 E. Fifth Street, Brooklyn, New York 11230; (718) 438-4878

Ohio

Association of Earth Religion Churches P.O. Box 141358, Columbus, Ohio 43214; (614) 263-7611

Church of Earth Healing 22 Palmer Street, Athens, Ohio 45701; (614) 592-6193

Green Dome Temple 1791 Westwood Avenue, Cincinnati, Ohio 45214

Temple of Wicca P.O. Box 2281, Lancaster, Ohio 43130

Rhode Island

The Society of the Evening Star, Inc. P.O. Box 29182, Providence, Rhode Island 02909; (401) 273-1176

Utah

Moonspun Circle 1603 South 1200 E., Salt Lake City, Utah 84105; (801) 467-3780

Vermont

Church of the Sacred Earth: A Union of Pagan Congregations R.R. 1, Box 239, Christian Hill Road, Bethal, Vermont 05032; (802) 234-9670

Washington

Aquarian Tabernacle Church P.O. Box 409, Index, Washington 98256; (206) 793-1945

Rowan Tree Church 9724 132 Avenue N.E., Kirkland, Washington 98033

West Virginia

Church and School of Wicca P.O. Box 297, Hinton, West Virginia 25951; (800) 407-6660

Free Association of Lillians P.O. Box 890, Morgantown, West Virginia 26505; (304) 296-3008; fax: (304) 296-3311

Wisconsin

Circle Sanctuary P.O. Box 219, Mount Horeb, Wisconsin 53572; (608) 924-2216; fax: (608) 924-5961

Re-Formed Congregation of the Goddess P.O. Box 6677, Madison, Wisconsin 53716; (608) 244-0072

Spiritpath P.O. Box 236, Gays Mills, Wisconsin 54631; (608) 735-4720

Canada

Congregationalist Witchcraft Association P.O. Box 2205, Clearbrook, British Columbia V2T 3X8

Covenant of Gaia P.O. Box 1742, Station M, Calgary, Alberta T2P 2L7; (403) 283-5719; Web site: www.cogcoa.ab.ca

The Wiccan Church of Canada 509 Saint Claire Avenue West, P.O. Box 73599, Toronto, Ontario M6C 1C0; (416) 656-6564

3

Schools

"Knowledge is power."

—BACON

The following list includes many schools that offer courses on Wicca, the magickal arts, natural healing, Voodoo, and herbalism, just to name a few. Most teach through correspondence courses; however, there are quite a few that offer public classes and even individual training to the serious seeker of knowledge.

Alaska

The Denali Institute of Northern Traditions
P.O. Box 671510
Chugiak, Alaska 99567

Offers lessons by mail in the Northern Spiritual Tradition, as well as a Rune Master program.

Arizona

Crossroads Lyceum
P.O. Box 19152
Tucson, Arizona 85731
Web site: http://members.aol.com/isislyceum/file.html

Founded in 1993, the Crossroads Lyceum is a contemporary mystery school and is one of the largest and most well established correspondence centers in the Fellowship of Isis. Its curriculum emphasizes basic skills and information gathered from inner knowledge that its members may assimilate and adapt to their own personal beliefs and traditions. It is an eclectic institution and its teachings reflect knowledge collected from various sources. The Fellowship of Isis honors the Goddess of Ten Thousand Names and follows in this tradition by honoring all pantheons and God/desses equally.

The Divine Circle of the Sacred Grove
16845 N. Twenty-Ninth Avenue, no. 1346
Phoenix, Arizona 85023
(602) 230-4186

This committed order of Druids and Wiccans offers instruction both by correspondence and through seminars on the Religion of the Old Ways. (Also performs legal handfastings and other rites of passage.)

Wicca, An Introduction Taught by Rik Johnson
c/o Desert Henge Coven
P.O. Box 40451
Tucson, Arizona 85717
(520) 323-8112

"Explore the mystery, magick, and beauty of Wicca (Witchcraft). Despite common misconceptions, Wicca is a joyous, life-loving nature religion that honors the God and Goddess, and encourages personal growth and living in harmony with the Earth. Held yearly since 1982, this is Arizona's oldest public class on Wicca. It emphasizes the traditional beliefs and practices of Wicca and explores the history, mythology, magick, and rituals of Wicca. The class uses slides, lectures, music, displays, handouts, and discussions to further illustrate the subject."

California

Builders of the Adytum

5101-05 N. Figueroa Street
Los Angeles, California 90042
(800) 255-0041; fax: (213) 255-4166

Established in 1922, this "foremost custodian of the Western Mystery Tradition" offers correspondence courses in the principles and practices of Tarot, Qabalah, alchemy, astrology, and the esoteric meaning and use of sound and color. A free brochure is available upon request.

Church of All Worlds

c/o Tony Navarro, Central Nest Liaison
P.O. Box 1542
Ukiah, California 95482
(415) 585-8228

This group, founded in 1962, offers classes on the following subjects: dance, healing, herbcraft, magick, massage, music, nature religions, and psychic development. Training for ordination into the Church of All Worlds priesthood is also available.

Circle of Aradia

P.O. Box 1608
Topanga, California 90290

This group sponsors classes and one-day workshops for women only on Feminist Witchcraft and Dianic Wicca.

The Hermetic Order of the Eternal Golden Dawn

14050 Cherry Avenue, Suite R-159
Fontana, California 92337
(909) 341-5628 or (310) 289-7214

A mystery school and fraternity that teaches the mysteries of Hermetics, Qabalah, Tarot, healing, ceremonial magick, Mystical Christianity, meditation, astral projection, Neopaganism, inner alchemy, and self-mastery. Members receive personalized instruction, temple work, and an opportunity to learn and share the Western Mystery Tradition with other like-minded people in a friendly atmosphere.

Metaphysics College

P.O. Box 728

Glendora, California 91740

Offers metaphysics and psychology courses. Write for a free brochure.

Priesthood

2110 Artesia Boulevard, Suite B-264

Redondo Beach, California 90278

(310) 397-1310

Offers "a complete and advanced metaphysical, magickal, and psychic power development correspondence course." Students can expect methods that are simple to understand and easy to apply. Write or call for a free brochure and rates.

Reclaiming Collective

P.O. Box 14404

San Francisco, California 94114

(510) 236-4645

This is a group that belongs to the American Neo-Witchcraft tradition called the Reclaiming Tradition. Write for more information regarding its classes, workshops, and retreats.

Rhiannon

20811-D Bear Valley Road, Suite 148

Apple Valley, California 92308

Correspondence training by a Wiccan Priestess. Affordable lessons on the tenets and practices of the Craft are offered. For more information, send a large self-addressed stamped envelope.

Shadowlight Institute

1965 Prince Albert Drive

Riverside, California 92507

Offers courses in Medicine Path, metaphysics, healing, and much more. For more information and a catalog listing descriptions of courses, faculty, certification opportunities, and methods of individual education design, send a check or money order in the amount of $2.00 to Shadowlight Products, Inc.

Temple Circle of Light
2110 Artesia Boulevard, Suite B-264
Redondo Beach, California 90278

A university of metaphysical arts and sciences offering a home study teacher training and certification programs. Write for a free brochure.

University of Egyptian Arts
P.O. Box 90062
San Diego, California 92109

Its home study course "now makes available much previously esoteric material." Send $1.00 for a detailed brochure and catalog.

Colorado

Fortress Temple
P.O. Box 172271
Denver, Colorado 80217
(303) 399-2971

A Wiccan-oriented group that offers weekly classes. Special training is offered to children (from ages five to twelve) of Pagan adults by the Education for Pagan Youth Committee.

Yero Wolo Spiritual Circle
3000 East Colfax, no. 355
Denver, Colorado 80206
(303) 754-2994

This group, founded on the "principles of traditional African spirituality," offers classes, workshops, and correspondence of "Neo-African spiritual practices."

Florida

As Always Coven
2568 E. Fowler Avenue
Tampa, Florida 33612
(813) 972-1766

Write or call for information regarding its one-year class in Wicca.

Church of the Seven African Powers

P.O. Box 453336
Miami, Florida 33245

Write for free information on its correspondence course and initiations. "Learn how to work with the gods and goddesses of West Africa to improve your life materially and spiritually."

Circle of the Moonlit Sea

649 S.W. Whitmore Drive
Port St. Lucie, Florida 34984
(407) 879-0578

This is a British-Traditional group that offers several eight-week introductory courses in Wicca throughout the year.

Inner Dimensional Pathways of Healing

2300 North Dixie Highway, Suite 203
Boca Raton, Florida 33431
(561) 392-1480

Center for hypnosis, shamanism, and metaphysical studies. Call for class schedule and a list of tapes and videos. A member of the Better Business Bureau.

Wiccan Religious Cooperative of Florida, Inc.

3936 S. Semoran Boulevard, Suite 116
Orlando, Florida 32822
(407) 725-4316; (407) 657-2182

Write or call for more information about educational classes, workshops, seminars, and other activities.

Georgia

Bangor Institute

P.O. Box 4196
Athens, Georgia 30605

Write for more information about the classes offered by this holistic college.

Delphi University
P.O. Box 70
McCaysville, Georgia 30555
(888) 335-7448; (706) 492-2772
E-mail: registrar@delphi-center.com

Knight of Runes
P.O. Box 2070
Decatur, Georgia 30031

A home study course in powerful rune magick taught by a European rune master.

Indiana

Circle of Isis Rising
Elkhart Branch, Indiana
(219) 262-3483

A multitraditional fellowship and Hermetic lodge offering classes on the following subjects: divination, magick, metaphysics, psychic development, and Wicca. Also offers counseling services. Call for more information.

Illinois

The Iseum of the Goddess of the Crystal Moon
P.O. Box 802
Matteson, Illinois 60443

Internationally recognized as an Iseum with the Fellowship of Isis (from Ireland), this group offers courses in Wicca through both classroom instruction and correspondence.

Temple of Kriya Yoga
2414 N. Kedzie Avenue
Chicago, Illinois 60647
(800) 248-0024

A center of spiritual study offering a wide selection of publications, audio- and videotapes, classes, and seminars, as well as a professional astrology course, Tarot, palmistry, the mysteries of ancient Egypt, astral projection, and more. Accepts Visa and Mastercard. Call or write for a free catalog.

Massachusetts

Full Circle
37 Clark Road
Cummington, Massachusetts 01026
(413) 634-0262

This is a center for spiritual and community development that offers both public and private instruction and various workshops in areas such as sacred mask making, meditation, exploring the Goddess within and among us, and the Wheel of the Year.

Michigan

Goddess Studies
1402 Hill Street
Ann Arbor, Michigan 48104
(313) 665-5550
Contact: Aurora

An eclectic Wiccan group that provides public classes.

New Hampshire

Our Lady of Enchantment
P.O. Box 1366
Nashua, New Hampshire 03061
(603) 880-7237

Five complete home study courses are available: Witchcraft, Sorcery, Egyptian Ritual Magick, Herbology, and Divination. Also offers on-campus training in the magickal arts at its metaphysical center in Nashua, New Hampshire. Open daily to all sincere seekers. Call or write for a free information package.

New Mexico

Ardantane
P.O. Box 1107
Los Alamos, New Mexico 87544
(505) 662-5333

Ardantane, a project of Our Lady of the Woods to create a Wiccan Seminary in New Mexico, offers evening lectures, weekend intensives, and week-long seminars in ritual design, coven leadership skills, herbal craft and healing, divination methods, Tarot, Qabalah, and others. Course description available upon request.

Our Lady of the Woods
P.O. Box 1107
Los Alamos, New Mexico 87544
(505) 662-5333

A British- and Celtic-oriented Wiccan coven and congregation that sponsors weekly classes in divination, magick, and other areas. Formal program from Dedicant to Third Degree. "Public Wicca 101," a six-week course, is offered annually. (See also Ardantane.)

New York

Lodge Uraeus/Servants of the Light
P.O. Box 4538
Sunnyside, New York 11104

For information regarding the course "Servants of the Light" send a self-addressed stamped envelope.

Second Sunday Mystery School
Source of Life Center
22 W. Thirty-Fourth Street, 5th Floor
New York, New York 10001
(800) 804-2184

Sponsored by The Tarot School, Second Sunday Mystery School offers day-long workshops and weekend intensives on such subjects as Qabalah, alchemy, Modern Witchcraft, Shamanism, ritual, and sacred dance. A course bulletin is available upon request.

Shadowfolk Teaching Collective
E-mail: breosaighit@juno.com

This New York-based organization sponsors groves for both beginning and advanced students.

Temple of the Eternal Light
928 E. Fifth Street
Brooklyn, New York 11230
(718) 438-4878

This group offers individual and group workshops and home study programs in "Thirteen Tools Towards Enlightenment," Qabalah, ceremonial magick, and Wicca.

North Carolina

The School of Wicca
P.O. Box 1502
New Bern, North Carolina 28563

Offers courses in Celtic Witchcraft, practical sorcery, Tantra, Yoga, prediction, astral travel, astrology, and healing, and a complete course on mystical awareness.

Stardust Circle
Seminary Admissions Office
P.O. Box 2474
Durham, North Carolina 27715

Offers a correspondence course that is "divided into five affordable units of six lessons each on cassette tape." For more information, send a long self-addressed stamped envelope.

Ohio

American Institute of Holistic Theology
5600 Market Street, Suite 10
Youngstown, Ohio 44512
(800) 650-HEAL

A private homestudy institution offering programs in divinity (the study of religion or theology), naturology (the study of nature as it applies to the health of man), metaphysics, parapsychic science, healthology, holistic ministries, and more. Write for free information or call to speak to an advisor.

The Center
P.O. Box 104
Sylvania, Ohio 43560

A Shaman-apprentice program with Owl Woman. Write for more information regarding its one-year guided cross-cultural program.

Church of Universal Forces
P.O. Box 03195
Columbus, Ohio 43203
(614) 252-2083

Offers a correspondence course in Wicca and Voodoo. Write or call for more information.

Oklahoma

Heartland Church and School of Wicca
P.O. Box 1945
Tulsa, Oklahoma 74101
(918) 743-0689

Traditional training and initiation for the modern Celtic Witch. Coveners and solitaries welcome.

Intuitive Mind International
6218 South Lewis, Suite 114
Tulsa, Oklahoma 74136
(918) 743-9492

Offers spiritual classes in visualization, meditation, dreams and healings. Also offers past life, health, relationships, and guide readings.

Virginia

The International Academy of Hermetic Knowledge
2150 Wise Street
P.O. Box 4384
Charlottesville, Virginia 22905

"A Qabalistic, Gnostic, Egyptian Magickal Organization," a function of the Holy Order of the Winged Disc. Write for more information.

Washington

The Hermit's Grove
9724 One Hundred Thirty-Second Avenue N.E.
Kirkland, Washington 98033
(206) 828-4124

A nonprofit educational center offering on-site classes, workshops, a Stone Circle for meditation and solitude, and facilities for student research. It is associated with the Rowan Tree Church and also offers a home study course. Classes average $10.00 to $15.00 per class. Work-study and barter are also available. Write for more information.

School of the Seasons
1463 E. Republican, no. 187
Seattle, Washington 98112

A correspondence course based on the idea of working with seasonal energies and metaphors. Packets available for each season suggesting tasks and readings in natural studies, personal growth, magickal skills, seasonal celebrations, festival foods, sacred crafts, and Goddess lore. Instructor Waverly Fitzgerald edits *The Beltane Papers: A Journal of Women's Mysteries* and studied with Starhawk. Send a self-addressed stamped envelope for information.

Uranus Publishing Company, Inc.
401 Pond Lane
Sequim, Washington 98382

Write for free information about its correspondence courses on astrology: Ove H. Sehested's Master Course in Basic Astrology and the Self-Teach Course.

West Virginia

Church and School of Wicca
P.O. Box 297
Hinton, West Virginia 25951
(800) 407-6660
E-mail: school@citynet.net

"The most complete instruction in Witchcraft and the Occult available today."

Wisconsin

Circle

P.O. Box 219

Mount Horeb, Wisconsin 53572

(608) 924-2216

Circle sanctuary is a Shamanic Wiccan church and multicultural Nature Spirituality resource center that offers education and training programs. For more information, write or call weekdays between the hours of 1 P.M. and 4 P.M. (Central Standard Time.)

SpiritSisters Learning Community

c/o RCG

P.O. Box 6677

Madison, Wisconsin 53716

(608) 244-0072

A program of spiritual development activities designed to further both personal and spiritual growth. It offers three weekend trainings a year, an RCG-trained Wiccan Priestess / teacher who assists with spiritual studies and provides support, and involvement with an ongoing group of spiritual women. After a year and a day in a SisterSpirits Community, you may, if you choose, be initiated as a Witch. Cost: $375.00 to $500.00 per year on a sliding scale.

WTI Cella Training Program

c/o RCG-I

P.O. Box 6677

Madison, Wisconsin 53716

(608) 257-5858

The Cella Program of the Women's Theological Institute, a course of study for women Witches, was developed to meet the needs of women who desire structured but not rigid assistance as students of the Craft. Cella Groups meet two weekends a year to share activities and progress. The third weekend is an intensive on a topic of your choosing (such as healing, ritual, divination, mythology, etc.). For enrollment materials and more detailed information, send $4.00.

United Kingdom

Eagle's Wing Centre for Contemporary Shamanism
58 Westbere Road
London NW2 3RU
England

Evening classes, weekend workshops, and year-long part-time courses are offered. Write for additional information.

The Institute for Progressive and Scientific Occultism
Attention: P. Cooper
670 Obelisk Rise
Kingsthorpe, Northampton NN2 8TG
England

Offers a home study course, with the advantage of personal tuition, that starts through a series of graduated exercises from the first principles to a full understanding of the science of magick. The course includes instruction in constructing the "Cosmic Inworld," dealing with symbols, the four elements, the planets, the cosmic tides, and more. There are no books to buy and payment can be spread out over a period of time at no extra cost.

Vivianne Crowley
BM DEOSIL
London WC1N 3XX
England

British coven elders offer correspondence training for newcomers to the Craft. Send $4.00 for more information or $20.00 for Part One.

New Zealand

The Australasian College of Herbal Studies
P.O. Box 35146
Browns Bay, Auckland
New Zealand
Phone: 64-9-473-5573

United States office:
P.O. Box 57
Lake Oswego, Oregon 97034
(503) 635-6652; fax: (503) 697-0615; voice mail: (800) 48-STUDY

At the present time the group offers eleven home study courses in natural healing. To receive a prospectus that outlines the courses, or if you need additional information, please call, write, or send E-mail.

4

Books and Publishers

"A good book is the precious life-blood of a master spirit,
embalmed and treasured up on purpose to a life
beyond life."

—MILTON

The companies listed below publish or sell New Age and Wicca books. Whether you are looking for a good book to read or are writing one yourself, chances are you will find exactly what you're looking for within the following pages. (Additional book dealers can be located in chapter 8, "Magickal and Metaphysical Shops," and in chapter 9, "Mail Order.")

Most of the publishers listed here are the major companies that deal with the subjects of Witchcraft, the New Age, psychic sciences, and the magickal arts. If you are considering writing such a book or have already written one and are in search of a publisher, you will find many to choose from.

Included in most publisher's listings are the types of books published along with basic guidelines for manuscript submissions. Even if not specified in the listing, it is always a good practice to include a self-addressed stamped envelope with adequate return postage whenever submitting a manuscript, outline, or query letter. If you are writing to a publisher outside of the United States, be sure to include the proper amount of international reply coupons (IRC's), which can be obtained at just about any U.S. post office. (Many publishing companies will not answer a query letter or return a rejected manuscript unless a self-addressed stamped envelope or return envelope with IRC's is provided.)

For more information about writing books and the publishing business, I recommend that you read a current edition of *Writer's Market.*

Acropolis Books, Inc.
747 Sheridan Boulevard, Suite 1A
Lakewood, Colorado 80214
(303) 231-9923; fax: (303) 235-0492

Alexandria Books
1342 Naglee Avenue
San Jose, California 95191
(800) 241-5422

Call or write for a free catalog of metaphysical and mystical books.

America West Publishers
P.O. Box 2208
Carson City, Nevada 89702
(702) 585-0700; fax: (702) 891-0704

Aquarian Press
77–85 Fulham Palace Road
Hammersmith, London W68JB
England
Fax: 081-307-4440

Publishes books (approximately fifty to sixty titles per year) on astrology, the divinatory arts, the New Age, psychic awareness, spirituality, and other subjects. Writers outside of England are advised to query first with a self-addressed envelope and international reply coupons (IRC's). Free book catalog available on request.

Aradia Books

P.O. Box 972-G

Burlington, Vermont 05402

Women's spirituality, priestess craft, Goddess studies, Earth religion, positive magick, and other topics. Catalog: $1.00.

Astro Communications Services (ACS Publications)

P.O. Box 34487

San Diego, California 92163

Publisher of astrology books. Writers are advised to query first. To receive a free book catalog or manuscript guidelines, send a 9″ × 12″ self-addressed envelope along with two first class stamps.

Bear and Co., Inc.

P.O. Box 2860

Santa Fe, New Mexico 87504

(505) 983-9868

A spiritually oriented publishing company interested in books on the New Age, Western mystics, ecology, and those that "heal and celebrate the Earth." Writers are advised to query first or submit an outline along with several sample chapters. To receive a free catalog, send a 9″ × 12″ self-addressed envelope along with three first class stamps.

Black Tower

P.O. Box 20699

Seattle, Washington 98102

(206) 729-1275

Web site: www.blktwr.com

E-mail: blacktower@hushmail.com

Publishing and distribution.

Blue Dolphin Publishing, Inc.

P.O. Box 1908

Nevada City, California 95959

(916) 265-6925; fax: (916) 265-0787

Publisher of "comparative spiritual traditions" and books for individuals interested in self-growth and planetary awareness. Writers are advised to submit an outline along with sample chapters and a self-addressed stamped envelope. Free book catalog available upon request.

Blue Star Productions
9666 E. Riggs Road, Suite 194
Sun Lakes, Arizona 85248
(602) 895-7995; fax: (602) 895-6991

Book Traders, Etc.
c/o Gloria Reiser
826 N. Fifth Street
Quincy, Illinois 62301
(217) 222-9082; fax: (217) 222-0513

A bimonthly mail order resource for new and used books (including many New Age and occult titles), tapes, CDs, videos, and Tarot and other divinatory supplies at bargain prices. It also affords paid subscribers the privilege of listing books, divinatory and magickal items, etc. for sale or wanted. One-year subscription: $8.00. (Those not wishing to advertise their own lists may be put on the mailing list to receive up to six issues at no charge.)

Citadel Press
850 Third Avenue
New York, New York 10022
(212) 407-1500

"For over thirty years, the Citadel Library of the Mystic Arts has been hailed as America's definitive line of works on occult sciences and personalities, magick, demonology, spiritualism, mysticism, natural health, psychic sciences, Witchcraft, metaphysics, and esoterica." Writers are advised to submit an outline or synopsis along with several sample chapters.

Cassandra Press
P.O. Box 868
San Rafael, California 94915
(415) 382-8507; fax: (415) 382-7758

Publisher of New Age, holistic health, and metaphysical books. Writers are advised to submit an outline along with sample chapters. Free book catalog and manuscript guidelines available upon request.

Celestial Arts/Ten Speed Press
P.O. Box 7123
Berkeley, California 94707
(510) 559-1600; fax: (510) 524-1052

Conari Press
2550 Ninth Street, Suite 101
Berkeley, California 94710
(510) 649-7175; fax: (510) 649-7190

The Crossing Press
97 Hangar Way
Watsonville, California 95019
(408) 722-0711; fax: (408) 722-2749

Crossquarter Breeze
P.O. Box 8756
Santa Fe, New Mexico 87504
(505) 438-9846

Publisher of Pagan books. Book catalogue: $1.75

Delphi Press, Inc.
P.O. Box 267990
Chicago, Illinois 60626
Fax: (312) 274-7912

Publishes books about divination, healing, magick, Nature and Earth religions, Paganism, Wicca, Witchcraft, women's spirituality, and men's mysteries. Writers are advised to submit a complete manuscript or an outline along with three sample chapters. Free book catalog and manuscript guidelines available upon request.

The Devil's Bookshelf
P.O. Box 666
Daytona Beach, Florida 32115
(904) 255-4346

Rare and out-of-print occult books, human skulls and skeletons, and more. Catalogue: $5.00.

E. J. M. Publishing, Inc.
976 Murfreesboro Road
Nashville, Tennessee 37217
(615) 781-8835

A small press that publishes books dealing with the paranormal and eyewitness accounts of UFO sightings.

Emerald Wave
Box 969
Fayetteville, Arkansas 72702
Contact: Maya Harrington

Hampton Roads Publishing Company, Inc.
976 Norfolk Square
Norfolk, Virginia 23502
(804) 459-2453; fax: (804) 455-8907

Publishes New Age books and occult fiction, among other subjects. Writers are advised to first submit a proposal and outline. To receive a free catalog, send a 9″ × 12″ self-addressed envelope along with two first class stamps.

Harper San Francisco
Division of HarperCollins
1160 Battery Street, 3rd Floor
San Francisco, California 94111
(415) 477-4400; fax: (415) 477-4444

Publishes books about new consciousness, spirituality, theology, and women's issues and studies, among other subjects. Writers are advised to query first or submit an outline along with sample chapters. Free catalog and manuscript guidelines available upon request.

Hay House, Inc.
P.O. Box 5100
Carlsbad, California 92018
(619) 431-7695; fax: (619) 431-6948

Among the various subjects published are New Age and philosophy, astrology, and books with "a positive self-help/metaphysical slant." Writers are advised to query first or submit an outline along with sample chapters. Free catalog upon request.

Heartsfire Books
500 N. Guadalupe Street
Suite G-465
Santa Fe, New Mexico 87501
(505) 988-5160

Holmes Publishing Group
P.O. Box 623
Edmonds, Washington 98020

Imprints: Alchemical Press, Sure Fire Press, Contra/Thought, and Alexandrian Press. Publishes occult and metaphysical fiction and nonfiction. Query with a self-addressed stamped envelope.

Humanics Publishing Group
1482 Mecaslin Street N.W.
Atlanta, Georgia 30309
Fax: (404) 874-1976

Publishes New Age books in addition to other subjects. Writers are advised to submit an outline with at least three sample chapters. Send a self-addressed stamped envelope for a free catalog or manuscript guidelines.

In Print Publishing
6770 W. State Route 89A, Suite 346
Sedona, Arizona 86336
(520) 282-4589; fax: (520) 282-4631

A small press with an interest in metaphysical how-to books.

Inner Traditions, International
P.O. Box 338
One Park Street
Rochester, Vermont 05767
(802) 767-3174; fax: (802) 767-3726

"For the past twenty years, Inner Traditions has been a leading publisher of quality books on alternative health and spirituality, metaphysics, and indigenous cultures of the world." Also publishes books on mythology, the New Age, esoteric philosophy, and women's issues and studies. Writers are advised to query first or submit an outline along with several sample chapters and a self-addressed stamped envelope. Free book catalog and guidelines available upon request.

International Guild of Occult Sciences
255 El Cielo Road, Suite 565
Palm Springs, California 92262

Publishes Witchcraft books and magickal grimoires, in addition to a bimonthly magazine filled with practical information. Also offers courses, professional ritual services, and rare products. Catalog: $4.00.

Llewellyn Publications
P.O. Box 64383
St. Paul, Minnesota 55164
(612) 291-1970; fax: (612) 291-1908

Publishes books dealing with the divinatory arts, alternative health, applied magick, herbs, metaphysics, Wicca-as-religion, Shamanic techniques, the occult, Paganism, Witchcraft, the New Age, and women's issues and studies. Writers are advised to submit an outline along with sample chapters. Free manuscript guidelines are available. To receive a book catalog, send a 9″ × 12″ self-addressed envelope along with four first class stamps.

Looking Glass Press
P.O. Box 8105
S-104 20 Stockholm
Sweden
E-mail: carl@lgc.se

Publishes books (in English) on such subjects as Thelemic magick, Pagan-Scandinavian religion, Satanism, and Aleister Crowley, as well as Swedish translations of famous occult classics.

Magickal Childe
35 W. Nineteenth Street
New York, New York 10011
(212) 242-7182

Publisher of occult nonfiction books.

Middle Earth Books
P.O. Box 81906
Rochester Hills, Michigan 48308
(313) 656-4989

Scarce and rare metaphysical titles. Catalog: $3.00.

Necronomicon Press
P.O. Box 1304
West Warwick, Rhode Island 02893
(401) 828-7161; fax: (401) 826-1151

Specializes in works by and about H. P. Lovecraft.

New Atlantean Press
P.O. Box 9638
Sante Fe, New Mexico 87504
(505) 983-1856

New Horizons Press
11659 Doverwood Drive
Riverside, California 92505

A small publishing house that specializes in New Age books.

Newcastle Publishing Company, Inc.
13419 Saticoy Street
North Hollywood, California 91605
(818) 787-4378; fax: (213) 780-2007

Publishes holistic health, metaphysical, New Age, and self-help books. Writers are advised to query first or submit an outline along with sample chapters. Free book catalog. To receive manuscript guidelines, send a self-addressed stamped envelope.

Night of Pan Books
> 347 Lisbon Avenue
> Buffalo, New York 14215
> (716) 833-5336

Rare and out-of-print occult, magickal, and Thelemic titles available. Catalog: $1.00.

Occult Bookstore
> 1561 N. Milwaukee Avenue
> Chicago, Illinois 60622
> (312) 292-0995

Specialist in metaphysics, featuring a large selection of books on all spiritual traditions. Also buys used books. Send a self-addressed stamped envelope to receive a free catalog.

One Spirit
> Camp Hill, Pennsylvania 17012
> (800) 998-1979

A book club offering "resources for the spirit, mind, and body." Offers New Age, Goddess religion, folklore, meditation, alternative healing, and many other subjects of interest to Wiccans and Pagans. Write or call for details on how to become a member.

Original Publications
> 22 East Mall
> Plainview, New York 11803
> (516) 454-6809; fax: (516) 454-6829

A publisher and distributor of books on Santeria, Voodoo, spiritualism, numerology, dreams, Qabalah, Wicca, magick, the occult sciences, healing, astrology, divination, and Tarot—many in Spanish. Complete catalog of more than 500 titles: $2.00.

Prometheus Books
> 59 John Glenn Drive
> Buffalo, New York 14228
> (800) 421-0351

Call or write for a free catalog.

Samuel Weiser, Inc.
P.O. Box 612
York Beach, Maine 03910
(207) 363-4393

Publishes books dealing with astrology, esoterica, the magickal arts, metaphysics, Oriental philosophy, Qabalah, and Tarot, but no poetry or novels. Writers are advised to submit a complete manuscript. Free catalog upon request.

Serpent's Occult Books
P.O. Box 290644
Pt. Orange, Florida 32129
(904) 760-7675

Top dollar paid for used occult books. Scarce editions and out-of-print titles offered. New and used book lists available. Write or call for a free catalog.

Sun Books
P. O. Box 5588
Santa Fe, New Mexico 87502

Publishes books on astrology, Earth changes, healing, the occult, and more. Write for a free book list.

The Theosophical Publishing House / Quest Books
P.O. Box 270
Wheaton, Illinois 60189
(708) 665-0130; fax: (708) 665-8791

Publishes books on the following subjects: astrology, comparative religion, Eastern and Western religions, health and healing, meditation, Native American spirituality, the New Age, women's and men's spirituality, and yoga. Also accepts nonfiction translations. Writers are advised to query first or submit an outline along with sample chapters. Free book catalog. Send a self-addressed stamped envelope to receive manuscript guidelines.

5

Periodicals

The following is an alphabetically arranged listing of most of the magazines, newspapers, literary journals, and newsletters published by and for members of the Wiccan, Pagan, or New Age communities. All efforts have been made to keep subscription rates, addresses, and editors up-to-date (though these sometimes seem to change as often as the Moon changes its phase).

Most of the periodicals listed here welcome the submission of articles, poetry, spells, ritual outlines, and artwork from freelancers. Write for guidelines (usually free if available) from the ones that interest you, and always have the courtesy of enclosing a self-addressed stamped envelope when submitting material for publication or whenever sending correspondence that requires a reply or forwarding. (If you are writing to periodicals outside of the United States, be sure to enclose a return envelope with the proper amount of international reply coupons [IRC's], which can be obtained at most U.S. post offices.)

Most of the periodicals listed here offer payment to writers in the form of free contributor's copies. A few pay in cash, but many of the smaller presses cannot afford to make a payment of any kind but will publish you and give you the opportunity and pleasure of seeing your work in print and sharing it with others of a like mind.

If you are searching for Pagan pen pals, new friends, or a soul mate, this section is an ideal place to begin, for many of the periodicals contain a section for contacts, networking, and ads. Rates vary from free to inexpensive to moderately priced.

Pagan journals and newsletters contain some of the best writing and poetry around, as well as traditional Witch recipes, information on magick and Sabbat ceremonies, reviews, announcements, and news to keep you updated on the events and changes constantly taking place throughout the Wiccan community.

Wherever your interests lie—Dianic feminist Wicca, gay spirituality, Thelema, Pagan political activism, modern Druidism, Goddess-oriented poetry, or Pagan parenting—there is a periodical here just for you.

Aamulet Newsletter
Nicole Everett, editor
P.O. Box 123
Coos Bay, Oregon 97420

A quarterly newsletter from Circle of Isis Rising. Sample copy: $2.50; one-year subscription: $10.00.

Aazari's Web
P.O. Box 1006
Texas City, Texas 77592

A Pagan "news 'zine" featuring an eclectic mixture of informative articles, poetry, art, and fiction. Sample copy: $4.95, $2.00 for shipping and handling; three issues: $15.00; one-year subscription (six issues): $30.00. Make money orders payable to Jolie E. Bonnette.

Accord
Lila Harman, editor
P.O. Box 33274
Austin, Texas 78764

A quarterly journal of the Council of the Magickal Arts (CMA). Established in 1980. Sample copy: $2.50; one-year subscription: $10.00.

Acorns
Lady Amethyst, editor
P.O. Box 6006
Athens, Georgia 30604
(706) 369-6813

A quarterly magazine of Wicca and Paganism. Sample copy: $2.50; one-year subscription: $12.00.

Aerious Journal
Mark S. McNutt, editor
93640 Deadwood Creek Road
Deadwood, Oregon 97430
(503) 964-5341

A quarterly magazine of Earth and Spirit. Networking, articles, letters, reviews, and more. Sample copy: $3.00; one-year subscription: $15.00; Canadian subscription: $20.00; back issues: $2.50.

Ancient Arts
P.O. Box 3127
Morgantown, West Virginia 26505
Sample copy: $4.00.

Ancient Religions Newsletter
Anna Nelson, editor
1157½ W. Thirtieth Street, Box B3
Los Angeles, California 90007
(213) 856-2824

A Pagan newsletter published eight times per year. Sample copy: 50¢; back issues: 75¢; one-year subscription: $5.00; Canadian subscription: $7.00; other countries: $10.00.

Anichti Poli
Sofia Mandilas, editor
P.O. Box 20037
Athens GR-11810
Greece

A quarterly "underground magazine" covering such topics as youth cultures, Paganism, Pantheism, poetry, and nature people. (This magazine is published only in Greek.) Sample copy: $4.00; one-year subscription: $22.00.

Arcanum: A Magickal Journal
Wald Amberstone, editor
57 E. Eleventh Street, Ninth Floor
New York, New York 10003
(800) 804-2184

A new magazine targeting the Wiccan, Pagan, magickal, and New Age communities. Published every two months for "readers who are just beginning to explore their spiritual path, as well as seasoned veterans who are looking for material that goes beyond the scope of introductory articles." Sample copy: $4.00; one-year subscription: $18.00. Make checks payable to The Tarot School.

Artemesia's Magick!
P.O. Box 144
Payette, Idaho 83661
(208) 454-2026

A quarterly publication celebrating "the Olde Ways" and featuring Goddess lore, rituals, formularies, Tarot, stones and herbs, meditations, ancient garb patterns, reviews, and original art by professional artists. Member of the Wiccan/Pagan Press Alliance. Sample copy: $7.00; one-year subscription: $15.00.

Asatru Today
Lewis Stead, editor
11160 Veirs Mill Road, L15-175
Wheaton, Maryland 20902

A quarterly journal of Germanic Paganism. Established in 1994 and digest size. One-year subscription: $15.00.

Asynjur
P.O. Box 567
Granville, Ohio 43023

A journal of the northern goddesses. Sample copy: $3.00.

At the Crossroads
Jeanne Neath, editor
P.O. Box 112
St. Paul, Arkansas 72760

"Feminism, spirituality, and new Paradigm Science exploring Earthly and unearthly reality." Sample copy: $6.50; one-year subscription (two biyearly issues): $24.00; Canadian and foreign subscriptions: $36.00.

Azrael Project Newsletter
Lorraine Chandler, publisher/editor
Westgate Press
5219 Magazine Street
New Orleans, Louisiana 70115
(504) 899-3077

"Dedicated to a macroscopic understanding of the Angel of Death." Published semi-annually. Sample copy: $5.00; one-year subscription: $10.00.

Baba Yaga News
Pamela Getner, editor
P.O. Box 330
South Lee, Massachusetts 01260
(413) 243-4036

"A celebration of creative expression." Free sample copy; one-year subscription: $8.00; Canadian subscription: $10.00.

Beltane Papers
P.O. Box 29694
Bellingham, Washington 98228

"A Pagan-Feminist journal of women's spirituality." Articles, interviews, rituals, herbal lore, book reviews, and more. *The Beltane Papers* exists to provide women with a safe place in which to explore the dimensions of our spiritual experience, and then to name it. Publishes quarterly. Submissions by women welcome; pays in copies. Sample copy: $8.50; one-year subscription: $21.00.

Beyond Bifrost
Lori Johnson, editor
P.O. Box 814
Douglas, Michigan 49406
(616) 857-4463

A quarterly newsletter for individuals who are new to Odinism and Asatru. Free sample copy; one-year subscription: $5.00.

Black Moon Publishing
P.O. Box 19469
Cincinnati, Ohio 45219

The "largest open occult archive of manuscripts in the Western world." Send $1.00 for a current list.

Body, Mind, and Spirit
P.O. Box 701
Providence, Rhode Island 02901

Bridge Between the Worlds
10 Royal Orchard Boulevard
Box 53067
Thornhill, Ontario L3T 7R9
Canada

An international contact newsletter, published four times per year, and "dedicated to older (pre-1970s) Witchcraft traditions." Sample copy: $3.00; one-year subscription: $10.00.

Calendar of Events
c/o Larry Cornett, editor
9355 Sibelius Drive
Vienna, Virginia 22182

A newsletter of festivals, contacts, workshops, and retreats of interest to or sponsored by Neopagans. One-year subscription: $4.50; Canadian subscription: $5.00.

Calendar of Moons
Ben Sargent, editor
Ninefold Press
P.O. Box 2215
Natick, Massachusetts 01760

A yearly "sacred lunar calendar in magazine format." It is available in Eastern, Central, and Pacific editions. Sample (one month): $1.00; one year: $9.00; Canadian subscription: $11.00.

Calling the Quarters
P.O. Box 4186
Dunellen, New Jersey 08812

A quarterly magazine published by the Living Wicca Foundation. It features articles of interest to the Wiccan community and information pertaining to the Living Wicca Foundation. Meditations, poetry, spellwork, recipes, gardening, and arts and crafts. Sample copy: $4.50; one-year subscription: $16.50.

Cauldron
Carol For Rites, editor
P.O. Box 14779
Long Beach, California 90803

"A quarterly publication committed to the unity of all women in celebration of our diversity."

The Cauldron
Mike Howard, editor
Caemorgan Cottage, Caemorgan Road
Cardigan, Dyfed, SA43 1QU
Wales

A "Pagan journal of the Old Religion, Wicca, and Earth Mysteries." One-year subscription: $20.00 (cash only; checks and money orders are not accepted).

Celtic Camper
P.O. Box 782
Tucson, Arizona 85702

"A quarterly journal of progressive Wiccan observation and opinion, and r/evolutionary eclectic Wiccan thought." One-year subscription: $7.00; two-year subscription: $13.00; foreign subscriptions: $10.00 (U.S. funds only).

Changing Men
Michael Biernbaum, editor
P.O. Box 908
Madison, Wisconsin 53701
(608) 256-2565

A profeminist magazine serving the national men's movement. Established in 1979 and published three times per year. Sample copy: $7.00; subscription (four issues): $24.00.

Cincinnati Journal of Magick
c/o Black Moon Publishing
P.O. Box 19469
Cincinnati, Ohio 45219

Sample copy: $6.00.

Circle Network News

Dennis Carpenter, editor
P.O. Box 219
Mount Horeb, Wisconsin 53572
(608) 924-2216 (1 P.M. to 4 P.M. weekdays, Central Standard Time)

A quarterly newspaper of contemporary Paganism, Nature Spirituality, Wicca, Shamanism, and Goddess religion. Provides news, views, announcements, rituals, networking, and a "Magickal Marketplace." Free sample copy; one-year subscription: $15.00; Canadian and Mexican subscriptions: $20.00 (U.S. funds only).

Coll of the Goddess

c/o Lilith
RR no. 3, Box 113
Cochranton, Pennsylvania 16314

A "home grown" bimonthly newsletter featuring an eclectic mix of positive Paganism. Articles, stories, art, poetry, networking, goods and services, and more. Sample copy: $1.00; one-year subscription: $6.00.

The Common Thread

111 Broadway, no. 133–143
Boise, Idaho 83702

A Silverwitch production, published occasionally by Elton Nesselrodt. Contains articles, poetry, ads, and a community directory. Member of the Witches' Anti-Defamation League.

Compost Newsletter

729 Fifth Avenue
San Francisco, California 94118

"A magazine of humor, satire, and bad taste, both in the Craft and out." Sample copy: $2.00 (please make all checks and money orders payable to V. Walker for CNL).

The Cosmic Calling

Raymond Mardyks, editor
P.O. Box 2841
Sedona, Arizona 86339

A galactic and Mayan astrology journal that offers its readers "a unique, expanded perspective regarding the relationship between the stars that make up our galaxy and the evolution of human consciousness as a part of the present planetary transformation." Sample copy: $5.00; one-year subscription: $18.00; all foreign subscriptions: $22.00.

Covenant of the Goddess Newsletter

P.O. Box 1226

Berkeley, California 94704

Established in 1975 and published eight times per year. Sample copy: $3.00; one-year subscription: $20.00.

Craft/Crafts

P.O. Box 441

Ponderay, Idaho 83852

"A publication of needlework and Craft designs, especially for Pagans, Wiccans, and those of the Earth religions." Published quarterly. One-year subscription: $13.00; foreign subscription: $20.00.

Crone Chronicles

Ann Kreilkamp, editor

P.O. Box 81

Kelly, Wyoming 83011

(307) 733-5409

A quarterly "journal of conscious aging" dedicated to reactivating the archetype of the Crone within modern Western culture. Named after the third aspect of the Triple Goddess, it "provides an open forum for exploring the range and depth of what the Crone evokes in us." Sample copy: $6.95; one-year subscription: $21.00.

Crystal Moon Metaphysical Digest

Firewalker and Talon, publishers/editors

P.O. Box 802

Matteson, Illinois 60443

An "international metaphysical Pagan digest, published by The Order of the Crystal Moon, an international Pagan fellowship." Sample copy: $6.50 (Canada and Mexico: $7.50); one-year subscription: $25.00 (Canada and Mexico: $30.00).

Curious Minds

Lady Hawke, editor

415 Campbell Avenue

West Haven, Connecticut 06516

(203) 932-1193

A quarterly newsletter "for Witches, by Witches." Sample copy: $2.00; one-year subscription: $8.00.

Dalriada Magazine

Sammy McSkimming, editor
Dun Na Beatha, 2 Brathwic Place
Brodick, Isle of Arran KA278BN
Scotland
Phone: 40-0770-302532

A quarterly magazine focusing on the native Celtic traditions of Ireland and Scotland. Sample copy: $7.00; one-year subscription: $15.00.

Daughters of Inanna

Teri Viereck, editor
P.O. Box 81804
Fairbanks, Alaska 99708

Established in 1987, this Pagan newsletter is published eight times per year. Sample copy: $2.00; one-year subscription: $10.00. Canadian subscription: $12.00.

Daughters of Nyx

Kim Antieau, editor
P.O. Box 1100
Stevenson, Washington 98648

A quarterly "magazine of Goddess stories, mythmaking, and Fairy Tales" from a feminist, matristic, nonpatriarchal point of view. Sample copy: $4.50; one-year subscription: $8.00; two-year subscription: $14.00; Canadian subscription: $24.00.

Dharma Combat

P.O. Box 20593
Sun Valley, Nevada 89433

"An unedited reader-written forum about religion, metaphysics, and spirituality." Sample copy: $2.00.

Diipetes (For the Defense of the Ancient Spirit)

D. Pastelakos, editor
P.O. Box 20037
Athens GR-11810
Greece

"The first openly Pagan journal to be published in Greece." (This magazine is published only in Greek.) Sample copy: $5.00; one-year subscription: $25.00 (United States and Canada); European subscriptions: $20.00; elsewhere: $22.00.

Dragon Chronicle
Moondancer and Star, editors
P.O. Box 3369
London, SW6 6JN
England

A Pagan journal of the Dragon Trust published twice each year. Sample copy: £2.50; one-year subscription: £7.00.

Dragon Whispers
1511 E. Commercial Boulevard, Suite 131
Fort Lauderdale, Florida 33334

Newsletter of the Dragonwhisper Coven. "Anyone can hear the Dragon roar. Only the chosen will learn to hear the Dragon whisper." Published eight times a year. One-year subscription: $18.00; two-year subscription: $34.00.

Dragon's Fire Magazine
1015 Rutledge Avenue
Phoenixville, Pennsylvania 19460

Published four times per year under the sanction of The Dragon's Hearth/CNW. Sample copy: $4.00; one-year subscription: $15.00. Make checks or money orders payable to Eric K. Moore.

The Dreamweaver
Ladyhawk, editor
P.O. Box 150692
Fort Worth, Texas 76108

"A positive life-path publication, featuring interests in self-healing, dreams, Wicca, Native American paths, crystals, vegetarianism, animal rights, environmental issues, and much more!" Published bimonthly. Sample copy: $3.00; one-year subscription: $15.00.

Earth Spirit
Azuel Crow, editor
P.O. Box 365
Medford, Massachusetts 02155
(617) 395-1023; fax: (617) 396-5066

A newsletter of Pagan culture. Articles, interviews, book reviews, letters column, announcement of Earth Spirit events, and other items of interest. Sample copy: $2.00; one-year subscription: $15.00 (includes membership in Earth Spirit).

Earth Spirit Star
P.O. Box 1965
Colorado Springs, Colorado 80901

The official magazine of Earth Spirit Pagans (ESP). Published quarterly. One-year subscription: $16.00 (U.S. funds only).

Egyptian Religion Newsletter
c/o Neter
P.O. Box 290011
Tampa, Florida 33687

Eidolon
P.O. Box 4117
Ann Arbor, Michigan 48106

Eklektikos
Jackie Ramirez, editor
788 Harrison Street
Lebanon, Ohio 97355

An "eclectic reader participation journal," published six times per year. Sample copy: $3.00; one-year subscription: $15.00; foreign subscriptions: $25.00.

Eldar's Cauldron
P.O. Box 28692
Columbus, Ohio 43228

"An international publication of magick, musings, and miscellaneous." Published eight times per year on the Greater and Lesser Sabbats. Sample copy: $1.50; one-year subscription: $12.00.

Emania
c/o Ford and Bailie
P.O. Box 138
Belmont, Massachusetts 02178

Emerging Self

Mary Paruszkiewicz, editor
129 C. Lucille Court
Bartlett, Illinois 60103

A quarterly newsletter "for anyone interested in alternative healing from all walks of life, including Pagan and Goddess spirituality." Send two first-class stamps for free sample copy; one-year subscription: $13.00.

Enchante

c/o John Yohalem, editor
30 Charlton Street, no. 6F
New York, New York 10014

"The journal for the urbane Pagan." Sample copy: $3.50; one-year subscription: $12.00.

Enchanting News

Frank Hedgecock, editor
P.O. Box 145
Marion, Connecticut 06444
(203) 621-3579

A quarterly Pagan magazine published in honor of the God and the Goddess. Sample copy: $2.50; one-year subscription: $14.00; Canadian subscription: $18.00.

Ever Changing

Carol Goodrich, publisher/editor
R.R. 1, Box 842
Hinesburg, Vermont 05461

"A magazine dedicated to personal and planetary healing and growth in body, mind, and spirit." Published bimonthly, it includes a directory of Vermont-based practitioners and businesses. Writer's guidelines furnished upon request. One-year subscription: $14.00.

Familiars

Winter Wren, editor
P.O. Box 247
Normal, Illinois 61761
(309) 888-4689

A quarterly magazine for eclectic Pagans of all ages, and a newsletter for the Illinois chapter of WARD. Write for more information and subscription rates.

Fertile Soil

Elizabeth B. J. Lord, publisher/editor
P.O. Box 503
Swanton, Ohio 43558
(419) 826-4414; fax: (419) 826-1062

A journal of writings that explore the spiritual nature of the universe. Each issue contains reader-written articles, channeled material from ascended masters, creative writing, and poetry. Sample copy: $1.00; one-year subscription: $20.00.

Free Spirit Rising

P.O. Box 5358
Laurel, Maryland 20726
(301) 604-6049

A quarterly newsletter of the Free Spirit Alliance. Established in 1986. Sample copy: $2.00; one-year subscription: $10.00.

From the Heart

c/o Kathryn Hinds, editor
728 Derrydown Way
Decatur, Georgia 30030

A journal of Pagan parenting published approximately six times per year. Send one fifty-two-cent stamp for a free sample copy; one-year subscription: $13.00; Canadian subscription: $15.00; back issues: $2.00 each.

Gnosis

Richard Smoley, editor
P.O. Box 14217
San Francisco, California 94114
(415) 974-0600; fax: (415) 974-0366

A "journal of the Western Inner Traditions." Published four times per year; approximately eighty-eight pages per issue. Send a self-addressed stamped envelope for free information. Sample copy: $9.00;

one-year subscription: $20.00; Canadian subscription: $25.00 (international money order or check drawn on a U.S. bank only).

The Green Egg
P.O. Box 1542
Ukiah, California 95482

The quarterly journal of the Church of All Worlds. "The 1970's foremost magazine of Neopaganism has returned to deliver an interdisciplinary treasure trove: Shamanism, Goddess lore, psychic development, Gaea and environmental activism, suppressed history, alternative sexuality, and an uncensored Readers Forum." Sample copy: $6.00; one-year subscription: $24.00; Canadian, Mexican, and Latin American subscriptions: $36.00.

Green Man
Diana Darling, editor
P.O. Box 641
Point Arena, California 95468
(707) 882-2052

"A magazine for Pagan men exploring the mysteries of Gods and Goddesses, rituals, and myth creation that celebrate men's connection with one another, with women, and with the natural world." Sample copy: $4.00; one-year subscription: $13.00; Canadian subscription: $18.00.

HAM (How About Magick?)
Nemeton
P.O. Box 488
Laytonville, California 95454

A journal for Pagan youth.

Hallows
William D. Calhoun, editor
P.O. Box 5807
Athens, Ohio 45701

A journal of the Ordo Arcanorum Gradalis—a Gnostic Christo-Pagan Order of the Grail Quest. Subscriptions are free but available only to students and members of the Order.

The Hawthorn Spinner
Endymion Vervaine, editor
P.O. Box 706
Monticello, New York 12701

A quarterly magazine of ancient and modern Paganism, particularly Wicca. To receive a sample copy, please send a self-addressed stamped envelope and a donation of any amount.

Hazel Grove Musings
Shirley Dawson-Myers, editor
1225 E. Sunset Drive, no. 304
Bellingham, Washington 98226

A "quarterly journal of Pagan musings." Sample copy: $2.00; one-year subscription: $8.00.

The Hazel Nut
Linda Kerr, editor
P.O. Box 186
Auburn, Alabama 36831
(334) 212-4683

A quarterly journal of "Celtic spirituality and sacred trees." This publication features the trees associated with the lunar calendar, folklore, herbcraft, historical research, poetry, artwork, and reviews. Sample copy: $4.50 (Canada: $4.75); one-year subscription: $13.00 to $22.00 (sliding scale); Canadian subscription: $14.00 to $23.00 (sliding scale).

Heart Dance
Oshara, editor
473 Miller Avenue
Mill Valley, California 94941
(415) 383-2525

A monthly events calendar for the San Francisco Bay Area's spiritual and New Age communities. Sample copy: $1.00; one-year subscription: $15.00 to $25.00 (sliding scale).

Hearth Circles
P.O. Box 95
Wauconda, Washington 98859

A bimonthly "interactive journal for Pagans who enjoy learning and growing alongside our children." A wide range of topics of interest to Pagan homeschooling families includes: networking, community resources, reviews, recipes, folklore and magick, online support, pen pals, and more. Sample copy: $2.00; one-year subscription: $18.00; Canadian subscription: $20.00.

Heartsong Review

Wahaba Heartsun, editor
P.O. Box 5716
Eugene, Oregon 97405

Reviews of Pagan and spiritually conscious music. Sample copy: $5.00; one-year subscription: $8.00; Canadian subscription: $10.00. (Subscribers receive a free hour-long sampler tape with each issue.)

Heavenly Fragrances

c/o Midnight Angel, Inc.
P.O. Box 951
Old Bridge, New Jersey 08857

A magazine about magickal and astrological fragrances, serving to inform customers of some of the oils and incenses offered from Midnight Angel.

Hecate's Loom

P.O. Box 5206, Station B
Victoria, British Columbia V8R 6N4
Canada
(604) 477-8488

"A Canadian Pagan quarterly celebrating the return of the Goddess. Includes articles, letters, prose, and more." Write for more information and subscription rates.

Heretic Hollow

Capella, editor
P.O. Box 5511
Pasadena, California 91117
(818) 584-0008

Established in 1996 and published monthly, this newsletter is "intended as a forum of expression for diverse magickal, Pagan and

Wiccan concerns, issues, facts, fantasy and opinion." Contains poetry, artwork, and ads. Payment to contributors: a free one-year subscription. Sample copy: $2.00 (make check payable to: Pat W.).

Hermit's Lantern
Rev. Paul V. Beyerl, editor
P.O. Box 0691
Kirkland, Washington 98083

A monthly educational newsletter, published by the Hermit's Grove, containing information on basic metaphysical sciences: herbalism, Tarot, astrology, gems and minerals, ritualism, and others. Sample copy: $2.00; one-year subscription: $20.00.

The Higher Choice
Salanda, publisher/editor
P.O. Box 65
Neotsu, Oregon 97364

A monthly journal featuring astrology, a question-and-answer forum, fiction, evolutionary discussions, and more. Sample copy: free. One-year subscription: $12.00; two-year subscription: $20.00.

Hole in the Stone: A Journal of the Wiccan Life
Rhiannon Asher and George Moyer, editors
2125 W. Evans
Denver, Colorado 80223

A national quarterly Pagan journal with a calendar of events serving the Colorado Pagan community. Contains poetry, art, reviews, rituals, and more. Sample copy: $2.00; one-year subscription: $12.00; Canadian subscription: $17.00.

Horns and Crescent
Meagan and Jennifer, coeditors
P.O. Box 622
Millis, Massachusetts 02054

"To create bridges, not build walls, within the Pagan community." Calendar listings are free, subject to space limitations and editorial policies. One-year subscription (eight issues): $5.00.

Idunna

Thorfinn Einarsson, editor

c/o The Troth

P.O. Box 25637

Tempe, Arizona 85285

This quarterly magazine is "the official journal of the Ring of Troth." Covers heathen gods and goddesses, runes, sagas, and mythology. Sample copy: $7.00; one-year subscription: $24.00.

Intuitive Exploration

Gloria Reiser, publisher/editor

826 N. Fifth Street

Quincy, Illinois 62301

A bimonthly newsletter offering "a wide range of metaphysical and New Age thought." Editorial content includes articles, reviews of books and products, interviews, true experiences of the mystical, and more. Sample copy: $3.00; one-year subscription (U.S., Canada and Mexico): $15.00; all other subscriptions: $25.00.

Is to Be!

P.O. Box 1055

Suisun City, California 94585

A quarterly newsletter for the sharing of ideas and information amongst practitioners of magick and those interested in magickal theory. For both the beginner and the advanced magician. Sample copy: $3.00; one-year subscription: $15.00; all foreign subscriptions: $25.00.

Ishpiming Magazine

Sage, editor

P.O. Box 340

Manitowish Waters, Wisconsin 54545

(715) 686-2372

An annual magazine for individuals who follow the path of Nature Spirituality. To receive a sample copy, send in a donation of any amount. One-year subscription: $12.00 donation is suggested.

Isian News
Lord Strathlock and Hon. Olivia Robertson, editors
Fellowship of Isis, Foundation Centre
Clonegal Castle, Clonegal Enniscorthy
Ireland

"Quarterly coverage of international Goddess-oriented Pagan news and contacts; available to members only. Apply for membership (no fees required)." Sample copy: $2.50 (£1.40); one-year subscription: $20.00 (£5.50).

Isis Connection
Isis, editor
P.O. Box 1636
Gresham, Oregon 97030

A monthly newsletter "to awaken, to expand consciousness, and to raise awareness of the reality of the oneness of all life." Editorial content includes channeled articles, essays, and reports of UFO sightings. Sample copy: $3.00; one-year subscription: $36.00 (sliding scale).

The Isis Papers
11666 Gateway Boulevard, no. 163
Los Angeles, California 90064

A journal of poems, stories, art, and meditations published by the Iseum of the Isis Pelagia (Isis of the Sea). Sample copy: $8.00. Make checks payable to Laura Janesdaughter.

KAM
P.O. Box 2513
Kensington, Maryland 20891

A journal of Traditional Wicca. Sample copy: $3.00.

Keltria: Journal of Druidism and Celtic Magick
Tony Taylor, editor-in-chief
P.O. Box 48369
Minneapolis, Minnesota 55448

"This quarterly journal provides insight into Druidism and Celtic Magickal religions, and promotes Druidic education and fellowship through articles concerning the three Druidic paths of the Bard, the Seer, and the Druid. Theme articles, as well as reviews and letters. Sample copy: $3.00; one-year subscription: $12.00; Canadian subscription: $13.00 (U.S. funds); all other countries: $20.00 (U.S. funds).

Lady Letter
   Cedar, editor
   P.O. Box 1107
   Los Alamos, New Mexico 87544

A quarterly, published by Ardantane (Our Lady of the Woods), containing educational and informational articles on Witchcraft, ritual design, history and tradition, magickal techniques, ethics, reviews, Pagan fiction, and more. Regular columns include "Ritual Toolbox" (tips), "Coven Clinic" (focus on topics that especially concern coven leaders), "Wicca 101" (basic skills), and "Ask Amber" (advice from author Amber K). Contains regular updates regarding the Ardantane Project, a Wiccan Seminary in New Mexico. Sample copy: $3.50; one-year subscription: $13.00. Editorial guidelines available upon request.

Leaves
   Michael Ragan, editor
   P.O. Box 765
   Hanover, Indiana 47243

A newsletter containing information on the activities and research of the Temple of Danann. One-year subscription: $13.00.

Littlest Unicorn
   c/o The Rowan Tree Church
   9724 One Hundred Thirty-Second Avenue N.E.
   Kirkland, Washington 98033

A publication for children (newborn to ten years old) and Pagan parents. Published eight times per year on the Greater and Lesser Sabbats. Contains stories, artwork, poetry, and more. Sample copy: $1.50; one-year subscription: $9.75; sample packet: $5.00 (includes *The Littlest Unicorn*, *The Unicorn* [a publication for adults], and information on the Rowan Tree Church and its Mystery School).

Llewellyn New Worlds of Mind and Spirit
P.O. Box 64383
St. Paul, Minnesota 55164
(800) THE-MOON

A magazine and catalog of astrology, magick, occult, Nature Spirituality and New Age books, tapes, and services. Reviews, articles, sales and events notices, calendar, answer column. Free sample copy upon request.

Llyr: The Magazine of Celtic Arts
3313 Northmont Road
Baltimore, Maryland 21244

"A small-press magazine established in 1993 and devoted to the culture and heritage of the Celts, focusing on the lands now known as Ireland, Scotland, and Wales. Features articles, interviews, reviews, folktales, and, occasionally, short fiction and poetry. Published several times a year." Sample copy: $2.50; one-year subscription (four issues): $10.00.

Lunar Awareness
P.O. Box 661673
Los Angeles, California 90066

A calendar and newsletter of myth, magick, and astrology that "follows the Moon daily through her cycles." Published once a month at the New Moon. One-year subscription: $21.00. (Make checks and money orders payable to Yolanda Valenzuela.)

Lunar News
WOC
P.O. Box 234
York, New York 14592

A Genesee Valley Wiccan newsletter. Published by the Wiccans of Can-a-wagus, a nonprofit religious organization. Sample copy: $1.00; one-year subscription (13 issues): $13.00. Make checks and money orders payable to: Laurie Voeltz.

Magical Blend Magazine
P.O. Box 600
Chico, California 95927
(917) 893-9037

Free sample copy.

The Magical Confluence
P.O. Box 230111
St. Louis, Missouri 63123
Sample copy: $3.00.

Magical Forest Gazette
Eileen Smith, editor
2072 N. University Drive
Pembroke Pines, Florida 33024

A quarterly newsletter of Wicca and Paganism. One-year subscription: $4.00.

Magical Star
1035 E. Boston Park Road, Unit 1–1
Mamaroneck, New York 10543

Pagan-related articles and classified ads. Sample copy: $2.00.

Maiden Moon
2-919 Tenth Avenue N.
Saskatoon, Saskatchewan S7K 3A3
Canada

A metaphysical quarterly published by a group of Neopagan spiritualists. Provides a forum for communication and sharing between all individuals and groups that abide by the Wiccan Rede. One-year subscription: $12.00; Canadian subscription: $15.00.

Merlana's Magickal Messages
Marjorie (Merlana) Navarro, managing editor
P.O. Box 1107
Blythe, California 92226
(888) 922-0835

Established in 1995, this "metaphysical, spiritual, New Age publication" is published three times per year in March, July and October. Send SASE for information about chapbook publishing of their ongoing poetry chapbook contest. Sample copy: $7.00; one-year subscription: $20.00 (make check or money order payable to Navarro Publications).

Meyn Mamvro
Cheryl Straffon, editor
51 Carn Bosavern, St. Just
Penzance, Cornwall TR19 7QX
England

A twenty-four page magazine of Paganism and Earth mysteries. Sample copy: $5.00 (cash); one-year subscription: $15.00 (cash). Personal checks and money orders are not accepted.

Mezlim
Kenneth Deigh, editor
P.O. Box 19566
Cincinnati, Ohio 45219
(513) 791-0344

A quarterly magazine of "Wicca, Shamanism, Ceremonial Magick, Neopaganism, and related New Aeonic practices." Sample copy: $6.00; one-year subscription: $20.00; Canadian subscription: $27.00.

Midwest Pagan Correspondence
Chris Thomas, editor
P.O. Box 160
Western Springs, Illinois 60558

The quarterly newsletter of the Midwest Pagan Council. Book reviews, recipes, articles, updates on council activities, and more. Free sample copy; one-year subscription: $3.00.

Milady's Enclave
Marisa
P.O. Box 68
Colonia, New Jersey 07067

A bimonthly Wiccan women's publication filled with articles, recipes, announcements, poetry, personals, calendar of events, artwork, ads, and Web connections. Women of all sexaul orientations are invited to participate.

Mnemosyne's Scroll
Helena Aislin Anderson, editor
P.O. Box 1137
Bryn Mawr, Pennsylvania 19010

Published quarterly by the Coven of Oak and Willow. Sample copy: $1.50; one-year subscription: $5.00.

Moira

M. Jean Louis de Biasi, editor
B.P. 68, 33034 Bordeaux Cedex
France
Phone: 56-94-73-99

A quarterly magazine of occult traditions, including Witchcraft and Paganism. Published in French by the Circle of the Dragon. Sample copy: $6.00; one-year subscription: $20.00.

The Muse

1800 Clay Street
Newport Beach, California 92663
(714) 646-1052

"A magazine honoring our Goddess and the source of creativity. Every issue is graced with beautiful art, informative articles, poetry, modern myths, ritual, magick, and womyn's herstory!" Published quarterly. One-year subscription: $18.00.

Mystagogue Magazine

c/o TCSC
P.O. Box 15955
Sacramento, California 95852

"A forum for worship and study of British Traditional Wicca that offers herbalism, reviews, theology, and other subjects of interest to the Wiccan-Pagan communities." Published eight times per year by the Temple of Cerridwen's Sacred Cauldron, which also provides group training and worship. One-year subscription: $10.00; foreign subscription: $14.00.

Mystic Magick

Lara Light, editor
P.O. Box 387
Springfield, Oregon 97477

No standard subscription price. Send a self-addressed stamped envelope for free sample copy and more information.

Newaeon Newsletter

G. M. Kelly, editor

P.O. Box 19210

Pittsburgh, Pennsylvania 15213

"A genuine Thelemic publication dedicated to the further establishment and defense of Thelema, which, in part, exposes the lies of the greatest threat to Thelema: those who misrepresent themselves as Thelemites to further their petty personal goals at the expense of the truth." For more information, send $1.00 and a self-addressed stamped envelope (deductible from first order). Sample (current volume): $6.66; back issues: $7.77 each. (U.S. funds only; please make checks and money orders payable to G. M. Kelly.)

New Moon Rising

Timothy Barker, editor

P.O. Box 1731

Medford, Oregon 97501

(541) 858-9404; fax: (541) 779-8815

"A quarterly magazine addressing magick, Paganism, and related fields." Member of the Wiccan/Pagan Press Alliance. Sample copy: $3.95; one-year subscription: $15.00; foreign subscriptions: $20.00.

Night-by-Night

Gerard Spring, editor

P.O. Box 318

Milton, Massachusetts 02186

(617) 698-8330

A daily astrological guide published once a month. Sample copy: $2.00; one-year subscription: $15.00; Canadian subscription: $18.00.

North Star

P.O. Box 878–887

Wasilla, Alaska 99687

"A newsletter for families who choose to teach their own while following a Wiccan-Pagan spiritual path. Features include children's forum, news watch, reviews, poetry, recipes, and networking." Sample copy: $1.00; one-year subscription (six issues): $12.00; Canadian and Mexican subscriptions: $18.00.

Of a Like Mind
    Lynn Levy, editor
    P.O. Box 6677
    Madison, Wisconsin 53716
    (608) 244-0072

"A women's spiritual newspaper and network dedicated to bringing together women following positive paths to spiritual growth. Its focus is on women's spirituality, Goddess religions, Paganism, and our Earth connections, all from a feminist perspective." Sample copy: $4.00; one-year subscription: $15.00 to $35.00 (sliding scale); two-year subscription: $25.00 to $60.00 (sliding scale). Canada or Mexico add $5.00/year; overseas add $10.00/year. Send a self-addressed stamped envelope for a free brochure.

Omega New Age Directory
    Rev. Dr. John Rodgers, editor
    6418 S. Thirty-Ninth Avenue
    Phoenix, Arizona 85041
    (602) 237-3213

A monthly New Age newspaper containing a calendar of events and a regional directory of groups and churches. Sample copy: $1.50; one-year subscription: $15.00.

Open Circle
    P.O. Box 060192
    Palm Bay, Florida 32906
    (407) 253-1473

A Wiccan newsletter based in central Florida. Information on events, networking, spirituality, Sabbat, herb lore, and more. To receive a free sample copy, send a self-addressed stamped envelope with two 32-cent stamps. One-year subscription: $10.00.

Open Ways
    P.O. Box 14415
    Portland, Oregon 97214
    (503) 239-8877

A newsletter for the Pagan communities in Oregon and the Pacific Northwest. Sample copy: $1.00; one-year subscription: $8.00.

Our Pagan Times

Clover Welsh, editor
P.O. Box 1471, Madison Square Station
New York, New York 10159
(212) 662-1080

A monthly newsletter for the Pagan community. Sample copy: $2.00; one-year subscription: $15.00.

Out of the Broom Closet

P.O. Box 2298
Athens, Ohio 45701
(614) 592-1755

A quarterly magazine of alternative spirituality published by Pentamerous Publishing, a nonprofit organization. Sample copy: $4.00; one-year subscription: $13.00; Canadian subscription: $15.00.

Outer Court Communications

Sabrina, editor
P.O. Box 1366
Nashua, New Hampshire 03061
(603) 880-7237

A ten-page newsletter established in 1980 and published once a year. Contains book reviews, rituals, information about Our Lady of Enchantment, and other material. One-year subscription: $12.00; Canadian subscription: $15.00.

Pagan Dawn

Pagan Federation
BM Box 7097
London WC1N 3XX
England

"A forty-page illustrated quarterly magazine," established in 1971 and focusing on "British Wicca, Paganism, and Druidism." Each issue contains research articles, news, poetry, contacts, and information about groups, gatherings, and rituals throughout Great Britain and Europe. Sample copy: $7.00; one-year subscription: $25.00 (cash preferred, U.S. or Canadian currency).

Pagan Free-Press Newsletter
PFP
Victor Brotte, editor
P.O. Box 55223
Tulsa, Oklahoma 74155

Pagan Nuus
P.O. Box 640
Cambridge, Massachusetts 02140

The newsletter of the Covenant of Unitarian Universalist Pagans. Articles, book and movie reviews, graphics, poetry, and more. Sample copy: $1.00 to $2.00 (sliding scale).

Pagans for Peace
Samuel E. Wagar, editor
P.O. Box 2205
Clearbrook, British Columbia V2T 3X8
Canada

A bimonthly newsletter of "Pagan theology, political networking, and resource reviews." Free sample copy; one-year subscription: $10.00.

Pagans in Recovery Quarterly
Bekki Shining BearHeart, editor
22 Palmer Street
Athens, Ohio 45701
(614) 592-6193

A quarterly, eclectic, Pagan publication for Pagans recovering from addiction, abuse, or a dysfunctional upbringing. Sample copy: $2.50; one-year subscription: $8.50.

PAN Pipes
Lyle A. Austin, editor
P.O. Box 17933
Phoenix, Arizona 85011

"The official publication of the Pagan Arizona Network." Contains articles, spells, book reviews, and more. Published six times per year. Sample copy: $3.00; one-year subscription: $15.00.

Panegyria
Pete Pathfinder, editor
P.O. Box 409
Index, Washington 98256
(206) 793-1945
"A journal of the Aquarian Tabernacle Church. Published eight times per year on the major holidays. News of interest to Pagans in the Pacific Northwest and beyond." Send three 32-cent stamps to receive a free sample copy. Back issues: $2.00 each.

Pangaia Magazine
P.O. Box 641
Pt. Arena, California 95468
(877) PANGAIA
www.pangaia.com
Sample copy: $6.00; one-year subscription: $18.00 (4 issues).

Pan's Grove
P.O. Box 124838
San Diego, California 92112
"A Pagan and New Age news magazine with a fantasy catalog." Ads, articles, information, spells, reviews, and more! Sample copy: $1.80; foreign: $2.50.

Psychic Pathways
P.O. Box 100
Valley Stream, New York 11582
A "*Now* Age newsletter." One-year subscription: $15.00; two-year subscription: $25.00.

Psychic Reader
2210 Harold Way
Berkeley, California 94704
(510) 644-1600

Quest
Marian Green, editor
BCM–SCL Quest
London WC1N 3XX
England

Established in 1970. A quarterly newsletter of modern natural and ritual magick, book reviews, events, divination, training, and more. Sample copy: $4.00; one-year subscription: $20.00/£8 (cash).

Raising the Sacred Serpent
Hanah Leia
5051 E. Highway 98, no. 212
Destin, Florida 34698

A "journal and guidebook from the Temple of Hanah Leia. Documents inspirational relationship between a priestess and her beloved snake. Includes firsthand information on the care and feeding of sacred serpents." To receive a copy, send $7.50 plus $1.50 for shipping. (Please make checks and money orders payable to Hanah Leia.)

Reclaiming
P.O. Box 14404
San Francisco, California 94114

A quarterly newsletter "dedicated to unifying spirit and politics." Sample copy: $2.00; one-year subscription: $6.00 to $25.00 (sliding scale); two-year subscription: $12.00 to $50.00 (sliding scale); free one-year subscription to those of minimal income.

Red Garters International
c/o NWC
P.O. Box 162046
Sacramento, California 95816

Public outreach newsletter published intermittently by the New Wiccan Church. News, editorials, articles, demagoguery, doubtful humor, controversy. Published since 1975. Sample copy: $3.00 plus seld-addressed stamped envelope with sufficient postage to cover two ounces; four-issue subscription: $10.00; foreign subscription: $13.00. Make check or postal money order payable to NWC.

The Red Queen
603 W. Thirteenth Street, no. 1A-132
Austin, Texas 78701

"A quarterly journal of Goddess religion, magick, Feminism, creativity, and more for women who never make bargains." Sample copy: $3.50; one-year subscription: $13.00.

Rosegate Journal
P.O. Box 5967
Providence, Rhode Island 02903

The Runestone
Stephen McNallen and Maddy Hutter, editors
P.O. Box 445
Nevada City, California 95959
A quarterly journal of the ancient northern European religion known as Asatru. Sample copy: $2.50; one-year subscription: $10.00.

Sacred Circle
Vilija Witte
Romuva/Canada
P.O. Box 232, Station D
Etobicoke, Ontario M9A 4X2
Canada
A journal focusing on Baltic Paganism.

Sacred Grove News
Janette Copeland and Kalman Mannis, editors
16845 N. Twenty-Ninth Avenue, no. 1346
Phoenix, Arizona 85023
"The official newsletter of the Divine Circle of the Sacred Grove Church and School of the Old Religion." Free sample copy upon request. One-year subscription: $2.00.

Sacred Heart Magazine
Bried Foxsong, editor
c/o Wyrdd Enterprises
P.O. Box 72
Kenmore, New York 14217

Sacred Record
Route no. 1, Box 7
Willcox, Arizona 85643
A publication of the Peyote Way Church of God. Write for information regarding sample copy and subscription rates.

Sacred Serpent

P.O. Box 232, Station D
Etobicoke, Ontario M9A 4X2
Canada

A quarterly publication focusing on the Baltic and Slavic traditions. One-year subscription: $10.00; overseas: $15.00. Please make checks and money orders payable to Iron Wolf.

Sage Woman

Anne Newkirk Niven, editor
P.O. Box 641
Point Arena, California 95468
(707) 882-2052; fax: (707) 882-2793

Established in 1986. An eighty-page quarterly magazine of women's spirituality celebrating the Goddess in every woman. Free sample copy upon request. One-year subscription: $18.00; two-year subscription: $33.00 (California residents add 7¼ percent sales tax).

Sanctuary Circles

P.O. Box 219
Mount Horeb, Wisconsin 53572

The newsletter of the Circle Sanctuary Community. It is edited by the staff of Circle and published eight times per year. Free sample copy upon request. One-year subscription: $10.00 minimum donation (free to those who are active members).

The Seeker

John Morris, editor
P.O. Box 3326
Ann Arbor, Michigan 48106
(313) 665-3522

A monthly newsletter focusing on Earth-centered religion based in southeast Michigan. Sample copy: $1.00; one-year subscription: $10.00; Canadian subscription: $15.00.

The Serpent's Tail

Karin Lorenz Clark, editor
P.O. Box 07437
Milwaukee, Wisconsin 53207
(414) 769-1785

A quarterly newsletter focusing on Earth and Goddess-oriented religion. Sample copy: $2.00; one-year subscription: $10.00; foreign subscription: $15.00.

Shamanka

Vee Van Dam, editor
53 Hallett Way
Bude, Cornwall EX23 8PG
England
Phone: (0288) 356457

A newsletter of Shamanism, androgyny, letters, Kaiana channelings, reviews, ads, and more. Sample copy: $1.00 (50 p.); one-year subscription: $4.00 (£2.75).

Shared Transformation

El Collie, editor
P.O. Box 5562
Oakland, California 94605

A newsletter for persons experiencing spiritual emergence and kundalini awakening. Editorial content includes such topics as astrology, cross-cultural traditions, dreams, folklore, healing and health, kundalini, meditation, mysticism, mythology, parapsychology, psychic phenomena, Shamanism, and spirituality. Send a self-addressed stamped envelope to receive a free sample copy. One-year subscription: $12.00.

Silver Chalice Magazine

Steven R. Smith, editor
P.O. Box 196
Thorofare, New Jersey 08086

A quarterly newsletter of Paganism and Wicca. Sample copy: $2.00; one-year subscription: $6.00; Canadian subscription: $7.00.

Silver Pentagram, The

Reed Dunwich, editor
P.O. Box 9776
Pittsburgh, Pennsylvania 15229

"A Witchcraft journal serving the Craft through its members." It contains ads, articles, poetry, and is a member of the Wiccan/Pagan Press Alliance. Sample copy: $1.50; one-year subscription: $6.00 (outside of the United States, add $3.00).

Societé
Courtney Willis, editor
c/o Technicians of the Sacred
1317 N. San Fernando Boulevard, Suite 310
Burbank, California 91504

A magazine of "Voudou and other Neo-African religious systems, magick, art, and culture." One-year subscription (three issues): $15.00.

Solitary, by Choice or by Chance
De-Anna Alba, editor
P.O. Box 6091
Madison, Wisconsin 53716

A quarterly journal published for solitary Wiccans and Pagans. Sample copy: $3.50; one-year subscription: $15.00 to $36.00 (sliding scale).

Solitary Path
Kazan Clark, editor
Route 1, Box 47-A
Havana, Arkansas 72842
(501) 476-2071

An eclectic bimonthly newsletter (formerly *Wiccan Times*) for the solitary practitioner. Sample copy: $1.00; one-year subscription: $13.00; Canadian subscription: $18.00.

Somnial Times
Mike Banys, editor
P.O. Box 561
Quincy, Illinois 63206
(217) 222-9082

A bimonthly publication focusing on dreams and related states. One-year subscription: $10.00; all foreign subscriptions: $12.00.

Songs of the Dayshift Foreman
Gwyneth Cathyl-Bickford, editor
P.O. Box 1607
Aldergrove, British Columbia V4W 2V1
Canada

A journal of modern Witchcraft. Wiccans are invited to submit material. Sample copy: $2.00 (cash only); one-year subscription: $15.00 to $20.00 (sliding scale). Please make checks and money orders payable to Susan Davidson.

Spinning in the Light
  850 S. Rancho Drive, no. 2-355
  Las Vegas, Nevada 89106

"A magazine for the New Age of spiritual enlightenment." Published eight times per year by the Guardians of Light and Life / Clan of the Spider. Articles, predictions, horoscopes, recipes, poetry, and more. One-year subscription: $18.00.

Spirit Link
  P.O. Box 50651
  Tulsa, Oklahoma 74150
  (918) 587-1237

A quarterly newsletter "distributed as a community service to more than 3,000 individuals and groups" and "offered as a communication link between our readership and the traditional, holistic, alternative, and progressive resources available in and around the Oklahoma area." Focuses on such topics as personal growth, self-empowerment, metaphysics, environmental and humanitarian issues, spiritual enlightenment, healing, and more. Also features a calendar of events section, reviews, interviews, and ads. One-year subscription: $5.00.

Spirit of the Moment
  Lance Lewey, editor
  P.O. Box 26778
  St. Louis Park, Minnesota 55426
  (612) 936-9562

A newsletter serving the Twin Cities Pagan community. Sample copy: $2.00; one-year subscription: $16.00.

Starlight
  c/o Sirius
  P.O. Box 452
  00101 Helsinki
  Finland

A quarterly publication from "Pagan Finland and nearby" that features news, reviews, articles, poetry, magick, and Finnish gods and goddesses. One-year subscription: $8.00 for surface or $10.00 for airmail. Cash only.

Strange Fire
  P.O. Box 1219
  Allston, Massachusetts 02134

A traditional small-press digest containing stories, poetry, artwork, reviews of occult books, and essays on subjects such as Witchcraft, Gnosticism, and Pandemonaeon. Sample copy: $3.00.

Symphony
Aline H. Simon, editor
P.O. Box 27465
San Antonio, Texas 78227

A quarterly Pagan-oriented magazine of magick and harmony. Sample copy: $3.50; one-year subscription: $12.00.

Talking Leaves
1430 Willamette, no. 367
Eugene, Oregon 97401

Talking Stick
Pandora and Babylon, editors
P.O. Box 3719
London SW17 8X7
England
Phone: (081) 707-3473

A quarterly magazine focusing on Paganism, occultism, magick, and mythology. Sample copy: $5.25 (£2.80); one-year subscription: $20.00 (£10.00).

Tamulet, The
c/o Carole J. Preisach, editor
5545 Mission Road
Fallon, Nevada 89406
(702) 423-5049

A quarterly eight-page newsletter published in connection with the Parapsychology Special Interest Group of American Mensa, Ltd. Sample copy: $1.50; one-year subscription: $7.00; Canadian subscription: $7.50.

Tarot Network News
Box 104
Sausalito, California 94966

Tarot News
Gloria Reiser and Lola Lucas, editors
P.O. Box 561
Quincy, Illinois
(217) 222-9082

A bimonthly newsletter for both the beginner and the advanced Tarot enthusiast. Sample copy: $3.00; one-year subscription (U.S., Canada, and Mexico): $15.00; all other subscriptions: $25.00.

Think
P.O. Box 286
Prides Crossing, Massachusetts 01965

"A Pagan magazine printing articles intended to provoke your thought processes." Published quarterly. Single issue: $3.75; photocopied sample: $1.00.

Thunderbow II
P.O. Box 185
Wheatridge, Colorado 80034

A monthly publication of Earth religion and spirit sciences from the Church of Seven Arrows. One-year subscription: $15.00.

True North
c/o The Denali Institute
P.O. Box 671510
Chugiak, Alaska 99567

A monthly journal that provides the reader with "practical techniques in the application of Northern spiritual traditions for freedom of mind and spirit." Six-month subscription: $11.00; one-year subscription: $19.00.

Tsujigiri
Greg Carden, editor
501 Kirkwood Drive
Northport, Alabama 35476

A newsletter, "Orthodox Discordian Zine," of religion and humor. Free sample copy or subscription.

UFO Newsclipping Service
Lucius Farish, publisher/editor
2 Caney Valley Drive
Plumerville, Arkansas 72127

A monthly publication reprinting current press reports on unidentified flying objects and other unexplained phenomena (such as Bigfoot, the Loch Ness Monster, cattle mutilations, and so forth.) Sample copy: $5.00; one-year subscription: $55.00; Canadian subscription: $70.00; all other subscriptions: $80.00.

Unarius Light Journal

Dr. Charles Spiegel, executive editor
145 S. Magnolia Avenue
El Cajon, California 92020
(619) 444-7062; fax: (619) 444-9637

A quarterly publication of the Unarius Academy of Science (established in 1954). It features articles about individual psychic experiences, reincarnation and consciousness. Sample copy: $7.00; one year subscription: $30.00.

The Unicorn

Rev. Paul V. Beyerl, editor
P.O. Box 0691
Kirkland, Washington 98083

Established in 1976. A Wiccan newsletter published eight times per year by the Rowan Tree Church. Member of the Wiccan/Pagan Press Alliance (WPPA). Contains letters, articles, poetry, ritual outlines, book reviews, and a few ads. One-year subscription: $10.00.

Unknown Newsletter

c/o Luna Ventures
P.O. Box 398
Suisun, California 94585

A newsletter about "various unexplained phenomena, UFOs, and Witchcraft." Sample copy: $2.00.

Up Close

P.O. Box 12280
Mill Creek, Washington 98082
Fax: (206) 485-7926

Articles and reviews of New Age and alternative publications. Published four times per year by Darla Sims Publications. Sample copy: $10.00; one-year subscription: $40.00; Canadian subscription: $45.00; all other subscriptions: $50.00.

Voice of the Anvil

P.O. Box 060672
Palm Bay, Florida 32906
(407) 722-0291

A monthly newsletter of Pagan and Wiccan networking in Florida for groups, gatherings, workshops, and seminars. Free sample copy available upon request. One-year subscription: $6.00.

The Web

Amber Vargringar, editor
P.O. Box 924
Springfield, Missouri 65801
(417) 865-5903

A monthly Wiccan and Pagan newsletter designed for networking. One-year subscription: $13.00.

Wicca-Brief

Arkana, editor
Georgstrasse 4
22041 Hamburg
Germany
Phone: 040-687623

A Wiccan newsletter, published in German, eight times per year. Established in 1988. Sample copy: $5.00; one-year subscription: $40.00.

The Wiccan

BM Box 7097
London WC1N 3XX
England

The quarterly journal of the Pagan Federation. Sample copy: $6.00 (cash only); one-year subscription: $18.00 (£10.00).

Wiccan Rede

Merlin and Morgana, editors
P.O. Box 473
Zeist, NL 3700 AL
The Netherlands

An "English/Dutch Craft magazine featuring in-depth articles on Craft Heritage, symbolism, archetypal images, natural magick, elemental forces, and seasonal tides, discussions about the Craft today, news, book reviews, and ads." Published quarterly. One-year subscription: $15.00 (airmail) or £8.00 (EEC countries). Cash only: personal checks are not accepted.

Wild and Weedy (A Journal of Herbology)
Doreen Shababy, editor
P.O. Box 508
Clark Fork, Idaho 83011
(208) 266-1492

A twenty-eight page, quarterly journal of herbology for Pagans and Wiccans interested in creative herbcraft, holistic healing, organic gardening, and other topics. Contains poetry, book reviews, contacts, and resources. Sample copy: $3.00; one-year subscription: $13.00; Canadian subscription: $15.00.

Wild Magick Bulletin
P.O. Box 1082
Bloomington, Indiana 47402

The official publication of the Elf Lore Family (ELF). Contains articles on ecology, Earth religion, Tao, and more. One-year subscription (four issues): $8.00.

Winged Chariot
c/o Tracey Hoover
P.O. Box 1718
Milwaukee, Wisconsin 53201

A newsletter devoted to the Tarot. Sample copy: $2.00; one-year subscription: $10.00.

Wisdom in the Wind
P.O. Box 92
Burley, Idaho 83318
(208) 678-4526

A magazine for "seekers and newcomers of the Beauty Way of Pagan enlightenment." Write for more information, sample copy, and subscription rates.

Witches' Almanac
P.O. Box 348
Cambridge, Massachusetts 02238

An annual almanac of occult lore and legend, astrology, rituals, spells, and recipes, including a "Moon Calendar" of Wiccan festivals and lunar phases; $7.45 for each issue (includes postage); Canadian orders: $8.45.

Witch's Brew

P.O. Box 9111
Mandeville, Louisiana 70470

A quarterly newsletter "for all of Mother's children." Articles, reviews, poetry, recipes, webweaving, and much more. Sample copy: $4.00; one-year subscription: $18.00. Make all checks and money orders payable to S. Oliver.

Wodenwood

P.O. Box 33284
Minneapolis, Minnesota 55433

"A quarterly Neopagan newsletter. Articles, rituals, book reviews, and more." Write for more information, sample copy, and subscription rates.

Wood and Water

Daniel Cohen and Jan Henning, editors
77 Parliament Hill
London NW3 2TH
England

A "Goddess-centered, feminist-influenced Pagan quarterly newsletter. Sample copy: $3.00 (£1.25); one-year subscription: $10.00 (£6.00). (Cannot accept checks or money orders not in pound sterling.)

Woman of Power

P.O. Box 2785
Orleans, Massachusetts 02653

A "quarterly magazine of feminism, spirituality, and politics. Features feminist visionaries and activists in articles, interviews, artwork, photography." Sample copy: $9.00; one-year subscription: $30.00. Write for information regarding Canadian and overseas rates.

Wyrd

Goldie Brown, editor
P.O. Box 624
Monroeville, Pennsylvania 15146

A quarterly newsletter of poetry relating to the occult, mysticism, and Nature Spirituality. Submissions should be no longer than forty-five lines (or one page) of previously unpublished material, preferably with a cover letter containing a brief biography. Poets whose work is published in *Wyrd* will receive a complimentary copy of that issue and may request additional copies at the special writers' discount of $3.00 each. Sample copy: $5.00; one-year subscription: $20.00.

Wyrrd Word
c/o Sandra McNally, editor
P.O. Box 510521
Melbourne Beach, Florida 32951

Published five times per year as "a bridge between Wiccans, eclectic Pagans, and the New Age community." Sample copy: $3.00; one-year subscription: $15.00; Canadian subscription: $18.00.

YAPN (Yet Another Pagan Newsletter)
Duncan, editor
P.O. Box 82089
Columbus, Ohio 43202
(614) 265-8862

A bimonthly magazine for the Pagan community. Calendar of events, poetry, astrology, editorials, and more. Sample copy: $2.00; one-year subscription: free with $15.00 membership in the Pagan Community Council of Ohio.

Yggdrasil
Prudence Priest, editor
537 Jones Street, no. 165
San Francisco, California 94102

"A quarterly journal focusing on heathen culture, ethos, religion, mythology, and runes." Sample copy: $2.00; one-year subscription: $6.00 (United States and Canada); foreign subscriptions: $8.00. (Please make checks and money orders payable to Freya's Folk.)

6

Astrology

"The contemplation of celestial things will make a man both
speak and think more sublimely and magnificently when he
descends to human affairs."

—CICERO

Astrology, also known as "the science of the stars," dates back to the
most ancient of times, but its popularity continues to remain strong in
the present day (and I'm confident that it will continue on into the
twenty-first century and probably beyond).

Many individuals, myself included, believe that the heavenly bodies
exert a mystical influence over the personalities, daily activities, and
even the destinies of all humans. If astrology didn't work, I'm sure
public interest in it would have died out centuries ago.

Astrology is perhaps the most mainstream of all the occult sciences,
to which the horoscope columns that appear in nearly every major
newspaper across the country give evidence. In most bookstores

astrology books abound, and even famous celebrities and presidents have been known to consult professional astrologers for guidance and advice pertaining to their careers and love lives. Throughout the world numerous astrological societies, dating services, and chart-preparing businesses have been established, and every effort has been made to include the listings of each and every one in this section. (If it's in the stars, chances are it's in here as well!)

Arizona

American Federation of Astrologers
P.O. Box 22040
Tempe, Arizona 85282
(888) 301-7630; (480) 838-1751; fax: (480) 838-8293

Arizona Society of Astrologers (ASA)
P.O. Box 9340
Scottsdale, Arizona 85252
(602) 952-1525
Contact: Charlotte Benson

Provides lectures and workshops, and holds monthly meetings.

Astro-Logic
P.O. Box 37053
Phoenix, Arizona 85069

California

American Federation for Astrological Networking (AFAN)
8306 Wilshire Boulevard, Suite 537
Beverly Hills, California 90211

Aspects
P.O. Box 260556
Encino, California 91426

A monthly periodical of astrology published by Aquarius Workshops.

Astro Communications Services, Inc.
5521 Ruffin Road
San Diego, California 92123
(619) 492-9919; fax: (619) 492-9917

Comprehensive computer services, books, and software.

Astro Connection
13448 Ventura Boulevard
Sherman Oaks, California 91423
(818) 789-2734

Astro Genetic Vision
22201 Sherman Way
Canoga Park, California 91303
(818) 346-5697

Astrology Consultants
16053 Devonshire Street
Granada Hills, California 91344
(818) 892-0828

California Astrology Association
(818) 340-9007

Cosmic Connections
P.O. Box 22
Corona Del Mar, California 92660

Write for information on "Star Talk" astrology tapes. Accepts Visa and MasterCard.

Gerina Dunwich
P.O. Box 4263
Chatsworth, California 91313

Affordable horoscopes, all hand-prepared the old-fashioned way by a Wiccan High Priestess. Tarot and pendulum divination, past-life readings, dream analysis, and spellcasting services also available. Reliable and strictly confidential. Send self-addressed stamped envelope for complete information.

International Society for Astrological Research
P.O. Box 38613
Los Angeles, California 90038

Sponsors conferences every two years and publishes a quarterly journal called *Kosmos*.

Moon Dance
6600 Topanga Canyon Boulevard
Canoga Park, California 91303
(818) 888-2744

Simply Astrological
P.O. Box 6894
Pico Rivera, California 90661

Colorado

The Luna Connection
P.O. Box 21164
Boulder, Colorado 80308

"Reclaiming archaic heritage through astrology." Woman-centered reports: natal, lunar, transit, or relationship (friends or lovers). Forecast horoscope. Catalog of custom reports and the meaning of the Luna Connection: $5.00 (credited to your first order).

The Mountain Astrologer
P.O. Box 17275
Boulder, Colorado 80308

Publishes an astrological magazine nine times a year, and sponsors a conference called "Planet Camp."

Connecticut

Astrological Society of Connecticut
P.O. Box 9346
Wethersfield, Connecticut 06109

Holds monthly meetings and frequently sponsors conferences.

Florida

Cosmic Corner / The Psychic Network
P.O. Box 499
Deerfield Beach, Florida 33443
Catalog: $2.00.

Maine

Star Sage
P.O. Box 342
East Machias, Maine 04630
(800) STARSAGE

A complete astrological service offering in-depth personal life readings, compatibility reports, progressed reports addressing a specific concern or area of life, and more. Using the latest in astrological technology, Star Sage constructs natal charts and carefully delineates the data to unfold the intricate pattern of a person's life as reflected by the heavens. Call or write for a free brochure and order form.

Massachusetts

ACA Inc.
Box 395
Weston, Massachusetts 02193

For price information regarding natal charts, please write to the above address.

Michigan

Visions
P.O. Box 7043
Marquette, Michigan 49855

Minnesota

Llewellyn's Computerized Astrological Services
P.O. Box 64383
St. Paul, Minnesota 55164

New Hampshire

Seacoast Astrological Association (SAA)
P.O. Box 4683
Portsmouth, New Hampshire 03801

This group holds monthly meetings and sponsors an annual conference called "Autumn Alchemy."

New Jersey

Astrological Society of Princeton
175 Harrison Street
Princeton, New Jersey 08540
(609) 924-4311

National Council for Geocosmic Research (NCGR)
105 Snyder Avenue
Ramsey, New Jersey 07446
(201) 818-2871

Holds monthly meetings, sponsors conferences, and has local chapters throughout the United States.

New Mexico

Stargazers
HC-75, Box 441
Lamy, New Mexico 87540
(800) 782-7497; (505) 466-3500

Founded in 1990, Stargazers is an international astrological dating service for individuals (both straight and gay) desiring to "meet others on a spiritual path." It publishes a quarterly newsletter every January, April, July, and October. Contributions of manuscripts are encouraged. Single copy: $3.50; one-year subscription: $12.00. Call or write for a free sample personals newsletter.

New York

Astral Vision
2214 Cotswold Court
Liverpool, New York 13088
(315) 622-0536

Astro-Analysis Research Center
P.O. Box 382
Guilderland, New York 12084
(518) 356-0848

Astrologer's Guild of America
54 Mineola Boulevard
Mineola, New York 11501

Gilda's Astrology
663 Bleecker Street
Utica, New York 13501
(315) 792-7777

Golden Trines
  7273 Hollywood Road
  Liverpool, New York 13088
  (315) 458-2605

New York Astrology Center
  350 Lexington Avenue
  New York, New York 12452
  (212) 949-7211

Ohio

Celestial Gateway
  15400 Pearl Road
  Strongsville, Ohio 44136
  (216) 238-5731

Northern Ohio Valley Astrologers
  c/o John Milam
  P.O. Box 1
  Lafferty, Ohio 43951

Oregon

Welcome to Planet Earth
  c/o The Great Bear
  P.O. Box 12007
  Eugene, Oregon 97440
  (503) 683-1760

A monthly periodical that looks at current events from an astrological point of view.

Vermont

Abbe Bassett
  P.O. Box 17
  Essex Junction, Vermont 05453

Personal astrology services.

Helia Productions
R. R. No. 3, Box 928
Montpelier, Vermont 05602
Sponsors an astrological conference each August.

Kathleen Johnson
Cedar Rail Farm
Brandon, Vermont 05733
(802) 247-3656
Professional astrologer offers life charts, progressions, and esoteric and past-life work.

Washington

Kepler College
4518 University Way N.E., Suite 213
Seattle, Washington 98105
The only liberal arts college in the United States offering a Bachelor of Arts degree in Astrology.

Rev. Paul V. Beyerl
The Hermit's Grove
9724 One Hundred Thirty-Second Avenue N.E.
Kirkland, Washington 98033
Professional astrologer since 1976. Offers natal chart interpretations, transit and progressed charts, relationship interpretations, and astrology courses. Write for fee scale (sliding fee and barter may be available).

Washington State Astrological Association
P.O. Box 45386
Seattle, Washington 98145

Canada

The Astrology Shop
c/o Becky Powell
49 St. Quentin Avenue
Scarborough, Ontario M1M 2M7

The Fraternity for Canadian Astrologers (FCA)
91 Bowmore Road
Toronto, Ontario M4L 3J1
This organization has affiliated groups throughout Canada and welcomes "astrologers at all levels of learning."

United Kingdom

The Astrological Lodge of London
BM Astrolodge
London WC1N 3XX
England
Founded in 1915, this group meets every Monday evening in London.

Faculty of Astrological Studies
Hook Cottage
Vines Cross, Heathfield
Sussex TN21 9EN
England

Computer Resources

Astrolabe
P.O. Box 1750
Brewster, Massachusetts 02631
(800) 843-6682
Call or write for information about their top-quality astrology software for IBM, Windows, MS-DOS, and Macintosh.

Halloran Software
P.O. Box 75713
Los Angeles, California 90075
(800) SEAGOAT (California residents: (818) 501-6515)
Astrology software for IBM, PC, and both DOS and Windows. For both the professional and the hobbyist. For a free catalog, write or call.

Matrix Software
(800) PLANETS
Call for a free catalog of astrology programs designed for home computers.

7

Herbs

Herbs are magickal indeed. From their use in the flying ointments and love philtres of olden times to their use in the healing remedies of modern Witches and Shamans, herbs have always had a strong tie to Paganism and the Craft of the Wise.

Herbs seem to "vibrate" with mystical properties. What Witch's kitchen would be complete without its herbs for potions, spellcraft, and rituals? Imagine a good old-fashioned cauldron brew without any herbs. You'd have to settle for something less appealing, such as eye of newt and wing of bat! Of course I'm joking, but seriously, herbs are an important part of the Craft; many of the more esoteric ones (mandrake, for example) can be quite difficult, if not downright impossible, to find at the local herb farm, health food store, gardening center, or in your supermarket's herbs and spices section. This is why I have included this section devoted entirely to herbs and where to obtain them.

For additional dealers who specialize in herbs (both the ordinary and Witchy types) see Chapter 8, "Magickal and Metaphysical Shops," and also Chapter 9, "Mail Order." There you will find many companies that carry a wide variety of herbs, as well as other items, and probably have exactly what you're looking for.

California

American Herbalists Guild
P.O. Box 1683
Soquel, California 95073

Write for information regarding its classes, conferences, and newsletter.

Botanica Mano Poderosa
7066 Van Nuys Boulevard
Van Nuys, California 91405
(818) 786-8377

Botanica Mistica
14534 Nordhoff
Panorama City, California 91402
(818) 830-0590

Dances with Herbs
54200 N. Circle Drive
Idyllwild, California 92549
(909) 659-0700

Ema's Herbs
695 E. Main Street
Ventura, California 93001
(805) 648-6426

The Herb Quarterly
P.O. Box 689
San Anselmo, California 94979
(814) 322-4996; fax: (814) 322-1536

Sample copy: $6.00; one-year subscription: $24.00; two-year subscription: $45.00.

Moon Maid Botanicals
P.O. Box 182
Sebastopol, California 95473
(707) 586-3971

Mother Earth Herbs
5272-A West Gold Court
Beale AFB, California 95903
(916) 788-0138

Catalog: $2.00.

Mountain Rose Herbs
20818 High Street
N. San Juan, California 95960
(800) 879-3337; fax: (916) 292-9138

Forty-eight page catalog: $1.00.

Nature's Herb Company
1010 Forty-Sixth Street
Emeryville, California 94608
٠ (510) 601-0700; fax: (510) 601-0726

Star Herb Company
38 Miller Avenue
Mill Valley, California 94941

Wild Weeds
302 Camp Weott Road
Ferndale, California 95536
(800) 553-9453

Free catalog.

Colorado

Cat Creek Herbs
P.O. Box 227
Florence, Colorado 81226

Green Mountain Herbs
P.O. Box 2369
Boulder, Colorado 80306

Motherlove Herbal Company
P.O. Box 101
Laporte, Colorado 80535
(970) 493-2892; fax: (970) 224-4844

Wish Garden Herbs
P.O. Box 1304
Boulder, Colorado 80306

Delaware

Renewal of the Spirit
P.O. Box 371
Delaware City, Delaware 19706
Catalog: $1.00 (refundable).

Florida

Daisy Way Herbs
213 S. Rosemary Avenue
West Palm Beach, Florida 33401
(561) 653-7157

The Emerald Garden
3111 Forty-Fifth Street, Suite 2
West Palm Beach, Florida 33407
(561) 683-7679; fax: (561) 683-2006

Illinois

Full Moon Botanicals
409 E. Church Street
Sandwich, Illinois 60548
(815) 786-6222

Indiana

American Herbs
P.O. Box 627
Ellettsville, Indiana 47429

Iowa

Frontier Cooperative Herbs
3021 Seventy-Eighth Street
Norway, Iowa 52318
(800) 669-3275

Louisiana

African Harvest
3212 Tulane Avenue
New Orleans, Louisiana 70119
(504) 822-2200

Brier Rose Herb, Inc.
8632 Highway 23
Belle Chasse, Louisiana 70037
(504) 392-7499

Coyote Creek
9382 Island Road
St. Francisville, Louisiana 70775
Catalog: $1.00.

Maryland

St. John's Herb Garden
7711 Hillmeade Road
Bowie, Maryland 20720
(301) 262-5302; fax: (301) 262-2489

Missouri

Blessed Herbs
Route 5, Box 1042
Ava, Missouri 65608

Willow Rain Herb Farm
P.O. Box 15
Grubville, Missouri 63041

New Hampshire

Willow Keep
R.R. No. 3, N. River Road
Milford, New Hampshire 03055

New Jersey

Herbalist and Alchemist
P.O. Box 553
Broadway, New Jersey 08803
(908) 689-9020

Well-Sweep Herb Farm
205 Mt. Bethel Road
Port Murray, New Jersey 07865
(908) 852-5390
Catalog: $2.00.

New Mexico

Seeds of Change
P.O. Box 15700
Santa Fe, New Mexico 87506
(505) 438-8080; fax: (505) 438-7052

New York

Angelica's Herbs
147 First Avenue
New York, New York 10003
(212) 529-4335

Aphrodisia
264 Bleecker Street
New York, New York 10014
(212) 989-6440; fax: (212) 989-8027

Green Terrestrial
Box 41, Route 9-W
Milton, New York 12547

Harvest Herb Company
R.R. 3, Box 51
Creighton Road
Malone, New York 12953
(518) 483-0030

The Herbal Bear
304 W. Seventy-Fifth Street, Suite 16-E
New York, New York 10023
(212) 532-9322

Workshops and apprenticeships in herbal studies. Classes offered in New York City and the northern Catskills.

Herbs From the Forest
P.O. Box 655
Bearsville, New York 12409

Monarda Herbal Apothecary
P.O. Box 505
Rosendale, New York 12472
(914) 658-7044

Free catalog.

Nature's Own
P.O. Box 563
Hogansburg, New York 13655

Westview Herb Farm
P.O. Box 3462
Poughkeepsie, New York 12603

Catalog: $1.00.

Wise Woman Center
P.O. Box 64
Woodstock, New York 12498

North Carolina

The Herbal Sage
P.O. Box 1324
Hamlet, North Carolina 28345
(910) 582-0792

Ohio

Equinox Botanicals
Route 1, Box 71
Rutland, Ohio 45775

Ohio Hempery
7002 Route 329
Guysville, Ohio 45735
(800) 289-4367; (614) 662-4367

Oklahoma

Tranquil Thymes
P.O. Box 721688
Norman, Oklahoma 73070
(405) 364-2041
Free catalog.

Oregon

Atlantis Rising
7915 S.E. Stark Street
Portland, Oregon 97215

Herb Pharm
P.O. Box 116
Williams, Oregon 97544

Starflower
885 McKinley Street
Eugene, Oregon 97402

The Thyme Garden Herb Company
20546 Alsea Highway
Alsea, Oregon 97324
(514) 487-8671
Catalog: $2.00.

Two Dragons Trading Company
4638 S.W. Beaverton
Hillsdale Highway
Portland, Oregon 97221
(800) 896-3724

Pennsylvania

Ageless Herbs
645 West Liberty Road
Slippery Rock, Pennsylvania 16057
(412) 794-8587

Penn Herb Company
603 N. Second Street
Philadelphia, Pennsylvania 19123

Village Herb Shop
P.O. Box 173
1151 Division Highway
Blue Ball, Pennsylvania 17506
(717) 354-6494

Vermont

Crystal Garden Herbs
438 Will Dean Road
Springfield, Vermont 05156
(802) 885-5500

Free sixteen-page catalog.

Herb Closet
P.O. Box 964
Montpelier, Vermont 05602

Northeast Herb Association
P.O. Box 146
Marshfield, Vermont 05658

Write for information regarding its classes, meetings, and newsletter.
It also offers a catalog of practitioners, teachers, and herb suppliers.

Purple Shutter Herbs
100 Main Street
Burlington, Vermont 05401
(802) 865-HERB

Virginia

Amrita Herbals
Route 1, Box 737
Floyd, Virginia 24380

Church Hill Herbs
608 Chimborazo Boulevard
Richmond, Virginia 23223

Catalog: $1.00.

Garden Medicinals and Culinaries
P.O. Box 320
Earlysville, Virginia 22936

Catalog: $1.00.

Washington

Herb Technology / Sunshine Oils
1305 N.E. Forty-Fifth Street, Suite 205
Seattle, Washington 98105
(800) 659-2077; (206) 547-2007; fax: (206) 547-4240

Hermit's Grove Herb Closet
9724 One Hundred Thirty-Second Avenue N.E.
Kirkland, Washington 98033

Mountain Spirit Herbals
P.O. Box 368
Port Townsend, Washington 98368
(800) 817-7233

Catalog: $1.00.

Pan's Forest Herb Company
411 Ravens Road
Port Townsend, Washington 98368

School of Herbal Medicine
P.O. Box 168
Suquamish, Washington 98392

Send a long self-addressed stamped envelope for information about its correspondence course.

Wisconsin

Avonlea Organic Herb Farm
Balsam Lake, Wisconsin 54810
(715) 857-5091

Harvest and Hearth Herb Farm
1964 Seventieth Avenue
Dresser, Wisconsin 54009
(715) 755-2130

Wyoming

Elk Mountain Herbs
214 Ord Street
Laramie, Wyoming 82070
(307) 742-0404

Canada

Herbally Yours
P.O. Box 612
Kamloops, British Columbia V2C 5L7

Richter's Herbs
357 Highway 47
Goodwin, Ontario L0C 1A0
(905) 640-6677; fax: (905) 640-6641

Wide World of Herbs
11 St. Catherine Street E.
Montreal, Quebec H2X 1K3

8

Magickal and
Metaphysical Shops

Where can a modern Witch go to buy dragon's blood ink, ready-made love potions, pentacle-embroidered capes, or handmade ritual tools that have been consecrated and charged with power during the correct phase of the Moon?

Wiccans, Pagans, and other magickal folks have very special needs. We cannot simply walk into the local Kmart, supermarket, or religious supply store and find the items we need and want for our worship and spellcraft.

Fortunately there are special shops designed just for us and our Witchy needs. These shops are listed alphabetically by state, and contain at least the basic magick paraphernalia (books, incense, candles, ritual tools, jewelry, and so forth). Many also carry handmade and rare, one-of-a-kind items. This section also lists shops located throughout Canada, Great Britain, and Germany.

If you do not live in an area that has (or is within reasonable driving distance to) a Witchcraft supply store, or if you are still in the "broom closet" and do not want to run the risk of having friends, coworkers, or family members spot you walking out of a New Age bookstore, shopping bags overflowing with magickal merchandise, then mail order is your best bet (see chapter 9).

Many of the shops and mail order businesses listed in the following two sections are owned and operated by practicing Pagans. They understand your needs, and if you are new to the Craft, more than likely they will be happy to offer you advice, recommend certain books and products, and even arrange for special orders (if they offer custom-made items and services).

Alabama

Enchanted Treasures   7914 Memorial Parkway SW. (E-14), Huntsville, Alabama 35802; (256) 650-0020

Ibis Books   1219-B Jordan Lane, Huntsville, Alabama 35816

Lodestar Books   2020 Eleventh Avenue S., Birmingham, Alabama 35205

Shadows and Light Shoppe   401 8th Street SE., Decatur, Alabama 35601; (256) 301-4507

Alaska

Black Elk   5911 Old Seward Highway, Anchorage, Alaska 99518; (907) 562-2703

The Source   329 E. Fifth Avenue, Anchorage, Alaska 99501; (907) 274-5850

Arkansas

Cauldron Bubbles   Corner of Main and Green, Havana, Arkansas 72842; (501) 476-2071

Dagda's Cauldron   101 W Hinkley Street, P.O. Box 416, Brookland, Arkansas 72417; (870) 932-2040

Enchanted Garden   404 S. Washington Street, El Dorado, Arkansas 71730; (870) 862-8900

Medea's Grove   Corner of N. Tenth and "B", Fort Smith, Arkansas 72901; (501) 783-4881

Mystic Encounters   1630 S. Eighth Street, No. 1 (Southgate Shopping Center), Rogers, Arkansas 72756; (501) 621-5910

Mystic Pleasures   1809 Fort Street, Barling, Arkansas 72923; (501) 452-9700

Arizona

Abby's Candles 'N' Things   6914 West Acoma Drive, Peoria, Arizona 85381; (623) 878-1910

Abracadabra   4613 E. Thomas Road, Phoenix, Arizona 85018; (602) 840-2041

Alpha Books and Gifts   1928 E. McDowell Road, Phoenix, Arizona 85006; (602) 253-1223

Arazmesa   2115 S Arizona Avenue No. 6, Yuma, Arizona 85364; (520) 539-9692

Divine Circle of the Sacred Grove   16845 Twenty-ninth Avenue No. 1346, Phoenix, Arizona 85023; (602) 433-7951

Eye of the Vortex Bookcenter   1405 W. Highway 89A, Sedona, Arizona 86336; (520) 282-5614

Fantasia—A Magickal Place   5108 North Seventh Street, Phoenix, Arizona 85014; (602) 265-4065

Illusions   1777 West Camelback Road, B-100, Phoenix, Arizona, 85015; (602) 265-2935

Jan Ross New Age Books and Gifts   3415 W. Glendale Avenue, Glendale, Arizona 85051; (602) 841-4933

Lady Sprite's Cupboard   3184 E. Indian School Road, Phoenix, Arizona 85016; (602) 956-3539

Magickal Moon   113 E. Southern Ave, Tempe, Arizona 85282; (480) 303-8368

Moon and Stars Unlimited   P.O. Box 97672, Phoenix, Arizona 85060; (602) 432-4357

MoonRise Herbs and Gifts   51420 Highway 60, Wickenburg, Arizona 85390; (520) 684-1077

New Age Books and Gifts   6019 N. Thirty-Fifth Avenue, Scottsdale, Arizona 85254; (602) 841-4933

New Age Emporium   Town and Country Shopping Center, Twentieth St and Camelback Road, Phoenix, Arizona, 85016; (602) 957-2956

Peace of Mind   6061 E. Broadway, Tucson, Arizona 85711; (800) 960-9695

Phoenix Rising Books and Gifts   2380 S. Madison Avenue, Yuma, Arizona 85364; (602) 997-0878

Rainbow Moods Metaphysical Bookstore   3532 E. Grant Road, Tucson, Arizona 85716; (520) 326-9643

Sacred Grove   5115 N. Twenty-seventh Avenue, Phoenix, Arizona 85017; (602) 789-1530

Tall Pines Bookshoppe   112 West Bonita, Payson, Arizona 85541; (520) 472-9700

Wizards World   432 W. Fry Boulevard, Sierra Vista, Arizona 85635; (520) 439-4833

Zodiac Cafe and Books   7611 W. Thomas (Desert Sky Mall), Phoenix, Arizona 85033; (602) 846-3437

California (Southern)

A Krystal Moon   21168 Beach Boulevard, Huntington Beach, California 92648; (714) 960-8798

Akashic Record Books   1414 E. Thousand Oaks Boulevard, Thousand Oaks, California 91362; (805) 495-5824

Alexandria II   567 S. Lake Avenue, Pasadena, California 91101; (818) 792-7885

Ancient Friends   38 E. Holly Street, Pasadena, California 91101; (818) 304-0589

Beyond Reality   21831 Sherman Way, Canoga Park, California 91303; (818) 888-0487

Bodhi Tree Books   8585 Melrose, Los Angeles, California 90069; (310) 659-1733

Botanica Momma Roots   3512 Adams Avenue, San Diego, California 92116; (619) 563-9110

Celtic Moon   3275-C Adams Avenue, San Diego, California 92116; (619) 640-4420

Controversial Books   3021 University Avenue, San Diego, California 92104; (619) 296-1560

Crystal Cave   891 Baker Street, Suite A16, Costa Mesa, California 92626; (714) 754-1151

The Crystal Cave   415 W. Foothill Boulevard, Claremont, California 91771; (909) 626-0398

Crystal Fantasy   264 N. Palm Canyon Drive, Palm Springs, California 92262; (760) 322-7799

Dark Delicacies   4213 W. Burbank Boulevard, Burbank, California 91505; (818) 556-6660; (888) DARKDEL

Desert Enchantments   74-800 Sheryl Drive, Suite 10-4, Palm Desert, California 92260; (619) 668-2074

Dragons Marsh   3744 Main Street, Riverside, California 92501; (909) 276-1116

Dream Merchant   3326 Adams Avenue, San Diego, California 92116; (619) 563-5591

Enchanted Herbs   6600 Gretna Avenue, Whittier, California 90601; (562) 699-1555

Eye of the Cat   3314 E. Broadway, Long Beach, California 90803; (562) 438-3569

Firdous-Abir Book Shop   320 E. Hillcrest Boulevard, Inglewood, California 90301; (310) 677-5110

Fourteen Angels Metaphysical Book Shop   10875 Washington Boulevard, Culver City, California 90230; (310) 842-9700

The Goddess Shop   8253½ Santa Monica Boulevard, West Hollywood, California 90046; (213) 848-8332

Good Scents   461-D Tennessee Street, Redlands, California 92373; (909) 335-6160

Harms None   2116 E. Fourth Street, Long Beach, California 90814; (562) 433-7181

House of Hermetic   5338 Hollywood Boulevard, Los Angeles, California 90027; (213) 466-7553

Journey Home   2950 Johnson Drive, Ventura, California 93001; (805) 650-8272

Karma Kandles   4279 Whittier Street, San Diego, California 92107; (619) 223-4509

Kindred Spirits   813 W. Foothill Boulevard, Claremont, California 91711; (909) 626-2434

Lady of the Lake   27326 Jefferson, Suite 19, Temecula, California 92590; (909) 694-0112

The Latest Thing   270 E. Seventeenth Street, Costa Mesa, California 92627; (949) 645-6211

Le Sorciere   1281 University Avenue, Suite A, San Diego, California 92103; (619) 29-WITCH

Lighthouse New Age Books   7856 Girard Avenue, La Jolla, California 92037; (619) 459-6062

Magic Bookstore   2306 Highland Avenue, National City, California 91950; (619) 477-5260

Malibu Shaman   23410 Civic Center Way, no. B-2, Malibu, California 90265; (310) 456-5617

Moon Gate Graphics   305 W. Torrance Boulevard, Carson, California 90745

Northern Mists   878 Jackman, no. 103, El Cajon, California 92020

Old Age Metaphysical Country Store   7152 Alabama Avenue, Canoga Park, California 91303; (818) 883-7115

Page One   1196 E. Walnut Street, Pasadena, California 91106; (626) 798-8694; outside of California: (800) 359-8694

Panpipes Magickal Marketplace   1641 Cahuenga Boulevard, Hollywood, California 90028; (323) 462-7078

Pathways Books and Gifts   2650 Jamacha Road No. 155, El Cajon, California 92019; (619) 660-3838

Pegasus Metaphysical Books   538 Redondo Avenue, Long Beach, California 90814; (310) 434-3869

Points of Light   4358 Stearns Street, Long Beach, California 90815; (562) 985-3388

Psychic Eye Bookshop   13435 Ventura Boulevard, Sherman Oaks, California 91401; (818) 906-8263

Psychic Eye Bookshop   21800 Ventura Boulevard, Woodland Hills, California 91364; (818) 340-0033

Psychic Eye Bookshop   1011 N. Olive Avenue, Burbank, California 91502; (818) 845-8831

Psychic Eye Bookshop   218 Main, Venice, California 90294;
(310) 396-0110

Psychic Eye Bookshop   3902 Pacific Coast Highway, Torrance,
California 90505; (310) 378-7754

Psychic Eye Bookshop   702 Pearl, La Jolla, California 92037;
(619) 551-8877

Psychic Reality   10240 Topanga Canyon Boulevard, Chatsworth,
California 91311; (818) 772-6862

Pyramid Book Shop   16727 Bear Valley Road No. 140, Hesperia,
California 92345; (760) 949-0055

Raven's Flight   5042 Vineland Avenue, North Hollywood,
California 91601; (888) 847-2836

Raven's Loft   252 East Grand Avenue, Escondido, California 92025;
(760) 746-5636

Shiva Imports   1335 Third Street, Santa Monica, California 90401;
(310) 394-1333

Sorcerer's Shop   8246½ Santa Monica Boulevard, Hollywood,
California 90046; (213) 656-1563

Starcrafts   1909 Cable Street, San Diego, California 92107; (619)
224-4923

The Temple of Good Things   6241 W. Eighty-seventh Street,
Westchester, California 90045; (310) 670-3772

Visions and Dreams Emporium   1804 Newport Boulevard, Costa
Mesa, California 92637; (949) 650-0730

Witches' Brew   711 West Lancaster Boulevard, Lancaster, California
93551; (661) 940-9902

California (Northern)

13—Real Magick   911 Cedar Street, Santa Cruz, California 95060;
(831) 425-1313

Ancient Ways   4075 Telegraph Avenue, Oakland, California 94609;
(510) 653-3244

As You Wish   8397 North Lake Boulevard, Kings Beach, California
96143; (530) 546-9474

Assembly of Wicca   4715 Franklin, Sacramento, California 95820; (916) 455-0109

Atlantis Metaphysical Tape, Record, and Book Store   1540 Union Street, San Francisco, California 94102; (415) 775-7166

The Brass Unicorn   845 E. Fern, Fresno, California 93701; (559) 441-7107

The Cauldron   3025 McHenry Avenue, Suite J, Modesto, California 95350; (209) 526-2134

Circle of the Raven   2141 W. Yosemite Avenue, Manteca, California 95337; (209) 824-8786

Claire Light Books   1110 Petaluma Hill Road, Santa Rosa, California 95404

Creative Awareness Books   1120-C Fulton Avenue, Sacramento, California 95825

Curios and Candles   289 Divisadero, San Francisco, California 94117; (415) 863-5669

Dolphin Dream   1437 N. Broadway, Walnut Creek, California 94596; (925) 933-2342

Earth Central   3726 Taylor Road, Loomis, California 95652; (916) 652-8084

Earthspirit Books   3315 Sacramento Street, no. 525, San Francisco, California 94118

East-West Books   1170 El Camino Real, Menlo Park, California 94025

East-West Bookshop   2216 Fair Oaks Boulevard, Sacramento, California 95825; (916) 920-3837

Enchanted Treasures   2185 Churn Creek Road, Suite J, Redding, California 96002; (530) 222-0673

Field's Books   1419 Polk Street, San Francisco, California 94109

Her Place   6635 Madison Avenue, Sacramento, California 95841; (916) 961-1058

Legends of Fantasy   5670 West End Road No. 4, Arcata, California 95521; (800) 322-6040

Minerva's Books   1027 Alma Street, Palo Alto, California 94301; (650) 326-2006

Open Secret Bookstore   923 C Street, San Rafael, California 94901; (415) 457-4191

Pandora's Legacy   624 Plumas Street, Yuba City, California 95991; (530) 751-7664

Planet Earth Rising   2931 Sunrise Boulevard, Suite 125, Rancho Cordova, California 95742; (916) 631-0249

Psychic Eye   301 Fell Street, San Francisco, California 94102; (415) 863-9997

The Rainbow Bridge   351 North Lake Boulevard, Tahoe City, California 96145; (530) 583-4323

Raven in the Grove   505 Lighthouse Avenue, Suite 103, Pacific Grove, California 93950; (408) 649-6057

The Sacred Grove   924 Soquel Avenue, Santa Cruz, California 95062; (831) 423-1949

San Jose Bookshop   1231 Kentwood, San Jose, California 95129; (408) 446-0590

Shambhala Booksellers   2482 Telegraph Avenue, Berkeley, California 94704; (415) 848-8443

Spellworks, Inc.   503 Elm Street, Westwood, California 96137; (530) 256-2248

Sunrise Bookshop   3054 Telegraph Avenue, Berkeley, California 94705

The Sword and Rose   85 Carl Street, San Francisco, California 94117

Town and Country Books   420 Town and Country Village, San Jose, California 95128

The Tree of Life   918 Twenty-Fifth Street, Sacramento, California 95816; (916) 447-3336

Whispered Prayers   932 Eighth Avenue, Suite D, Chico, California 95926; (530) 894-2927

Colorado

Alternate Realities   3170 E. Fourth Avenue, Durango, Colorado 81301; (800) 801-9943

Celebration   2209 W. Colorado Avenue, Colorado Springs, Colorado 80904; (719) 634-1855

Coven Gardens   P.O. Box 1064, Boulder, Colorado 80306

Crystalight Psychic Center   1562 S. Parker Road, Denver, Colorado 80231

Herbs and Arts   2015 E. Colfax Avenue, Denver, Colorado 80206; (303) 388-2544

Isis Bookstore   5701 E. Colfax Avenue, Denver, Colorado 80220; (303) 321-0867; (800) 808-0867

Kristin's Creations   1113 Mathews Street, Fort Collins, Colorado 80524; (970) 493-6035

Lighthouse New Age Books   1201 Pearl, Boulder, Colorado 80302; (303) 939-8355

Lighthouse New Age Books   1842 Thirtieth Street, Boulder, Colorado 80302; (303) 444-6989

Metaphysical Bookstore   9511 E. Colfax Avenue, Aurora, Colorado 80010

Pandora's Box   1135 N. Lincoln, no. 3, Loveland, Colorado 80537

The Phoenix   451 Main Street, Delta, Colorado 81416; (970) 874-4723

Quantum Alchemy   1209 Ninth Avenue, Denver, Colorado 80218; (303) 863-0548

Spirit Ways   3301 E. Colfax Avenue, Denver, Colorado 80206; (303) 331-1070

Snowy Creek Studios   620 Main Street, Fairplay, Colorado 80440; (719) 836-2050

So What?   506 Fifth Street, Georgetown, Colorado 80444

Spirit Wise   6590 S. Broadway, Littleton, Colorado 80121; (303) 730-2974

Wings Metaphysical Books and Gifts   3559 W. Forty-fourth Avenue, Denver, Colorado 80211; (303) 561-0387

Connecticut

Avalon   9 N. Main Street, South Norwalk, Connecticut 06854; (203) 838-5928

Calista's Curios   8 Salem Marketplace, Salem, Connecticut 06420; (860) 885-1191

The Cosmic Cat   30 Front Street, Putnam, Connecticut 06260; (860) 963-9500

Curious Goods Witchcraft Shop   415 Campbell Avenue, West Haven, Connecticut 06516; (203) 932-1193

Edge of the Woods Grocery   279 Edgewood, New Haven, Connecticut 06511; (203) 787-1055

Gaian Goods   222 Bradley Avenue, Bldg. 8, Unit 8B, Waterbury, Connecticut 06708; (203) 757-0102

The Goddess Shoppe   829 Main Street, Manchester, Connecticut 06040; (860) 533-1466

The Goddess Shoppe II   1264 Main Street, Coventry, Connecticut 06238; (860) 742-4178

Incantations   16 Ann Street, Meriden, Connecticut 06450; (203) 238-9097

The Magik Mirror   321 Boston Post Road, Milford, Connecticut 06460; (203) 876-8832

Moon Beams   17 W. Main Street, Rockville, Connecticut 06066; (860) 870-1001

Mystical Horizons   Route 27 N., P.O. Box 536, Old Mystic, Connecticut 06355; (860) 572-9191

New Age Books and Games   1131 Tolland Turnpike, Suite 0-210, Manchester, Connecticut 06040

Pandora's Box   209 W. Thames Street (Route 32 South), Norwich, Connecticut 06360; (860) 887-4501

Purple Moon   45 Padanaram Road, Danbury, Connecticut 06811; (203) 730-2412

Serendipity   328 E. Main Street, Unit 3, Branford, Connecticut 06405; (203) 481-1213

Delaware

Ancient Treasures   406 S. Governors Avenue, Dover, Delaware 19904; (302) 735-4757

Bell, Book, and Candle   114 B Loockerman Street, Dover, Delaware 19901; (302) 678-4545

Book Thrift   Tri-State Mall/Lower Level, I-95 and Naamans Road, Claymont, Delaware 19703

Hen's Teeth Bookstore   214 N. Market Street, Wilmington, Delaware 19801

Soulstice   276 E. Main Street, Suite 11, Newark, Delaware 19711; (302) 456-1939

Trinket's   4377 Highway One, Rehoboth Beach, Delaware 19971; (302) 226-2466

Florida

Aquarian Center for Body, Mind, and Spirit   5600 Tamiami Trail North, Naples, Florida 34108; (941) 597-3241

Athene   6851 Bird Road, Miami, Florida 33155

Awakenings Book and Gift Store   12189 U.S. Highway 1, no. 11, North Palm Beach, Florida 33480; (561) 691-0701; fax: (561) 691-0702

Blue Moon Spiritual Accessories   1560 N.W. Ninety-Ninth Avenue, Plantation, Florida 33322; (954) 370-8968; (888) 483-9399

Brigit Books and Gifts for the Spirit   3434 Fourth Street North, St. Petersburg, Florida 33704; (813) 522-5775

Center of Metaphysical Study   8683 Griffin, Cooper City, Florida 33328

Changing Times   911 Village Boulevard, Suite 806, West Palm Beach, Florida 33409; (561) 640-0496; fax: (561) 640-0286

Crystal Connection   1401 Gulf Boulevard, Indian Rocks Beach, Florida 33785; (813) 595-8131

Crystal Fantasy Bookstore (of the Sacred Light Temple)   5111 Coconut Creek Parkway, Margate, Florida 33063; (954) 973-0903

The Crystal Garden   2610 N. Federal Highway, Boynton Beach, Florida 33435; (561) 369-2836

Earth Gifts   1027 Park Street, Jacksonville, Florida 32204; (904) 356-3073

Earth Wisdom   5775 S. University Drive, Davie, Florida 33328; (954) 680-4008

Earth's Aura Metaphysical Center   5385 Stirling Road, Davie, Florida 33314; (954) 321-3477

The Emerald Garden   3111 Forty-Fifth Street, Suite 2, West Palm Beach, Florida 33407; (561) 683-7679; fax: (561) 683-2006

Gladstar Books   154 Cone, Ormand, Florida 32074

Inner Light House   228 Sixth Avenue S., Jacksonville Beach, Florida 32250; (904) 249-6307

Inner Light Metaphysical Center and Bookstore   5425 N. State Road 7, Tamarac, Florida 33317; (954) 730-7790

Iris Moon   1401 S. Military Trail, West Palm Beach, Florida 33415: (561) 357-0230

Jeani's Secrets New Age Bookstore   4469 S. Congress Avenue, Suite 121, Lake Worth, Florida 33461; (561) 642-3255

Kemet House   4315 Brentwood Avenue, Jacksonville, Florida 32206; (904) 356-3922

Kenley Gifts and Books   4966 N. University Drive, Lauderhill, Florida 33351; (954) 749-9409

The Lighthouse Bookstore   505 Fifth Avenue S., Naples, Florida 33940; (941) 261-6619

Magical Forest   2072 N. University Drive, Pembroke Pines, Florida 33024; (954) 438-9399; (954) 438-9398

Magickal Forest   5725 Hollywood, Hollywood, Florida 33021

Merlin's Books   2568 E. Fowler Avenue, Tampa, Florida 33612; (813) 972-1766

Mi-World   9808 N.W. Eightieth, no. 10-N, Hialeah Gardens, Florida 33016

Momma's Medica   444 Brickell, Miami, Florida 33131

Mystic Goddess Metaphysical Center   12041 Sixty-Sixth Street N., Largo, Florida 34643; (813) 530-9994

Mystical Creations   4410 W. Hillsborough Avenue, Tampa, Florida 33614; (813) 877-8177; fax: (813) 871-5127

New Age Books and Things   4401 N. Federal Highway, Fort Lauderdale, Florida 33308; (954) 771-0026

The 9th Chakra   817 Lincoln Road, South Beach, Miami, Florida 33133; (305) 538-0671

A Novel Thought   1227 E. Mohawk, Tampa, Florida 33604

Other Worlds   722 Pasadena Avenue S., St. Petersburg, Florida 33707; (813) 345-2800; (888) 967-5370

Planet Earth Book Center   Royal Palm Square, Fort Myers, Florida 33907; (941) 939-3969

Rainbow Bridge   7593 S. Dixie Highway, West Palm Beach, Florida 33405; (561) 585-2000

Road to Enlightenment   5522 Hanley Road, Tampa, Florida 33612; (813) 885-4948

Secret Garden   321 Northlake Boulevard, Suite 104, North Palm Beach, Florida 33480; (561) 844-7556

Shining Through   426 E. Atlantic Avenue, Delray Beach, Florida 33483; (561) 276-8559

Spiral Circle   750 N. Thornton, Orlando, Florida 32803; (407) 894-9854

Tomes and Treasures Books   408 S. Howard Avenue, Tampa, Florida 33609; (813) 251-9368

Treasures Metaphysical Bookshop   4355 W. Kennedy Boulevard, Tampa, Florida 33609; (813) 287-BOOK (2665)

Under the Stars   1760 N.W. Thirty-Eighth, Lauderhill, Florida 33311

Vortech   (407) 327-0050 (Call for address and business hours.)

WHVH Psychic Bookshop   4578 St. John's Avenue, Jacksonville, Florida 32210; (904) 387-2064

The Wizard's Attic   560 Southard Street, Key West, Florida 33040; (305) 294-6180; fax: (305) 294-2807

Georgia

The Black Cauldron   Apple Valley Drive, Augusta, Georgia 30906; (706) 560-1121

Crystal Blue   1168 Euclid Avenue N.E., Atlanta, Georgia 30307; (404) 522-4605

Isis Metaphysical Center   1400 Third Avenue, Columbus, Georgia 31901; (706) 561-7844

Mark My Words Magick Happens   4048 Belair Road (Dyess Pkwy), Augusta, Georgia 30909; (706) 854-8653

Mother Wolf's Magickal Designs   314 Stations Avenue, Woodstock, Georgia 30189; (770) 517-5990

Phoenix and Dragon Bookstore   5531 Roswell Road, Sandy Springs, Georgia 30342; (404) 255-5207

The Silver Lotus   155 Powers Ferry Road, Marietta, Georgia 30067; (800) 874-5704; (770) 973-7000; fax (770) 973-1400

Touch of Magick   1722 Watson Boulevard, Warner Robins, Georgia 31093; (478) 929-3437

Hawaii

The Broom Closet   118 Kam Avenue, Rm 2 Upstairs, Hilo, Hawaii 96720; (808) 933-1043

Prosperity Corner   3619 Waialae Avenue, Honolulu, Hawaii 96816; (808) 732-8870

Sedona   Ward Centre, 1200 Ala Moana Boulevard, Honolulu, Hawaii 96814; (808) 591-8010

Sirius Books   2320 Young Street, Honolulu, Hawaii 96826; (808) 947-4910

Serendipity   2885 S. King Street, No. 202, Honolulu, Hawaii 96826; (808) 949-4711

Idaho

The Blue Unicorn   107 N. Ninth Street, Boise, Idaho 83702; (208) 345-9390

Crone's Cupboard   3013 Overland Road, Boise, Idaho 83705; (208) 333-0831

Moonrise Mountain   1609 N. Orchard, Boise, Idaho 83706; (208) 323-6085

The Mystic Topaz   6419 W. Ustick, Boise, Idaho 83704; (208) 323-4557

The New Stone Age   701 S. Latah, Boise, Idaho 83705; (208) 338-1328

Purple Moon Crystal Company   50 E. Main Street, P.O. Box 549, Lava Hot Springs, Idaho 83246; (208) 776-5475

Totem   1214 E. Main Street, Burley, Idaho 83318; (208) 678-4526

Illinois

Alchemy, The Eclectic Rock and Metaphysical Shop   815 Plainfield Road, Joliet, Illinois 60436; (815) 722-7467

Arum Solis Books and Supplies   5113 N. Clark Street, Chicago, Illinois 60640; (312) 334-2120

Augustine's Spiritual Goods   3114 S. Halsted Street, Chicago, Illinois 60608; (312) 326-3088; fax: (312) 326-6010

Awakenings   3006 Georgetown Road, Suite A, Westville, Illinois 61883; (217) 267-3227

Back to the Source   610 E. State Street, Rockford, Illinois 61104; (815) 987-0181

Eclectic Soul   38305 N. Sheridan Road, Beach Park, Illinois 60087; (847) 263-3030

Explorations   934 N. Bourland, Peoria, Illinois 61606; (309) 674-1242

Golden Spiral   205 S. Arlington Heights Road, Arlington Heights, Illinois 60006; (800) 357-2719

Insight Books   505 S. First, Champaign, Illinois 61820

Isis Rising   7005 N. Glenwood Avenue, Chicago, Illinois 60657

Light of the Moon   809 Dempster Street, Evanston, Illinois 60201; (708) 492-0492

Little Shop of Incense   1210 W. Granville, Chicago, Illinois 60660

Little Shoppe of Auras   109 E. Bethalto Drive, Bethalto, Illinois 62010; (618) 377-9055

Minor Arcana   1852 N. Damen Avenue, Chicago, Illinois 60647; (773) 252-1389

Moon Mystique   614 W. Belmont Avenue, Chicago, Illinois 60657; (312) 665-9016

Mystical Isle   116 N Main Street, Creve Coeur, Illinois 61610; (309) 698-0406

Occult Bookstore   1561 N. Milwaukee Avenue, Chicago, Illinois 60622; (312) 292-0995

Practical Magick   633 North LaGrange Road, Frankfort, Illinois 60423; (815) 464-4817

Sacred Space   603 S. Wright Street, Champaign, Illinois 61820; (217) 367-2070

Sanctuary Crystals   5524 Cal-Sag Road, Alsip, Illinois 60658; (708) 396-2833

The Sunshine House   1504 N. Eighth, Vandalia, Illinois 62471

Wings of Wisdom   Pinetree Plaza, 1117 Plainfield Road, Suite 4, Joliet, Illinois 60435; (815) 727-7863

Indiana

Crystal Cove   1831 Wells Street, Ft. Wayne, Indiana 46808; (219) 422-3582

Dreamweaver   104 W. Walnut Street, Kokomo, Indiana 46901; (317) 868-0343

Illuminations   300 S. Fourth Street, Richmond, Indiana 47374; 765-939-0939

The Mind's Eye   5022 Madison Avenue, Indianapolis, Indiana 46227; (317) 783-2788

Moonshadows   504 Main Street, Beech Grove, Indiana 46107; (317) 784-8951

Quarter Moon Curios   304 S. Walnut Street, Muncie, Indiana 47305; (317) 284-5489

White Raven   201 Front Street, Lawrenceburg, Indiana 47025; 812-537-1544

World of Wisdom   5142 Madison Avenue, Suite 4, Indianapolis, Indiana 46227; (317) 787-3005

Iowa

The Atlantean   315 E. Fifth Street, Des Moines, Iowa 50309; (515) 883-1227

Happy Medium Bookstore and Coffee Bar   1251 Seventy-third
Street, Suite C, Des Moines, Iowa 50311; (515) 279-6888

Inner Dimensions   555 Walnut Street, Suite 206B, Des Moines, Iowa
50309; (515) 244-5596

Moon Mystique   114½ E. College Street, Iowa City, Iowa 52240; (319)
338-5752; fax, (319) 337-6761

RA Enterprises   1022 Mount Street, Davenport, Iowa 52803; (319)
322-0803

Kansas

The Crystal Window   2003 S.W. Gage Boulevard, Topeka, Kansas
66604; (913) 271-5338

The Enchanted Willow Alchemy Shoppe   418 S.W. Sixth Street,
Topeka, Kansas 66603; (785) 235-3776

Journey Books and Gifts   120 N. Hillside Street, Wichita, Kansas
67214; (316) 684-6951

Life and Light   10920 Shawnee Mission Parkway, Shawnee, Kansas
66203; (913) 268-1460

Magical Mystical Connection   1728 S. Seneca Street, Wichita, Kansas
67213; (316) 262-3512

The Renaissance Shoppe   127 E. Fourth Avenue, Hutchinson, Kansas
67501; (316) 662-4170

Kentucky

Babylon's End Percussion   8830 E. Bend Road, Burlington, Kentucky
41005; (606) 689-5275

Moonbeams and Angels Wings   Highway 53, Shelbyville, Kentucky
40601; (502) 223-5276

Nature's Magic   2018 Brownsboro Road, Louisville, Kentucky 40206;
(502) 895-5848

The Obsidian Horse   1058 Bardstown Road, Louisville, Kentucky
40204; (502) 589-5665

Peace Offerings   1370 Center Street, Bowling Green, Kentucky
42101; (502) 846-2674

Louisiana

Barksdale Enterprises   7877 Jefferson Highway, Baton Rouge, Louisiana 70809; (504) 927-2385

Bottom of the Cup Tea Room   616 Conti Street, New Orleans, Louisiana 70130; (504) 524-1997

Bottom of the Cup Tea Room and Gifts   732 Royal Street, New Orleans, Louisiana 70116; (504) 523-1204

Cosmic Crystal Bookstore and Emporium   7815 Maple, New Orleans, Louisiana 70118; (504) 861-3303

The Crescent Moon   736 Orleans Avenue, New Orleans, Louisiana 70116; (504) 528-9400

Life's Journey Bookstore   3313 Richland Avenue, Metairie, Louisiana 70001; (504) 885-2375; fax: (504) 454-5122

Marie Laveau House of Voodoo   739 Bourbon Street, New Orleans, Louisiana 70116; (504) 581-3751

Mystic Curio   831 Royal Street, New Orleans, Louisiana 70116; (504) 581-7150; orders: (888) 211-4754, (800) 728-7460; fax: (504) 581-7171

The Witches' Closet   521 St. Philip Street, New Orleans, Louisiana 70116; (504) 593-9222

Maine

Enchantments   16 McKown Street, Boothbay Harbor, Maine 04538; (207) 633-4992

Gulf of Maine Books   61 Main, Brunswick, Maine 04011

Kindred Spirits   6 Pleasant Street, Brunswick, Maine 04011; (207) 725-6140

Light of the Moon   324 Fore Street, Portland, Maine 04101; (207) 828-1710

Maryland

Cauldron Crafts   6611 Baltimore National Pike, Baltimore, Maryland 21228; (410) 744-2155

Celtic Renaissance   1922-A Fleet Street, Fells Point, Maryland 21231; (410) 327-1234

Circle West Books   38 West Street, Annapolis, Maryland 21401

Concatentions   8032 Main Street, Ellicott City, Maryland 21043

The Crystal Fox   366 Main Street, Laurel, Maryland 20707; (301) 317-1980

Crystal Visions   377A Gambrills Road, Gambrills, Maryland 21054; (410) 923-1191; fax: (410) 923-1192

Fire and Spirit Candles   36 W. Twenty-Fifth Street, Baltimore, Maryland 21218

Foxcraft   343 N. Market Street, Frederick, Maryland 21701; (301) 663-5463

Grandma's Candles Shop   113 W. Saratoga Street, Baltimore, Maryland 21201

Keepers of the Moon Garden   23905 Mervell Dean Road, Hollywood, Maryland 20636; (301) 373-4388

Legends Books   8101 Main Street, Ellicott City, Maryland 21043; (410) 465-0010; (800) 235-8097

North Door Books   4906 Berwyn, no. D, College Park, Maryland 20740

Port Market Place   1715 Eastern Avenue, Baltimore, Maryland 21231

Renaissance Books   8101 Main Street, Ellicott City, Maryland 21043; (410) 465-0010; (800) 235-8097

The Shaken Tree   1331-S Rockville Pike, Rockville, Maryland 20852; (301) 217-0884

The Turning Wheel Bookstore   Putty Hill Plaza, 7942-A Bel Air Road, Baltimore, Maryland 21236; (410) 882-8060

Massachusetts

Angelica of the Angels   7 Central Street, Salem, Massachusetts 01970; (508) 745-9355

Arsenic and Old Lace   318 Harvard Street, no. 10, Brookline, Massachusetts 02146; (617) 734-2455; (800) 279-7785

Black Cat Book Guild   131 Essex Street, Salem, Massachusetts 01970; (508) 744-9522

The Broom Closet   3–5 Central Street, Salem, Massachusetts 01970; (508) 741-3669

Celtic Shaman   462 Winthrop Street, Winthrop Old Farm, Rehoboth, Massachusetts 02769; (508) 252-6919

Center of Illumination   209 Main Street, Buzzards Bay, Massachusetts 02532; (508) 759-7359

Crow Haven Corner   125 Essex Street, Salem, Massachusetts 01970

Featherstones   Twinboro Crossing Plaza, Route 20 West, Marlboro, Massachusetts 01752; (508) 460-8048

Food for Thought   67 N. Pleasant, Amherst, Massachusetts 01002

Gypsy Moon   1780 Massachusetts Avenue, Cambridge, Massachusetts 02140; (617) 876-7095; fax: (617) 876-6203

Hare and Tortoise Bookery and Womynplace Gifts   92 Washington Street, Fairhaven, Massachusetts 02719; (508) 994-2408

Infinity   955 Ashley Boulevard, New Bedford, Massachusetts 02745; (508) 995-2221

The Magic Attic   251 W. Central, no. 189, Natick, Massachusetts 01760

Magic Circle   12 Main Street, Northampton, Massachusetts 01060; (413) 584-5016

Magick N' Mail   67 Washington Street, Haverhill, Massachusetts 01832; (508) 374-5340

Mysterious Wonders: A New Age Gift and Craft Shop   25 Park Street, Adams, Massachusetts 01220; (413) 743-9176

The New Moon   262 Main Street, Marlboro, Massachusetts 01752; (508) 481-7533

Of All Ages New Age Store and Cafe   289 Salem Road (Route 60), Medford, Massachusetts 02155; (617) 391-1313; (617) 391-3131

Open Doors Metaphysical Books and Gifts   351 Washington Street, Braintree, Massachusetts; (617) 843-8224

Pyramid Books: The New Age Store   214 Derby Street, Salem, Massachusetts 01970; (508) 745-7171

Ritual Arts   153 Harvard Avenue, Brighton, Massachusetts 02135; (617) 787-4157

Seven Stars   (formerly Shambalah Books), 58 John F. Kennedy Street, Cambridge, Massachusetts 02140; (617) 547-1317

Solstice Sun   10 Nason Street, Maynard, Massachusetts 01754; (508) 461-0040

Tarr and Feathers   74 Federal Street, Greenfield, Massachusetts 01301; (413) 733-3921; (800) 428-5126

Unicorn Books   1210 Massachusetts Avenue, Arlington, Massachusetts 02174

Wandering Moon   59 Bridge Street, Shelburne Falls, Massachusetts 01370; (413) 625-9667

The Wizard's Workshop   37 Rose Street, Watertown, Massachusetts 02172

Woman of Wands   Route 2 (in the River House), South Lee, Massachusetts 01260; (413) 243-4036

Your Last Chance   Museum Place Mall, Salem, Massachusetts 01970; (508) 745-9687

Michigan

Capricorn Moon   210½ Petoskey Street, Suite A, Petoskey, Michigan 49770; (616) 347-2235

Crazy Wisdom Books   206 N. Fourth, Ann Arbor, Michigan 48106; (734) 665-2757

Gundella's Witch Ways and Ware   6248 Middlebelt Road, Garden City, Michigan 48135; (313) 525-6666

Lite the Way   8161 Secor Road, P.O. Box 156, Lambertville, Michigan 48144; (313) 854-1514

Mayflower Books   2645 W. 12 Mile, Berkeley, Michigan 48072

New Age Metaphysical Bookstore   3920 N.W. River Road, Sanford, Michigan 48657; (517) 687-2271

Omni Spectrum   12083 Weiman, Hell, Michigan 48169

Roots and Wings   980 Winchester Avenue, Lincoln Park, Michigan 48146; (313) 388-9141

Sacred Sparks   5071 Mount Bliss Road, East Jordan, Michigan 49727; (616) 536-2704

Minnesota

Amazon Books   1612 Harmon Place, Minneapolis, Minnesota 55403

Crystals and Wolf   414 Division Street, Northfield, Minnesota 55057; (507) 663-7720

Evenstar Bookstore   2401 University Avenue W., St. Paul, Minnesota 55114; (612) 644-3727

Magus Books and Herbs   1316 S.E. Fourth Street, Minneapolis, Minnesota 55414; (612) 379-7669

Many Voices   727 Grand, St. Paul, Minnesota 55105

Mother Lode Book and Women's Center   813 W. Fiftieth Street, Minneapolis, Minnesota 55419; (612) 824-3825

New Age Bookstore   122 E. Second Street, Winona, Minnesota 55987; (507) 454-3947

Star Lightrider's Curious Goods   113 Pioneer Street, Detroit Lakes, Minnesota 56501; (218) 847-7872

Sunsight Books   616 W. Lake Street, Minneapolis, Minnesota 55408

Symbios: Art and the Arcane   125 S.E. Main Street, no. 148, Minneapolis, Minnesota 55414; (612) 331-7412

Mississippi

Bayou Magick   229 Highway 90, Waveland, Mississippi 39576; (228) 467-9527

Lemuria Books   238 Highland Village, 4500 I-55 North, Jackson, Mississippi 39211; (601) 366-7619; fax: (601) 366-7784

Silver Moon Shop   3709 Beachview Drive, Suite C, Ocean Springs, Mississippi 39564; (228) 872-0506

Summerland Magickal Shoppe   345 Ulman Avenue, Bay St. Louis, Mississippi 39520; (228) 467-5550

Missouri

The Alchemist Shop   2519 Woodson, Overland, Missouri 63114

Celestial Horizons   5337-F S. Campbell Avenue, Springfield, Missouri 65807; (417) 889-9940

Gypsie's Tea Room   Route 1, Box 23A, Carl Junction, Missouri 64834; (417) 649-7982

Renaissance Books and Gifts   1337 E. Montclair, Springfield, Missouri 65807; (417) 883-5161

White Light New Age Books   1607 W. Thirty-Ninth Street, Kansas City, Missouri 64111; (800) 340-0116

Montana

Barjon's   2718 Third Avenue N., Billings, Montana (59101); (406) 252-4398

Earth Spirit Books, Etc.   135 E. Main Street, Missoula, Montana 59802; (406) 721-2288

Odyssey   2 W. Main Street, Bozeman, Montana 59715; (406) 587-5521

Sacred Spaces   119 N. Twenty-ninth Street, Billings, Montana 59101; (406) 245-8820

Three Pheasants   710 Central Avenue, Great Falls, Montana 59401; (406) 452-6221

Nebraska

Heavenly Scentsations   7914 W. Dodge Road, No. 282, Omaha, Nebraska 68114; (402) 551-3828

My Sweet Angel Gift Shop   1502 W. Sixteenth Street, Scottsbluff, Nebraska 69361; (308) 632-7764

New Realities   1026 Howard Street, Omaha, Nebraska 68102; (402) 342-1863

The Next Millennium Book Center   2308 N. Seventy-second Street, Omaha, Nebraska 68134; (402) 393-1121

Synchronicity   4711 Huntington Avenue, Suite 3, Lincoln, Nebraska 68504; (402) 464-9163

The Way Home   3231 S. Thirteenth Street, Lincoln, Nebraska 68502; (402) 421-1701

Nevada

Bell, Book, and Candle   1725 E. Charleston Boulevard, Las Vegas, Nevada 89104; (702) 386-2950

Catz Eye   2784 E. Charleston Boulevard, Las Vegas, Nevada 89104; (702) 384-3330

Psychic Eye Book Shop   953 E. Sahara, Las Vegas, Nevada 89104; (702) 369-6622

Psychic Eye Book Shop   4810 Spring Mountain Road, Las Vegas, Nevada 89101; (702) 368-7785

Psychic Eye Book Shop   3315 E. Russell Road, Las Vegas, Nevada 89420; (702) 451-5777

Psychic Eye Book Shop   6848 W. Charleston, Las Vegas, Nevada 89117; (702) 255-4477

New Hampshire

The Dragon's Hoard   41 Greely, Nashua, New Hampshire 03061

Isis   38 N. Main Street, Concord, New Hampshire 03301

Open Sesame Books   13 Rumford Street, Concord, New Hampshire 03301

Our Lady of Enchantment Gift Shop   39 Amherst Street, Nashua, New Hampshire 03060; (603) 880-7237

Stuff 'n' Such / The Wishful Witch   1 Stoneybrook Lane, Finch Plaza, Exeter, New Hampshire 03833; (603) 778-7630

Willow Keep   R.R. No. 3, N. River Road, Milford, New Hampshire 03055

The Witchery   101 Manchester, Manchester, New Hampshire 03101

The Witches' Brew   206 Market, Portsmouth, New Hampshire 03801

New Jersey

Aquarius Rising   234 S. Broad Street, Woodbury, New Jersey 08096; (609) 384-1614

Botanica Che   336 State Street, Perth Amboy, New Jersey 08861; (732) 442-7884

Botanica Santa Barbara   6 Jersey Avenue, New Brunswick, New Jersey 07501; (732) 545-5373

The Equinox Books and Curios   108 Brighton Avenue, Long Branch, New Jersey 07740; (732) 222-0801

The Lion's Thorn   302 Somerset Street, North Plainfield, New Jersey 07060; (908) 769-5694

Merchant Street Booksellers   120 W. Merchant Street, Audubon, New Jersey 08106

The Middle Pillar   430 Bloomfield Avenue, Montclair, New Jersey 07042; (973) 744-2282

Mr. Bargain   291½ McClellan Street, Perth Amboy, New Jersey 08861; (732) 324-1974

Mystical Crossroads   604 White Horse Pike, Atco, New Jersey 08004; (609) 768-9868

The Philosopher's Stone   557 Route 46, Kenvil, New Jersey 08106

New Mexico

Abitha's   3906 Central Avenue S.E., Albuquerque, New Mexico 87108; (505) 262-0401

Blue Eagle Book and Metaphysical Center   8334 Lomas Boulevard N.E., Albuquerque, New Mexico 87102; (505) 268-3682

Brotherhood of Life Metaphysical Bookstore   110 Dartmouth S.E., Albuquerque, New Mexico 87106; (505) 255-8980

Crystal Gazer   301 San Pedro Drive N.E., Albuquerque, New Mexico 87108; (505) 260-1485

Full Circle Books   2205 Silver Avenue S.E., Albuquerque, New Mexico 87106; (505) 266-0022

Heaven on Earth   119 Harvard Drive S.E., Albuquerque, New Mexico 87106; (505) 262-0066

Just Imagine   481 E. Highway 66, Tijeras, New Mexico 87059; (505) 281-9611; Fax: (505) 281-0505

Moonrise Books   2617 Juan Tabo Boulevard N.E., Suite D, Albuquerque, New Mexico 87112; (505) 332-2665

Mystic Colors   1429 San Mateo Boulevard N.E., Albuquerque, New Mexico 87110; (505) 232-9851

Ochun and Company   506 W. Second Street, Roswell, New Mexico 88201; (505) 623-5597

Open Mind Metaphysical Booksellers   119 Harvard Drive S.E., Albuquerque, New Mexico 87106; (505) 262-0066

New York

Altar Egos Gallery   110 W. Houston Street, New York, New York 10012; (212) 677-9588

The Awareness Shop   180 Main Street, New Paltz, New York 12561; (914) 255-5756

Bell, Book, and Candle Esoterica   33 Lebanon Street, Hamilton, New York 13346; (315) 824-5409

Between the Worlds / Fe Fi Faux Studio   276 City Island Avenue, Bronx, New York 10464; (718) 885-2024

Blue White Rainbow   10 New Karner Road, Albany, New York 12203; (518) 869-6915

Botanica   327 W. Fayette, Syracuse, New York 13202; (315) 476-1442

Botanica Esoterica   712 Broadway, Brooklyn, New York 11206; (800) 567-5555

Camelot   94 St. Marks Place, New York, New York 10003; (212) 995-2185

Candle Therapy   213 W. Eightieth Street, New York, New York 10024; (212) 799-3000

Cosmic Vortex East   The Commons (107-A), Ithaca, New York 14850

Crystal Gardens   21 Greenwich Avenue, New York, New York 10014; (212) 366-1965

Curious Goods   4025 Bailey Avenue, Eggertsville, New York 14226; (716) 835-3157

Dreams East   1 Tower Place, Roslyn, New York 11576; (516) 484-5384

E and R Gifts and Graphics   215 Main Street, Binghamton, New York 12204; (607) 729-5305

Earth Emporium   511 Ridge Road, Lackawanna, New York 14218;
(716) 827-0623

Earthly Creations   401 First Street, Liverpool, New York 13088;
(315) 451-5484

Earth Magic Productions, Inc.   2166 Broadway, New York, New York
10024; (212) 873-2170

Earth Sea   315 E. Ninth Street, New York, New York 10003;
(212) 529-5353

Eden's Garden   28 Main Street, Box 33, Freeville, New York 13068

Enchanted Candle Shoppe   2321 Westchester Avenue, Bronx, New
York 10462; (718) 892-5350

The Enchanted Mystical Psychic Place   220 E. Fifty-Third Street,
New York, New York 10022; (212) 755-3999

Enchantments, Inc.   341 E. Ninth Street, New York, New York 10003;
(212) 228-4394

Esoterica   81 Main Street, New Paltz, New York 12561; (914) 855-5777

Herbs 'n' Trends   495 Jewett Avenue, Staten Island, New York 10302;
(718) 815-1260

Indio Products, Inc. / Lama Temple   2637 Webster Avenue, Bronx,
New York 10458; (718) 933-7700; fax: (718) 933-8500

Instant Karma   14 S. Village Avenue, Rockville Centre, New York
11570; (516) 763-0833

Lady in the Moon   111 St. Marks Place, New York, New York 10003;
(212) 473-8486

Leigh's Sanctuary   1539 Central Avenue, Colonie, New York 12205;
(518) 452-9774; fax: (518) 452-9329

Little Turtle Trading Company   3932 Fifty-Eighth Street, Woodside,
New York 11377

Long Island Rock Shop   104 Bedford Avenue, Bellmore, New York
11710; (516) 868-4853

The Magik Herb   138 Jay Street, Schenectady, New York 12305; (518)
377-2873

Mama Donna's Tea Garden and Healing Haven   P.O. Box 380403,
Brooklyn, New York 11238; (718) 857-2247

Meadowsweet Herbal Apothecary   77 E. Fourth Street, New York, New York 10003; (800) 879-4161; (212) 254-2870

Moon Magic   97 Main Street, Geneseo, New York 14554; (716) 243-0750

Moonstar Magic Healing Gifts   300 E. Fortieth Street, New York, New York 10016; (212) 818-0689

Morgana's Chamber   242 W. Tenth Street, New York, New York 10014; (212) 243-3415

Mystic Earth   179 Grand Street, New York, New York 10013; (212) 343-0854

Mystic Warrior   10 Wall Street, Huntington Village, New York 11743; (516) 547-8418

The Mystical Moon Shop   5086 Amboy Road, Staten Island, New York 10312; (718) 227-2212

Myth and Magick   212 River Street, Troy, New York 12180; (518) 274-5403

New Alexandrian Bookstore   110 N. Cayuga Street, Ithaca, New York 14850; (607) 272-1163

The New Voyage Bookstore   1712 Monroe Avenue, Rochester, New York 14618; (716) 461-2137

Nirvana of New York   829 Ninth Avenue, New York, New York 10019; (212) 489-9457

Oasis Metaphysical Center   Route 9, Garrison, New York 10524; (914) 424-3801

Original Products Botanica   2486-88 Webster Avenue, Bronx, New York 10458; (718) 367-9589/9591; fax: (718) 367-3613

Other Worldly Waxes and Whatever, Inc.   131 E. Seventh Street, New York, New York 10009; (212) 260-9188

Pastimes   5 Continental Avenue, Forest Hills, New York 11375; (718) 263-4747

Pillars of Light   16 Elm Street, Huntington, New York 11743

Psychic's Thyme   16 Edmonds Street, Rochester, New York 14607; (716) 473-4230

The Quest Bookshop   240 E. Fifty-Third Street, New York, New York 10022; (212) 758-5521

Rivendell   109 Saint Mark's Place, New York, New York 10003

Rozelisa   28 Kings Highway, Sugar Loaf, New York 10981; (914) 469-9923

Rutland Road Religious Store   1043 Rutland Road, Brooklyn, New York 11212

Seven Rays Book Store, Inc.   508 Westcott, Syracuse, New York 13210; (315) 424-9137

Six Rays of Gold   230 Mulberry Street, New York, New York 10012; (212) 431-8348

Spiritual Essence   519 Front Street, Vestal, New York 13850; (607) 786-3456

The Stone Age   133–36 Forty-One Road, Store CS-4, Flushing, New York 11355; (718) 358-3484

Strange Brew   2826 Elmwood Avenue, Kenmore, New York 14217; (716) 871-0282

The Three Marias   76 Havemeyer Street, Brooklyn, New York 11211; (718) 599-0417

Three of Cups   115 Tinker Street, Woodstock, New York 12498

Video Haven / Pagan Community Center   61 Fourth Avenue, New York, New York 10003; (212) 475-4223

The Wild Rose   2 Market Street, Potsdam, New York 13676; (315) 265-0160

Wizard's Wonderland   451 Jewett Avenue, Staten Island, New York 10302; (718) 816-1234

Womankind Books   5 Kivy, Huntington Station, New York 11746

North Carolina

Ancient Wisdom Centre   1158-A Highway 105, Boone, North Carolina 28607; (828) 268-2684

Anything's Possible   142 N. Main Street, Morrisville, North Carolina 28115; (704) 664-9557

Central Sun Storehouse/Celtic Connection 1825 E. Seventh Street, Charlotte, North Carolina 28210; (704) 333-9200

Crystal Connection 15 S. Water Street, Wilmington, North Carolina 28430; (910) 251-0439

Crystal Visions 5920 Asheville Highway, Naples, North Carolina 28760; (828) 687-1193

The Dancing Moon 614 W. Johnson Street, Raleigh, North Carolina 27603; (919) 834-6644

Dancing Moon Earthway Bookstore 553 W. King Street, Boone, North Carolina 28607; (828) 264-7242

Earth and Spirit 754 Ninth Street, Durham, North Carolina 27705; (919) 286-4250

Enchanted Journeys 2508 Freeman Street, Winston-Salem, North Carolina 27127; (336) 748-0100

Energy Emporium and Academy 119 Chestnut Street, Wilmington, North Carolina 28401; (910) 763-8220

The Fifth Element 7517 Kisco Road, Fayetteville, North Carolina 28303; (910) 609-0980

The Goddess Store 382 Montford Avenue, Asheville, North Carolina 28806; (704) 258-3102

Indian Dreams 1159 Pearl Court, Jacksonville, North Carolina 28540; (910) 938-3804

Infinity's Images 3714 E. Independence Boulevard, Charlotte, North Carolina 28205; (704) 536-7642

Jewels of the Spirit 425 Hathaway Drive, Winston-Salem, North Carolina 27103; (336) 760-1146

Lightworks 63 Brook Street 9, Asheville, North Carolina 28815; (828) 274-9840

Magickal Arts 129 Brogden Road, Stem, North Carolina 27581; (919) 528-1879

The Mystic Dragon Highway 70 E. Morehead City, North Carolina 28560; (252) 637-2527

Mystic Eye 30 N. Lexington Avenue, Asheville, North Carolina 28801; (704) 251-1773

Mystic Moon   321 Flea Market Building No. 2, Dallas, North Carolina 28016; (704) 629-0955

Mystical Impressions   20 Alexander Road, Havelock, North Carolina 28532; (252) 447-2523

Pan's Collection   930 Burke Street, Winston-Salem, North Carolina 27101; (336) 725-4233

The Rainbow Path   1412 East Boulevard, Suite G, Charlotte, North Carolina (28203); (704) 332-3404

Rising Moon   316 East Boulevard, Charlotte, North Carolina 28203; (704) 332-7473

Seventh Heaven   40 Westgate Parkway, Asheville, North Carolina 28806; (704) 253-8070

Sheer Magic   1420 Dewitt Smith Road, Pittsboro, North Carolina 27312; (919) 542-4316

The Silver Cord   29 Barnes Road, Sylva, North Carolina 28724; (828) 631-0008

Silver Moon   209 East Main Street, Elkin, North Carolina 28621; (336) 526-5822

Silver Stars Moon   912 Hope Mills Road, Fayetteville, North Carolina 28304; (910) 426-7451

Sleeping Dragon   911 N. Marine Boulevard, Jacksonville, North Carolina 28540; (910) 347-7421

Stargate Books and Gifts   4405-B Wrightsville Avenue, Wilmington, North Carolina 28403; (918) 395-9933

The Sylver Cyrcle   853 W. Morgan Street, Raleigh, North Carolina 27606; (919) 832-3132

Temple of Mystical Faiths   127 Coot Davis Road, Jacksonville, North Carolina 28540; (910) 455-0399

World Junkets   704 Brookstown Avenue, Winston-Salem, North Carolina 27101; (336) 722-0105

North Dakota

Silver Hoofs, Inc.   114 Broadway, Elm Tree Square Mall, Fargo, North Dakota 58102; (701) 293-3868

Ohio

Ambergram Metaphysical Center   8071 Broadview Road, Cleveland, Ohio 44147; (440) 526-3011

Athens Book Center   753 E. State Street, Athens, Ohio 45701

Book of Shadows   116-C Maryland Avenue S.W., Canton, Ohio 44710; (330) 456-8368; fax: (330) 453-9848

Crazy Ladies Books   4039 Hamilton Avenue, Cincinnati, Ohio 45223; (513) 541-4198

Curiosity Shop   118 E. Northern Avenue, Lima, Ohio 45801; (419) 222-1335

Earth Rhythm Workshop   2488 Nadine Circle, Hinckley, Ohio 44233; (216) 273-6260

Epic Books   118 Dayton, Yellow Springs, Ohio 45387; (937) 767-7997

Fly By Night   2275 N. High Street, Columbus, Ohio 43201; (614) 299-7930

House of Astrology   1449 Messenger, South Euclid, Ohio 44121

House of Circe   27 Broadway, Toledo, Ohio 43602; (419) 243-0002

Library Books   4836 Hills and Dales N.W., Jackson Township, Ohio 43030

Manifestations   31 Colonial Arcade, Cleveland, Ohio 44155

Moonstar   38422 Lake Shore Boulevard, Willoughby, Ohio 44094; (216) 942-5652

My Enchanted Garden   Lima Mall, no. 158, 2400 Elida Road, Lima, Ohio 45805; (419) 229-0290

New World Books   336 Ludlow, Cincinnati, Ohio 45220

Northern Spirits: A Magickal Place   452–454 W. Delaware, Toledo, Ohio 43610; (419) 255-0595

Rainbow Connection   1449 Messenger Court, Cleveland, Ohio 44121; (440) 291-0523

Salem West   1209 N. High Street, Columbus, Ohio 43201; (614) 421-7557

Seventh Ray Books   13670 York Road, Cleveland, Ohio 44133; (440) 582-2299

The Shadow Realm   3347 N. High Street, Columbus, Ohio 43202;
(614) 262-1175

Star Spectrum   1484 Roycroft, Lakewood, Ohio 44107

Tradewinds   1652 N. High Street, Columbus, Ohio 43201

Woodsprite   923 Vine Street, Cincinnati, Ohio 45202; (513) 651-2231

Oklahoma

Beyond Your Dreams   8124 S. Harvard, Tulsa, Oklahoma 74137;
(918) 491-2085; fax: (918) 491-2087

Curious Goods   1319 W. Lee Boulevard, Lawton, Oklahoma 73502;
(405) 353-5355

The Four Winds   761 Asp, Norman, Oklahoma 73069

Peace of Mind   1401 E. Fifteenth Street, Tulsa, Oklahoma 74120;
(800) 523-1090

Starwind   3015 Classen Boulevard, Oklahoma City, Oklahoma 73106

Oregon

Grass Roots Books   227 S.W. Second, Corvallis, Oregon 97333

Peralandra Books and Music   1016 Willamette Street, Eugene,
Oregon 97401; (503) 485-4848

Rosebud and Fish Community Bookstore   524 State Street, Salem,
Oregon 97301; (503) 399-9960

Witch Hazel and Broom   258 A Street, Ashland, Oregon 97520;
(541) 482-9628

Woman's Place Books   2349 S.E. Ankeny, Portland, Oregon 97214

Pennsylvania

Cosmic Visions, Ltd.   956 Hamilton Street, Allentown, Pennsylvania
18102; (610) 433-3610

The Divine Light   110 N. Front Street, Steelton, Pennsylvania 17113;
(717) 939-7071

Earth Magic   c/o Elaine's, Great Valley Shopping Center, Route 30
(Lincoln Highway), North Versailles, Pennsylvania 15137

Emporium of Curious Goods   15 Broadway, Jim Thorpe, Pennsylvania 18229; (717) 325-4038

Gypsy Heaven   115 S. Main Street, New Hope, Pennsylvania 18938; (215) 862-5251

Hands of Aries   620 S. Fourth Street, Philadelphia, Pennsylvania 19147; (215) 923-5264

Harry's Occult Shop   1238 South Street, Philadelphia, Pennsylvania 19147

Inner Connections   308 W. Market Street, New Cumberland, Pennsylvania 17070; (717) 774-4874

Kasapov Company   P.O. Box 243, Cresco, Pennsylvania 18326; fax: (717) 695-3289

Mystickal Tymes   127 S. Main Street, New Hope, Pennsylvania 18938; (215) 862-5629

Obscurity   9 E. Northampton Street, Wilkes-Barre, Pennsylvania 18701; (717) 821-0818

Perceptions Bookstore   328 W. Sixth Street, Erie, Pennsylvania 16507; (814) 454-7364

Ray's New Age Curio Shop   1358 South Street, Philadelphia, Pennsylvania 19147; (215) 545-3135

Sagittarius Books   87 S. Main Street, New Hope, Pennsylvania 18938

Solomon's Seal OSC   9 E. Main Street, Kutztown, Pennsylvania 19530; (610) 683-0822

Spider Herbs   111 Branch, Pittsburgh, Pennsylvania 15215

Rhode Island

Amethyst Readings   Route 146 North, North Smithfield, Rhode Island 02064; (401) 762-4062

Crystal Enchantment   29 State Street, Bristol, Rhode Island 02809; (401) 254-1130

Estas Elemental   257 Thayer Street, Providence, Rhode Island 02906; (401) 831-2651

Herbal Magick   72 Washington Street, West Warwick, Rhode Island 02893; (401) 826-2573

The Mind's Eye   182 Thames Street, Newport, Rhode Island 02840; (401) 849-7333

Starling's Harvest Moon   515 Armistice Boulevard, Pawtucket, Rhode Island 02862; (401) 728-5788

South Carolina

The Atlantean Connect   900 Bacons Bridge Road, Summerville, South Carolina 29485; (843) 851-0069

A Circle of Light   116 South Murray Avenue, Anderson, South Carolina 29621; (864) 964-0863

Dark Eagle's Forest   931 Augusta Street, Laurens, South Carolina 29390; (864) 983-2401

The Dragon's Treasure   1922 Cedar Lane Road, Greenville, South Carolina 29617; (864) 294-0094

East of Eden   6 Wall Street, Yemassee, South Carolina 29945; (843) 589-8031

Good Scents   40 N. Market Street, Charleston, South Carolina 29401; (803) 723-6933

Green Dragon   7671 Northwoods Boulevard N., Charleston, South Carolina 29406; (843) 797-2052

Healing Rays   57 Broad Street, Charleston, South Carolina 29401

The Keep   127 Central Avenue, Summerville, South Carolina 29483; (843) 873-2320

Kenaz Services   69 Lucas Avenue, Laurens, 29360; (864) 984-2820

LunaSeas Metaphysical Gifts and Spiritual Supplies   1215-H Augusta Highway, West Columbia, South Carolina 29169; (803) 796-4048

Mother Earth   1051 Oakland Avenue, Rock Hill, South Carolina 29732; (803) 328-0203

Out of Bounds   219 F W. Antriam Drive, Greenville, South Carolina 29607; (864) 239-0106

Pan's Garden   P.O. Box 7055, Sumter, South Carolina 29150; (404) 978-1267, ext. 1220

Quicksilver and Fireflies   Meeting Street, Charleston, South Carolina 29401; (803) 723-0106

Stardust Books   2000 Blossom Street, Columbia, South Carolina 29205; (803) 771-0633

Tenagis   116 South Murray Avenue, Anderson, South Carolina 29621; (864) 231-7246

South Dakota

Luna Line   1817 Shellynn Drive, Sioux Falls, South Dakota 57103; (605) 371-8753

Tennessee

The Arcane Connection   East Ridge Flea Market, No. 224-A, 6725 Ringgold, Chattanooga, Tennessee 37412; (423) 664-4021

The Backdoor Store   109 Towne Road, Oak Ridge, Tennessee 37830; (865) 483-9115

Crystal Visions   The Knoxville Center, 3017-B N. Mall Road, Knoxville, Tennessee 37924; (423) 546-0210

Dilly's Curiosity Shop   3009 N. John B. Dennis Highway, Kingsport, Tennessee 37660; (423) 288-4666

Ebbo Spiritual Supply   1331 Madison Avenue, Memphis, Tennessee 38104; (901) 278-1915

The Elven Door   5415 Kingston Pike, Knoxville, Tennessee 37919; (423) 602-2384

Goddess and the Moon   512 Heather Place, Nashville, Tennessee 37204; (615) 383-3039

Green Earth Emporium   4451 Kingston Pike, Knoxville, Tennessee 37919; (423) 588-9882

Little Sisters Silver Jewelry   4901 Jackson Pike, Knoxville, Tennessee 37918; (865) 688-3991

Magical Journey   203 Louise Avenue, Nashville, Tennessee 37203; (615) 327-0327; fax: (615) 322-1235

New Age Emporium   1500 Southside Avenue, Bristol, Tennessee 37620; (423) 968-1313

The New Moon Gallery   36 Frazier Avenue, Chattanooga, Tennessee 37405; (423) 265-6321

Ramona's Rock Room   308 W. Castle Street, Murfreesboro, Tennessee 37129; (615) 898-0832

Sacred Space   4615 Brainerd Road, Chattanooga, Tennessee 37411; (423) 629-9100

Scarab In-Scents   4615 Brainerd Road, Chattanooga, Tennessee 37411; (423) 622-0690

Spice Island Specialty Shop   5100 N. Broadway, Knoxville, Tennessee 37918; (865) 689-9799

Stonehenge Metaphysical Bookstore   5425 Highway 153, Suite A-4, Hixson, Tennessee 37343; (423) 875-0065

Stonekeepers   1403-B Greenland Drive, Murfreesboro, Tennessee 37130; (615) 849-1792

Violet Moon   521 N. Main Street, Greeneville, Tennessee 37745; (423) 638-4589

The Wicca Basket   1500 Southside Avenue, Bristol, Tennessee 37620; (615) 968-1313

Zephyr's   4921 Homberg Drive, Knoxville, Tennessee 37919; (423) 588-8061

Texas

Aquarian Age Books   5603 Chaucer, Houston, Texas 77005

Bell, Book, and Candle   2505 W. Berry Street, Fort Worth, Texas 76109

Book People   4006 S. Lamar Boulevard, Suite 250, Austin, Texas 78704

Botanica Perez Drugstore   311 N. Zaramora Street, San Antonio, Texas 78207; (210) 433-9001

Celebration   108 W. Forty-Third Street, Austin, Texas 78751; (512) 453-6207

The Constellation   2829 W. Northwest Highway, Suite 846, European Crossroads, Dallas, Texas 75220; (214) 352-4847

Cosmic Cup Cafe   2912 Oak Lawn Avenue, Dallas, Texas 75207; (214) 521-6157

Devonshire Apothecary   2105 Ashby, Austin, Texas 78704
(512) 444-5039

Flight of the Phoenix   1034 N. Carrier Parkway, Grand Prairie, Texas
75050; (214) 642-6363

A Gift From the East   4701 University Oaks, Houston, Texas 77004

House of Avalon/Papa Jim Botanica   5630 S. Flores Street, San
Antonio, Texas 78214; (210) 922-6665

House of Power   2509 Canal Street, Houston, Texas 77003

Lucia's Garden   2942 Virginia Street, Houston, Texas 77098;
(713) 523-6494

M. Z. Nita's Candle, Incense and Herb Shop   5521 E. Grand Avenue,
Dallas, Texas 75223; (214) 823-5471

Magick Cauldron   2214 Richmond Avenue, Houston, Texas 77098;
(713) 468-8031

New Age Books   1006 S. Lamar Boulevard, Austin, Texas 78704

The Occult Shop   2222 Yale, Houston, Texas 77076

OLSF Metaphysical Center   5304-A Bellaire Boulevard, Bellaire,
Texas 77401

Overtones Books and Gifts   14902 Preston Road at Beltline, Dallas,
Texas 75240; (214) 458-0404

Rosario's-Mystic   5314 Canal Street, Houston, Texas 77011

Sweet Remembrance   107 E. Avenue E, Copperas Cove, Texas 76522;
(817) 542-1555

Stanley Drug Company   2819 Lyons, Houston, Texas 77020

Unlimited Thought Bookstore   5525 Blanco Road, San Antonio,
Texas 78212; (210) 525-0693

Ye Seekers   9336 Westview, Houston, Texas 77055

Utah

Aswattha Books   4700 S. Nine Hundred E., Salt Lake City, Utah
84117; (801) 268-3841

Capricorn's Lair   2456 Washington Boulevard, Ogden, Utah 84401

The Eclectic   2651 Washington Boulevard, no. 15, Ogden, Utah 84401; (801) 334-7675

Fertile Ground   274 E. Nine Hundred S., Salt Lake City, Utah 84111; (801) 521-8124

Gypsy Moon Emporium   1011 E. Nine Hundred S., Salt Lake City, Utah 84105; (801) 521-9100

Jeweled Maidens   1765 W. 4160 S., West Valley City, Utah 84119; (801) 967-0590

Lost Arts   4699 Holladay Boulevard, Salt Lake City, Utah 84117; (801) 278-9505

Nizhoni Trading Company   Fashion Place Mall, 6191 S. State Street, Murray, Utah 84107; (801) 262-7345

Vermont

The American Society of Dowsers Bookstore   101 Railroad Street, St. Johnsbury, Vermont 05819; (800) 711-9497; (802) 748-8565

Bubastis Moon   19 Church Street, no. 2, Burlington, Vermont 05401; (802) 864-2495

The Dragon's Leyr   Rutland Mall, Woodstock Avenue, Rutland, Vermont 05701; (802) 775-0610

The I Wonda Book Shoppe   63 Main Street, Lower Level, Windsor, Vermont 05089; (802) 674-5503

Merkebah   3 N. Main Street, Randolph Center, Vermont 05061; (800) 413-3730

Mystic Trader   23 Langdon Street, Montpelier, Vermont 05602; (802) 229-9220

Paperback Exchange   Towne Marketplace, Susie Wilson Road, Essex Junction, Vermont 05452; (802) 879-0340

The Spiral   5 Merchants Row, Middlebury, Vermont 05753; (802) 388-7477

Spirit Dancer   22 Church Street, Burlington, Vermont 05401; (802) 660-8060; fax: (802) 660-8088

Virginia

Alchemists   3066 Stony Point Road, Richmond, Virginia 23235; (804) 323-5563

Aquarian Bookshop   3519 Ellwood Avenue, Richmond Virginia 23221; (804) 353-5575

Aquarius   6653 Arlington Boulevard, Falls Church, Virginia 22042

Divine Magic and Novelties   5943 Midlothian Turnpike, Richmond, Virginia 23225; (804) 232-1345

The Monster Museum New Age Shop   Route 3, Box 678, Stuart, Virginia 24171; (540) 694-3794

Mystique   3130 Tidewater Drive, Norfolk, Virginia 23509; (757) 627-5354

Phoenix Rising   19 N. Belmont Avenue, Richmond, Virginia 23221; (804) 355-7939

Starbound   Box 210, Ruther Glen, Virginia 22546

Washington

Akasha Metaphysical Books   1124 State, Bellingham, Washington 98225

Astrology Et Al   4728 University N.E., Seattle, Washington 98115; (206) 548-9128

Aum-Nee Books   Twenty-Fifth and D, Freighthouse Square, Tacoma, Washington 98404

Dawn Horse   918 Sixty-Fourth N.E., Seattle, Washington 98115; (206) 527-2979

Earth Magic   205 E. Fourth Avenue, Olympia, Washington 98501; (360) 754-0357

Goddess Rising   4006 First Avenue N.E., Seattle, Washington 98105

The Golden Age   5445 Ballard, Seattle, Washington 98107

Illusions   113 S.W. Legion, Olympia, Washington 98501

Imprint Books   917 N. Second Street, Tacoma, Washington 98403

Lodestar Center   11049 Eighth Avenue N.E., Seattle, Washington 98105; (206) 548-9128

Magical Garden   2407 Sixth Avenue, Tacoma, Washington 98406; (253) 627-5417

Mandala Books and Gallery   918 Sixty-Fourth Street N.E., Seattle, Washington 98115; (206) 527-2979

Odyssey Books   321 Main Street, Edmonds, Washington 98020; (425) 672-9064

Pan's Forest Herb Company   411 Ravens Road, Pt. Townsend, Washington 98368

Passages   310 W. Champion, Bellingham, Washington 98225

Psychic Energy Center   1912 E. Seventy-Second Street, Tacoma, Washington 98404

Quest Bookshop   717 Broadway East, Seattle, Washington 98102; (206) 323-4281

The Sage   10846 N.E. Second Street, Bellevue, Washington 98004

Stargazer   12727 N.E. Twentieth Street, Bellevue, Washington 98005

Tenzing Momo and Company   93 Pike Street, Seattle, Washington 98101; (206) 623-9837

Visionary Books   2203 Sixty-Fifth Street N.E., Seattle, Washington 98115

Wortcunning   2915½ First Avenue (rear), Seattle, Washington 98121

Zenith Supplies   6319 Roosevelt N.E., Seattle, Washington 98115

West Virginia

As You Wish   Inwood Center, Inwood, West Virginia 25430; (888) 838-8098

Full Moon Rising   219 Eighth Street, Marlinton, West Virginia 24954; (304) 799-2246

Oasis of the Spirit   2255 Market Street, Wheeling, West Virginia 26003; (304) 232-5768

Wildflowers Unique Books and Gifts   1512 Oakhurst Drive, Charleston, West Virginia 25314; (304) 746-0100; fax: (304) 746-0113

Wisconsin

Aquarian Sun Books   6469 W. Fond du Lac, Milwaukee, Wisconsin 53218

Astrum Argentum   325 N. Plankinton Avenue, Milwaukee, Wisconsin 53203; (414) 276-6966

Autumn's Moon Bookstore   167 Liberty Avenue, Beloit, Wisconsin 53511; (608) 365-2597

By the Light of the Moon   212 N. Henry Street, Madison, Wisconsin 53711; (608) 250-9810

Earthsong Bookstore   2214 Kennedy Road, Janesville, Wisconsin 53545; (608) 754-3933

High Wind Books   2625 N. Downer Avenue, Milwaukee, Wisconsin 53211; (608) 332-8288

House of Scorpio   5922 W. Burnham Street, Milwaukee, Wisconsin 53219; (608) 545-7470

Microcosm Books   301 W. Lakeside, Madison, Wisconsin 53715

Mimosa Community Bookstore   210 N. Henry, Madison, Wisconsin 53703; (608) 256-5432

New Earth   Ishpiming Retreat Center, Box 340, Manitowish Waters, Wisconsin 54545; (715) 686-2372

Of a Like Mind Store   P.O. Box 6677, Madison, Wisconsin 53704; (608) 257-5858

Prisca Magica   815 E. Johnson Street, Madison, Wisconsin 53703

Red Oak Books   610 Main Street, LaCrosse, Wisconsin 54601

Room of One's Own Bookstore   307 W. Johnson Street, Madison, Wisconsin 53703; (608) 257-7888

Shakti Books   320 State Street, Madison, Wisconsin 53703; (608) 255-5007

The Three Fates   1233 E. Brady Street, Milwaukee, Wisconsin 53202; (414) 276-3282

Windows of Light / Angels Forever   229 E. College Avenue, Appleton, Wisconsin 54911; (920) 738-6636

Witches Brew and Extras   517 Forest Street, Green Bay, Wisconsin 54302; (920) 437-6988

Wyoming

Abundance   1809 Warren Avenue, Cheyenne, Wyoming 82001; (307) 632-8237

Crystal Clear   342 W. K Street, Casper, Wyoming 82601; (307) 266-4742

The Marigold Merchant   137 Bear River Drive, Suite 3–4, Evanston, Wyoming 82930; (307) 789-4671

Pan's Grove   458 S. Walnut Street, Casper, Wyoming 82601; (307) 577-6411

Spiritual Apothecary   2134 E. D Street, Torrington, Wyoming 82240; (307) 532-2366

Canada: Alberta

Dragon Child Metaphysical   916-A Sixteenth Avenue N.W., Calgary, Alberta T2M 0K4; (403) 275-8556; (413) 275-8556

A Flash of Insight, Ltd.   10441–82 Whyte Avenue N.W., Edmonton, Alberta T6E 2A1; (780) 431-1981

Isis Metaphysical Books   8217 104th Street, Edmonton, Alberta T6E 4E7; (780) 433-9373

Sanctuary   10310 Eighty-first Avenue N.W., Edmonton, Alberta T6E 1X2; (403) 944-2654

Where Faeries Live   10991A 124th Street, Edmonton, Alberta T5M 0H9; (780) 454-0187

The Witches' Cottage   11819–135 Street, Edmonton, Alberta T5L 1W7; (780) 452-4370

Canada: British Columbia

Aunt Agatha's Magickal Emporium   46 Begbie Street, New Westminster, British Columbia V31 3M9; (604) 516-6959

Avalon Metaphysical Center   62–560 Johnson Street, Victoria, British Columbia V8W 3C6; (250) 380-1721

Bell, Book, and Candle   1479 Third Avenue, Prince George, British Columbia V2L 3G1; (250) 562-2255

Books and Beyond   1561 Ellis Street, Kelowna, British Columbia V1Y 2A7; (250) 763-6222

De Ja Vu Psychic Services   49386 Yale Road, Chilliwack, British Columbia V2P 6H4; (604) 794-7205

Greenstone Concepts   7141 Griffiths Avenue, Burnaby, British Columbia V5E 2Y1; (604) 526-7783

Hub of the Wheel   207 Main Street, Penticton, British Columbia V2A 5B1; (250) 490-8837

Merlyn's Grove   250–520 Rithet Street, Victoria, British Columbia V8V 1E2; (250) 381-3513

Reflections Books   1111 Austin Avenue, Coquitlam, British Columbia V3K 3P4; (604) 939-6000

Serendipity's Backyard   120–12031 First Avenue, Richmond, British Columbia V7E 3M1; (604) 275-1683

Spirit Lodge   20270 Industrial Avenue, Langley, British Columbia V3A 4K7; (604) 533-6592

Spirit Quest Gifts   3828 Cadboro Bay Road, Victoria, British Columbia V8N 4G2; (250) 472-1712

Winds of Change   441 Cliffe Avenue, Courtenay, British Columbia V9N 2J3; (250) 338-5095

Witch Town   Rosehill Street, Nanaimo, British Columbia V9R 2SE; (250) 753-8117

Canada: Manitoba

Genesis Books   130 Osborne Street, Winnipeg, Manitoba R3L 1Y5; (204) 452-0982

Oracle Grove Bookstore   264 McDermott Street, Winnipeg, Manitoba R3B 0S8; (204) 989-2688

Triskele Pagan Supply   295 Blight Street, Miami, Manitoba R0G 1H0; (204) 435-2500

Canada: New Brunswick

Lapsilla IV   390 Queen Street, Fredericton, New Brunswick E3B 1B2; (506) 455-2455

Shakti's Haven   11 Canterbury Street, Saint John, New Brunswick E2L 4S4; (506) 657-1100

Tranquility Books and Gifts   1111 Regent Street, Unit 13, Fredericton, New Brunswick E3B 3Z2; (506) 450-7915

Canada: Nova Scotia

Little Mysteries Books   1663 Barrington Street, Halifax, Nova Scotia B3J 1Z9; (902) 423-1313

Zelda's Mystique Shop   56 Water Street, Digby, Nova Scotia, B0V 1A0; (902) 245-5812

Canada: Ontario

The Ancient Earth   314 St. Paul Street, St. Catharines, Ontario L2R 3M9; (905) 688-0111

The Cosmic Cookie Company   Suite 141, 314 Queen Street S., Bolton, Ontario L7E 4Z9; (416) 446-7400; (888) 826-8758; fax: (905) 880-3061

The Crystal Dawn   330 Cumberland Street, Ottawa, Ontario K1N 7J2; (613) 241-2262

Dragon's Lair Myth Shoppe   1971 Salem Road, RR No. 1, Consecon, Ontario K0K 1T0; (613) 394-2147

Flashbacks Metaphysical Shop   574 Talbot Street, St. Thomas, Ontario N5P 1C5; (519) 633-1294

Forest Dreams   422 Donald B. Munro Drive, Carp, Ontario K0A 1L0; (613) 839-2400

The Magick Box Book Shop   169 South Mitton Street, Sarnia, Ontario N7T 3C8; (519) 383-8708

Mystasia   901 King Street West, Hamilton, Ontario L8S 1K5; (905) 525-2401

Pagan Playground   70 George Street, Second Floor, Ottawa, Ontario K1N 5V9; (613) 241-2227

Pandora's Books   3332 Yonge Street, P.O. Box 94009, Toronto, Ontario M4N 2L0

Phenomena   170 Wyndham St N., Guelph, Ontario N1H 4E; (519) 763-5211; fax (519) 763-7803

Spiritually Speaking   R.R. 2, Concession 24, Wiarton, Ontario N0H 2T0; (519) 534-5539

Wiccashoppe   2211 Queen E., Toronto, Ontario M4E 1E8; (416) 693-9422

Winds of Change   441 Cliffe Avenue, Beachburg, Ontario K0J 1C0; (613) 338-5095

Zodiac Circle   640 Queen Street E., Paul Mall, Sault Ste. Marie, Ontario P6A 2A4; (705) 254-5209

Canada: Quebec

A la Maison Sciences Occultes   11083 Boul Saint-Vital, Montréal-Nord, Quebec H1H 4T7; (514) 323-7017

Arbre Enchante Enr   201 Rue Saint-Marcel, Drummondville, Quebec J2B 2E1; (819) 475-5065

Boutique Aux Mille Symboles   1025 Boul Du Seminaire N., Saint-Jean-sur-Richelieu, Quebec J3A 1R7; (450) 349-0882

Boutique Esotherique Puits   562 Rue St-Georges, Saint-Jérome, Quebec J7Z 5B8; (450) 438-2593

Boutique l'Intuition   155 Rue Notre-Dame, Repentigny, Quebec J6A 5L3; (450) 585-2658

Boutique Magie Blanche   561 Soixieme Avenue, Grand-Mère, Quebec G9T 2H4; (819) 538-7887

Centre Du Cadeau Esoterique   147 St. Paul, Joliette, Quebec J6E 5G2; (450) 755-4989

Chatelet Des Chevaleries   919 Av Laurier E., Montréal, Quebec H2J 1G4; (514) 279-9312

Chrysalide Enr   50 Rue Principale E., Sainte-Agathe-des-Monts, Quebec J8C 1J6; (819) 326-2945

Editions de l'Atlantide   2188 Rue Chambly, Montréal, Quebec H1W 3J4; (514) 524-1344

Etoile Brillante Enr   317 Boul Boivin, Granby, Quebec J2G 2K5; (450) 776-6323

Eye of Horus   270 St. Catherine Street West, Montreal, Quebec H2X 1A2; (514) 866-5036

Foret Enchantee   5175 Rue Belanger, Montréal, Quebec H1T 1E1; (514) 376-3308

L'Etoile Doree Senc   955 Rue Royale, Trois-Rivières, Quebec G9A 4H7; (819) 379-4652

L'Ilot Tresor   230 Principale, St-Sauveur-des-Monts, Quebec J0R 1R0; (450) 227-7561

Librairie Banque Du Livre   864 Troisieme Avenue, Val-d'Or, Quebec J9P 1T1; (819) 825-8787

Librairie Esoterique l'Ere   447 Rue Notre-dame, Le Gardeur, Quebec J5Z 1S9; (450) 654-5927

Librairie Esoterique Source   400 Boul Du Seminaire N., Saint-Jean-sur-Richelieu, Quebec J3B 5L2; (450) 359-4273

Librairie l'Essence Ciel   41 Rue Jacques-Cartier, Gatineau, Quebec J8T 2W3; (819) 568-2643

Librairie Quintessence   275 Rue Principale, St-Sauveur-des-Monts, Quebec J0R 1R0; (450) 227-5525

The Magical Blend   1928 St. Catherine Street West, Montreal, H3H 1M4; (514) 938-1458

Maison Du Cadeaux Esoterique   748 Rue St-Francois Xavier, Terrebonne, Quebec J6W 1G7; (450) 961-0011

Melange Magique   1928 Rue Sainte-Catherine, Montréal, Quebec H3H 1M4; (514) 938-1458

Mouvement Gnostique Chrêtien   4235 Rue Saint-Jacques, Montréal, Quebec H4C 1J5; (514) 935-2635

Mouvement Gnostique Chrêtien   3993 Rue Wellington, Verdun, Quebec H4G 1V6; (514) 766-4667

Pikottine   3880 Rue Ontario E., Montréal, Quebec H1W 1S6; (514) 522-5189

Royaume Des Christaux   17 Place Bourget N., Joliette, Quebec J6E 5E3; (450) 752-1731

Societé de Transformation   1062 Rue Berri, Montréal, Quebec H2L 4X2; (514) 843-8430

Uranie Muse de l'Astrologie   4147 Rue Sainte-Catherine E., Montréal, Quebec H1V 1X1; (514) 522-5775

Canada: Saskatchewan

A Wee Witches' Nook   2206 Dewdney Avenue, Regina, Saskatchewan S4R 1H3; (306) 565-3757

Atlantis 2000   115 Third Avenue S., Saskatoon, Saskatchewan S7K 1L7; (306) 653-0845

Brighter Horizons Wholeness   P.O. Box 26014, RPO Lawson Height, Saskatoon, Saskatchewan S7K 8C1; (306) 978-7277

Earth Echoes Gift Gallery   614 Broadway Avenue, Saskatoon, Saskatchewan S7N 1A8; (306) 933-4989

Eveningstar Metaphysical Supplies   A119 Second Avenue N., Saskatoon, Saskatchewan S7K 2A9; (306) 978-1313

Mind Games   2105 Broad Street, Regina, Saskatchewan S4P 1R1; (306) 757-8544

Spiritworks Books and Gifts, Inc.   1814 Lorne Avenue, Saskatoon, Saskatchewan S7H 1Y4; (306) 653-7966

Witch's Brew   126 Twentieth Street W., Saskatoon, Saskatchewan S7M 0W6; (306) 665-6612

Great Britain

Ace of Wands   128 Macklin Street, Derby, United Kingdom

Arcana   151 Fortuneswell, Portland, Dorset, United Kingdom

Atlantis Bookshop   49-A Museum Street, London, England

Awareness Shop   25 High Street, Bishop's Castle, Shropshire, England

Craefte Supplies   33 Oldridge Road, London, England

Fate and Fortune   35 Wellington Street, Batley, West Yorkshire, England

Gothic Image   High Street, Glastonbury, Somerset, United Kingdom

Merlin's Cave Bron-Y-Craig, Glan-Y-Wern, Talsarnau, Gwynedd County, Wales

The Mushroom 10 Heathcote Street, Nottingham, England

Occultique 73 Kettering Road, Northampton, England

Prince Elric 498 Bristol Road, Selly Oak, Birmingham, England

The Sorcerer's Apprentice 418 Burley Lodge Road, Leeds, Yorkshire, England

Germany

Mega Cooperation Versand c/o H. Schuren, Lindenweg 3, 59192 Bergkamen

Merlin Mineralien, Mystik, und Esoterik Friedrich-Ebert Strasse 143, 34119 Kassel, Germany; 49-561-777439

9

Mail Order

Shopping at home from a catalog is easy, discreet, and fun. (It also saves gas and keeps you from having to deal with traffic, going out in bad weather, and other inconveniences.) And like stores, mail order companies also offer merchandise ranging from the basic items to the most unique specialties. (Be sure to tell them you saw their listing in this book!)

Abyss Distribution/Azure Green
P.O. Box 48
Middlefield, Massachusetts 01243
Web site: www.azuregreen.com
(413) 623-2155; fax: (413) 623-2156

Free occult catalog. Over 2,400 books, plus 5,000 other ritual items. Amulets, jewelry, herbs, perfumes, incense, burners, candles, statues, and more. Magickal one-stop shopping. Retail and wholesale.

Alternatives/Golden Spiral
P.O. Box 433
Arlington Heights, Illinois 60006
(800) 357-2719

Carries thousands of products for all your magickal needs. If they don't list it, they will try to locate any item you need—just give a call. Catalog: $3.00.

Amulets by Merlin

P.O. Box 2643
Newport News, Virginia 23609

A complete line of original design jewelry and hand engraving. Specializes in custom design work in silver, bronze, and gold for groups or individuals. Also available, a one-of-a-kind Tarot casting set, the result of thirteen years of research. This set encompasses the Tarot, Qabalistic, and astrological correlation in each amulet, resulting in a revolutionary form of divination. Catalog: $1.00.

Ancient Circles/Open Circle

P.O. Box 610
Laytonville, California 95451
(800) 726-8032

Symbolic jewelry of Celtic design, pendants in Goddess and God images, temple formula perfumes, and exclusive "new classics" such as the Celtic Pentagram, Bamburg Green Man, and more. Catalog: $2.00.

Arachne's Web

P.O. Box 9106
Chapel Hill, North Carolina 27515

Handcrafted Witchy items, including cloaks, pouches, runes, wands, jewelry, Tarot, books, and more. Catalog: $2.00 (credited to your first order).

Ars Obscura

P.O. Box 20695
Seattle, Washington 98102
(206) 448-2048

Bookbinding and restoration. Publisher of grimoires, specializing in fine leather bookbindings. Manufactures a line of full-leather blank journals and Tarot boxes. Publisher of occult classical visual art. Catalog: $2.00.

Aunt Agatha's Occult Emporium

46 Begbie Street
New Westminster, British Columbia V31 3M9
Canada
(604) 516-6959

Catalog: $3.00 (refundable with first purchase).

The Bead Tree
P.O. Box 682
West Falmouth, Massachusetts 02574
(508) 548-4665

Earrings and pendants taken from ancient images of the Goddess. Medicine card earrings and pendants with your totem animal and other charms. All contain symbols of Earth, Air, Fire, and Water. Send $1.00 for brochures.

Bell, Book, and Candle
5886 Rocky Point
Long Island, New York 11778

Candles, oils, incense, herbs, sachets, pyramids, Tarot cards, Voodoo dolls, books, tapes, and more. Free catalog.

Bell, Book, and Candle
2505 W. Berry Street
Fort Worth, Texas 76109

Celtic catalog. Hundreds of books, cassettes, and compact discs, and jewelry. Catalog: $1.00 (refundable with first order).

Blue Earth Dream Trading Co.
8215 S.E. Thirteenth Avenue
Portland, Oregon 97202
(503) 231-1146

Shamanistic-oriented tools, smudging herbs, crystals, feathers, Tibetan bowls, lunar and animal totems, and other items. Catalog: $2.00.

The Brass Unicorn
845 E. Fern
Fresno, California 93728
(209) 441-7107

Books, incense, herbs, jewelry, art, crystals, ritual accessories, New Age music, and more.

Brigid's Fire
P.O. Box 800482
Santa Clarita, California 91380

A catalog of symbolic jewelry. Wholesale inquiries welcome.

Capestries
P.O. Box 549
Appleton, Maine 04862

Specializes in hats and capes. "Fun, functional, flowing, soft, and sensual." Catalog: $1.00.

Celestial Sights and Sounds, Inc.
P.O. Box 195
Sayville, New York 11782

A variety of Priestess designs on T-shirts, notecards, and ebony plaques. Send $10.00 for catalog (includes eight Egyptian notecards by Thor and four Priestess notecards).

Celtic Folkworks
R.D. no. 4, Box 210
Willow Grove Road
Newfield, New Jersey 08344

Celtic Folkworks is a family-run business specializing in traditional Celtic design handcrafts and jewelry. Catalog: $1.00.

Cere's Garden
Route 3, Box 305
Alvin, Texas 77511

Feminist Witchcraft accessories: silk altar cloths, Tarot wraps and spread cloths, velvet Tarot, amulet and crystal bags embroidered in gold and silver with symbols of the Goddess, herb-filled dream pillows, custom-made necklaces for healing purposes, and more. Catalog: $1.00.

Church of Universal Forces
P.O. Box 03195
Columbus, Ohio 43203
(614) 252-2083

Magickal, ritual, and occult supplies. Catalog: $5.00.

Cloister Wear
P.O. Box 541
Park Forest, Illinois 60466
(708) 747-5173

"Clothing and other things for the enlightened."

The Conjured Night
P.O. Box 16844
Chapel Hill, North Carolina 27516

"Witchy crafts for rituals, altars, Full Moons, celebrations, Moon-bloods, dreaming ... for the Wise One, gods or goddesses, lovers, nymphs, fairies, healers, maids, mamas, crones, consorts, and the wild night's creature in us all!" Catalog: $1.00 (credited to your first order).

Cornelius Antiquities
P.O. Box 1787
Scottsdale, Arizona 85252

Cosmic Corner
Box 499
Deerfield Beach, Florida 33443
Catalog: $2.00.

Cosmic Vision, Ltd. (formerly The Occult Emporium)
956 Hamilton Street
Allentown, Pennsylvania 18102
(610) 433-3610

Ancient wisdom archive and supply—retail and illustrated mail order catalog: $2.00. Books, herbs, incense, jewelry, minerals, candles, altar attire and equipment, brasses, Tarot, consultations, magick-on-contract, experts in right and left traditions, oils, powders, antiques, and arcane specialties. UFO museum on premises. Open Monday to Friday, 11 A.M. to 6 P.M., Saturday 11 A.M. to 5 P.M. Since 1975.

Coven Gardens
P.O. Box 1064
Boulder, Colorado 80306
(303) 444-4322

Occult supplies: incense, oils, bath products, herbs, candles, and more. Western Traditional ancient recipes; also Wiccan, Druidic/Celtic, Egyptian, Greco-Roman, Middle and Near Eastern, Macumba, and Voodoo upon request. All planetary and Zodiacal blends are Qabalistic. Supplies to aid practitioners from Paganism to High Ceremonial ritual work. All products are made by planetary placements, lunar cycle phase, and during ritual circle.

Crescent Moongoddess

P.O. Box 153

Massapequa Park, New York 11762

Magick supplies for Wiccans. Send $2.00 for a nineteen-page catalog (refundable with first purchase). Make checks and money orders payable to Bonnie Thompson.

The Crystal Moon

P.O. Box 802

Matteson, Illinois 60443

Send $3.00 (refundable with first purchase) for catalog of astrology and occult supplies.

Crystal Moon Curio Shoppe

72 Van Reipen Avenue, Suite 11

Jersey City, New Jersey 07306

Witch supplies, including books, spell kits, herbs, oils, incense, Tarot cards, mojo bags, candles, amulets, and talismans. Catalog: $2.00.

The Crystal Rose

P.O. Box 8416

Minneapolis, Minnesota 55408

(612) 488-3715

Hand-wrapped crystal pendants, gemstone jewelry, magick wands with spell scrolls, amulet bags, runestones, New Age stationery, and much more. Send a self-addressed stamped envelope to receive a free catalog.

Curious Goods Witchcraft Shoppe

415 Campbell Avenue

West Haven, Connecticut 06516

(203) 932-1193

Offers handmade magickal crystal gemstone charms for those seeking love, money, healing, or protection. Catalog: $2.00; newsletter: $2.00.

Dark Moon Designs

20 Bristol Road

Brighton, BN2 1AP

England

Phone: (01273) 623321; fax: (01273) 607711

Full-color cards, prints, and posters in designs that "celebrate the cycles of nature, the ever-changing moon, and the ancient festivals." Call or write to request a catalog or if you have any suggestions for new designs.

Dunraven House
P.O. Box 403
Boulder, Colorado 80306

"Superior quality incenses, perfume, oils, and metaphysical books. Serving Wicca, Ceremonial, Qabalistic, Celtic, and Dianic Traditions." Catalog: $2.00 (refunded with first order).

Earth Emporium
R.R. no. 1, Box 236
Friendship, New York 14739

Send $2.00 to receive the "big bulk list of over 1000 items," or $4.00 for the complete catalog (refunded with order). Make checks payable to Betsy Daggett.

Earth Magic Productions
2166 Broadway
New York, New York 10024
(800) 662-8634

Write or call for a free catalog.

Enchantments
341 E. Ninth Street
New York, New York 10003
(212) 228-4394

Witchcraft supply store and catalog. Herbs, Shaman goods, chalices, daggers, incense, books, crystal balls, oils, candles, Tarot cards, Wiccan study groups, lectures, classes, and workshops. Tarot and astrology readings by appointment. Catalog: $2.00.

The Enlightened Path
P.O. Box 618001
Dallas, Texas 75261

"Creators of the world's most potent and successful talismans." Visa and MasterCard accepted. Free catalogue.

The Excelsior Incense Works
P.O. Box 853
San Francisco, California 94101
(415) 822-9124

Incense from around the world, religious statues from India, raw materials to make incense, crystals, and candles, and many gift items. Catalog: $1.00.

Eye of the Day
P.O. Box 21261
Boulder, Colorado 80308
(800) 717-3307

"A circle of prosperity." For a free retail catalog of quality products at reasonable prices, write or call.

Eye of the Goddess
P.O. Box 2507
Chula Vista, California 91912

Handmade metaphysical gifts and supplies. Catalog: $1.00.

Feng Shui Warehouse
1130 Scott Street
San Diego, California 92106
(800) 399-1599

Call for a free catalog of Feng Shui products: mirrors, chimes, flutes, compasses, books, and tapes.

The Formulary
P.O. Box 5455
Grants Pass, Oregon 97527

Astrologically correct incense, bath salts, oils, candles, books, jewelry, and many other occult supplies. Catalog: $2.50.

Gary's Gem Garden
404 Route 70 East
Cherry Hill, New Jersey 08034

Quartz crystals, hundreds of polished stones and mineral specimens from amber to zircon, books, charts, and pouches. Send a self-addressed stamped envelope for a free catalog (outside of the United States, send $1.00).

Gemstone Crafts
P.O. Box 621165
Littleton, Colorado 80167

Offers sacred and mystical gemstones and gemstone gifts. Write for more information.

Goddess Design Enterprises
No. 150-1917 W. Fourth Avenue
Vancouver, British Columbia V6J 1M7
Canada

Clothes made for the Goddess in you: ancient-style robes, hooded capes, sheer gowns, metallics, sequins, velvets, satins, evening wear, and everyday wear. For a current season catalog, send a check or money order for $5.00 (Canadian funds).

Goddess Wares
4128 Holmes Boulevard
Kansas City, Missouri 64110

Batiked, ancient goddess, animal, and cave painting inspired images on cotton clothing and T-shirts. To receive a free brochure, send a self-addressed stamped envelope.

Grand Adventure
R.D. 6, Box 6198
Stroudsburg, Pennsylvania 18360

Handmade Goddess statuettes of artstone. Make your own selection among the powerful images of the goddesses that have evolved over twenty-five thousand years. Catalog: $1.00.

Gypsy Heaven
115 S. Main Street
New Hope, Pennsylvania 18938
(215) 862-5251

"The Witch Shop of New Hope!" Specializing in books, herbs, oils, incense, and much more. Catalog: $3.00 (refundable with first purchase).

Gypsy Moon

1780 Massachusetts Avenue, Dept. GI
Cambridge, Massachusetts 02140

"Our clothes exist for special people who feel as though they were born to another age. Our styles are transformative, designed to flow as you move. Clothing that is magic you can take with you into the larger world, where magic is sorely lacking." Catalog: $2.00.

Halloran Software

P.O. Box 75713
Los Angeles, California 90075
(800) SEA-GOAT (California residents call (818) 501-6515).

Astrology software for PC, both DOS and Windows. For both the professional and the hobbyist. For a free catalog, write or call.

Hamilton

P.O. Box 1258
Moorpark, California 93021
(805) 529-5900

Books, crystals, talismans, herbs, essential oils, incense, Tarot, videos, candles, robes, and more. Catalog: $3.00.

Harmony Ministries

Box 1568
Overgaard, Arizona 85933

"Personalized musical healing tapes for your mind, body, and soul." Write for more information.

HeartArt Greeting Cards

659 Liberty Street
Ashland, Oregon 97520
(541) 552-1510; fax: (541) 552-1516

Goddess greeting cards celebrating the Wheel of the Year and all occasions. Personalized custom orders welcome. Receive two sample cards and catalog for $7.00 (payable to Raphaella Vaisseau).

Hypno Vision Occult Shop

P.O. Box 2192
Halesite, New York 11743

Over three thousand New Age and self-help titles. Custom-made subliminal tapes upon request. Large selection of King Solomon's amulets, talismans, and pentacles, crystal balls, jewelry, and many more great magickal things. Sixty-five page brochure: $3.00 (refundable with first order).

Indio Products

236 W. Manchester Avenue
Los Angeles, California 90003
Web site: www.indioproducts.com

Manufacturer and distributor of spiritual, religious, and New Age products. Catalogue: $5.00.

Infinity

955 Ashley Boulevard
New Bedford, Massachusetts 02745
(508) 995-2221

Offers metaphysical books, Craft supplies, gifts, workshops, and readings. Please write or call for a catalog.

International Guild of Occult Sciences Research Society

255 El Cielo Road, Suite X565X
Palm Springs, California 92262
(619) 327-7355

Huge catalog of rare books, courses, products, psionic helmets and boxes, Witchcraft Radionics, time travel, hidden technology, alchemical money boxes, exorcism, PSI warfare, and invisibility. Teacher, researcher, or publisher memberships available. Bimonthly magazine and more. Complete information and catalog: $3.00.

Isis

5701 E. Colfax Avenue
Denver, Colorado 80220
(303) 321-0867

Metaphysical New Age center. Candles, books, incense, herbs, jewelry, tapes, crystals, stone pendulums, artwork, and more. Catalog: $3.00.

Isiscraft

3305 Adams Avenue no. 48
San Diego, California 92116

"A unique catalog of Great Goddess gifts, rubber stamps, mugs, T-shirts, oils, incense, handcrafts, books and statues." Catalog: $2.00 (includes a free lucky scarab).

J. L. Enterprises
P.O. Box 1069
Lakewood, California 90714

Spiritual, New Age, and American Indian items; spell kits for love, money, success, and more; oils, incenses, candles, books, runes, and Tarot cards. Catalog: $3.00.

Jane Iris Designs
2260 El Cajon Boulevard, No. 452
San Diego, California 92104
(619) 294-9332
(800) 828-5687
Web site: www.janeirisdesigns.com

Images of empowerment, guidance, protection, and self-expression. Jewelry, pendulums, sculpture, and candles from Jane Iris Designs, Inc. Free catalog.

Joan Teresa Power Products
P.O. Box 442
Mars Hill, North Carolina 28754
(704) 689-5739

Large selection of hard-to-find herbs and roots. Some plants available shipped live from their nursery. Herbs, fine quality handmade oils, incense, powders and bath items, candles, books, jewelry, and more. Written lessons and personal instruction. Ten percent discount on all Wiccan products. Catalog: $2.00.

KLW Enterprises
3790 El Camino Real, no. 270
Palo Alto, California 94306

Unique designs: "Born Again Pagan" and "Howl at the Moon" buttons, bumper stickers, 8″ diameter iron-on transfers. Catalog: $1.00.

Lady Moon Graphics
P.O. Box 601
Oconomowoc, Wisconsin 53066

An inspiring collection of classic and contemporary fine art prints reflecting the magical beauty and power of the Goddess in Her many guises. Catalog: $2.00 (credited to your first order).

Ladyslipper, Inc.
P.O. Box 3124
Durham, North Carolina 27715
(800) 634-6044; fax: (800) 577-7892

A catalog of music by women, including a wide selection of women's spirituality, New Age, Celtic, native American, and drumming/percussion cassette tapes and compact discs. Also lists attractive Pagan notecards and calendars. Free catalog.

Lea's Light
P.O. Box 33272
Charlotte, North Carolina 28233

Handmade candles—over twenty-five shapes to choose from, plus unlimited colors. Design your own. For more information, send $1.00 or a self-addressed stamped envelope.

Llethtovar Creations
P.O. Box 855
Urbana, Ohio 43078

Images of the archetypal Earth Mother and Her Priestess, hand-carved in various types of stone and available in many styles and sizes. Rainbow necklaces, Minoan breast beads, and amulet bags. Catalog: $1.00.

Llewellyn's New Worlds of Mind and Spirit

New book excerpts, readers' forum, horoscopes, weather and earthquake forecasts, New Age marketplace, and more. For a free issue, call: (800) THE MOON.

Lori Baratta Artworks
26 Dalbert Street, Bldg. L-2
Carteret, New Jersey 07008
Phone/Fax: (732) 969-0932 (twenty-four hours)

Notecards, keychains, and silver and gold Gothic treasure boxes (great for holding Tarot cards, crystals, etc.) available in your choice of full-color designs: Goddess, Egyptian, Green Man, Celestial, Angels, and more. Specializing in Earth religions and mystickal people. All designs have been researched to assure history and accuracy of symbols, hieroglyphics, etc. Color catalog: $1.00 (refundable with order). Specify retail or wholesale.

Lotions, Potions and Jewels
P.O. Box 610387
Newton Heights, Massachusetts 02161

Send $1.00 to receive a descriptive catalog of their unique aromatherapy products, "handcrafted, using the purest herbs and oils individually blended for your needs."

Magickal Creations
1024 McClendon Street
Irving, Texas 75061
(214) 438-2072

Runeboards, incense, oils, scrying mirrors, robes, wands, banners, and more. Retail or wholesale catalog: $3.00.

The Magickal Mind
P.O. Box 7838
Alhambra, California 91802
(626) 282-7255

Incense, oils, candles, tools for divination and psychological development, books, handmade jewelry, crystals, and more. Catalog: $2.00.

Magickal Moments
12 Pine Street
Easthampton, Massachusetts 01027
(413) 529-0760

"Products for the magick in your life!" Candles, incense, oils, solid pewter figurines, and gemstones. Free wholesale catalog upon request.

Magus Books and Herbs
1316 S.E. Fourth Street
Minneapolis, Minnesota 55414
(800) 99-MAGUS; (612) 379-7669

Occult books, incense, oils, and supplies. Catalog: $2.00.

Mainely Magick
P.O. Box 293
Hampden, Maine 04444
(207) 234-2633

Specialists in the manufacture and crafting of the finest jewelry and ritualware. Explore its complete line of hand-cast Sterling silver and gold jewelry, or allow Mainely Magick to cast your own custom design in most any type of metal. Customwork can be done on the day and planetary hour of your choice. Wholesale inquiries welcome.

Marah
P.O. Box 948
Madison, New Jersey 07940

Learn magickal herbalism and make incenses to enhance your rituals with Marah's *The Magic of Herbs*, $29.95 postpaid. Full line of Wiccan herbs also available, plus flower oils, handcrafted incense, candles, books, Wicca course, and other enchantments. Send $1.00 for catalog, incense sample, and a free issue of *Marah's Almanac*.

Metatools
P.O. Box 8027
Santurce, Puerto Rico 00910

Metaphysical software for IBM and compatibles. "Great selection and prices." Free catalog.

Miller's Curios and Lucky Items
87 Broad Street
Atlanta, Georgia 30303
(800) 863-5654

"The home of hard-to-find items since 1965." For a free consultation, call: (404) 523-8481.

Moondance
P.O. Box 593
Varysburg, New York 14167

Twenty-one varieties of fragrant stick incense, forty-eight kinds of oils, handmade earthenware incense burners, and other items of interest to magickal folk. Catalog: $1.00.

Moonscents and Magickal Blends
P.O. Box 381588
Cambridge, Massachusetts 02238
(800) 368-7417

Incense and oils, books, Tarot, capes, robes, herbs, jewelry, crystals, cauldrons, and more. Call or write for a free full-color magickal catalog.

Moonstar Psychic and Spiritual Center
38422 Lake Shore Boulevard
Willoughby, Ohio 44094
(216) 942-5652

Candles, books, cards, incense, tapes, herbs, oils, powders, jewelry, crystal balls, and more. Catalog: $2.00.

Mother's Magick
P.O. Box 82174
Portland, Oregon 97282

"Gourmet goods for the Craft connoisseur." Essential oils, herbs, incense, ritual items, spell kits, athames, and more. Catalog: $2.00.

Mysteria Products
P.O. Box 1147
Arlington, Texas 76004

"We have something for everybody—crystals, books, herbs, incense, jewelry, oils, candles, spell kits, stones, and talismans." Free catalog.

Mysteries
9 Monmouth Street
London, WC2
England
Phone: 01-240-3688

The largest store in the United Kingdom stocking New Age and occult books and products. Free catalog.

Mystic Arts
105D Town Square, Suite 47
Copperas Cove, Texas 76522

Books, incense, magick tools, and much more. Catalog: $2.00.

Mystical Essence
P.O. Box 169
Kearny, New Jersey 07032
(201) 991-5388

Books, Tarot cards, oils, herbs, tapes, handmade incenses, buttons, and more. Ask about first-time order specials. Ninety-page catalog: $2.00 (refundable with first order).

Mystical Swan Products
Goldfox, Inc.
P.O. Box 726
Forest, Virginia 24551

A small New Age company dedicated to serving the Wiccan, Pagan, and eclectic occult communities. Specializes in herbal, instructional, and ritual-oriented supplies and products. Thousands to choose from. Catalog: $2.00 (discounted from first order).

Mystique Impressions
E. 81 No. B Daniels Road
Shelton, Washington 98584
(360) 427-9504

Athames, books, candles, cauldrons, chalices, crystals, herbs, incense, ritual tolls, and wear. Retail catalogue: $3.50; wholesale packet: $5.00.

Mythic Images Altar Figurines
P.O. Box 982
Ukiah, California 95482
(707) 485-7787

Exquisite sculptures of goddesses and gods, both museum-quality replicas and original interpretations. Created by Oberon and Morning Glory Zell. Send a self-addressed stamped envelope to receive a free catalog.

Natural Indulgence
P.O. Box 102
Methuen, Massachusetts 01844
(800) 610-3674; (508) 686-6155

Call or write for a wholesale/retail catalog of professional massage products, aromatherapy kits, moon oils, bath oils, anoints, chakra oils, and other "thoughtfully handcrafted" items.

Nemeton

  P.O. Box 1542
  Ukiah, California 95482
  (707) 463-1432

  Books, tapes, and songbooks (especially the music of Gwydion Pendderwen), videos, and more. Publishing arm of the Church of All Worlds. Send a self-addressed stamped envelope to receive a free catalog.

The Northern Light

  P.O. Box 130
  Kattskill Bay, New York 12804

  Books, incense, stones, jewelry, and more. Catalog: $1.00.

Nuit Unlimited

  249 N. Brand Boulevard, no. 482
  Glendale, California 91203
  (213) 258-5734

  Abundance of magickally charged, sensual, and practical products honoring all paths of ceremonial and personal work is offered in this informative, unique mail order catalog. Oils from A to Z, stick and powder incense, massage oil blends, bath salts, formulations for Wiccan, Qabalistic, and special purposes, ceremonial, meditation, and tantric tapes, statuary, books, and robes. All with total personal service and love of the Goddess. Send $3.00 for a catalog and oil or incense of your choice.

The Occult Emporium

  P.O. Box 5342
  Blue Jay, California 92317
  (909) 336-1263
  Web site: www.theoccultemporium.com

  Books, candles, herbs, incense, occult antiques, oils, and ritual supplies. Catalog: $3.00.

Original Magick Designs

  P.O. Box 132229
  Tyler, Texas 75713–2229
  Web site: www.originalmagick.com

Our Lady of Enchantment / Eden Within

P.O. Box 667

Jamestown, New York 14702

"A catalog for all your magickal needs: ritual tools, candles, oils, books, herbs, robes, talismans, and much more." Catalog: $2.00 (refundable with first order).

Panda Ink

P.O. Box 5129

West Hills, California 91308

(818) 340-8061; fax: (818) 883-6193

They carry a line of products called "Wynda's Wiccan Ways," which includes Sabbat greeting cards, bookmarks, clocks, mouse pads, and other items with a design of a cute Witch on them.

Panpipes Magickal Marketplace

1641 N. Cahuenga Boulevard

Hollywood, California 90028

(323) 462-7078

Complete line of occult supplies, handmade robes, Tarot pouches, jewelry, books, crystals, hand-blended incense and oils, and more. Tarot, palmistry, and numerology readings given on premises. Catalog: $5.00.

Pan's Forest Herb Co.

411 Ravens Road

Port Townsend, Washington 98368

Offers Tarot decks, unique books, and bulk herbal tinctures. Free catalog.

Pan's Grove Catalogue and Newsletter

P.O. Box 124838

San Diego, California 92112

Send $1.80 for information.

Paul Beyerl

9724 One Hundred Thirty-Second Avenue N.E.

Kirkland, Washington 98033

Noted herbalist and astrologer offers books, tapes, and study materials. Send $2.00 for a sample of *Hermit's Lantern.*

POTO (Procurer of the Obscure)
11002 Massachusetts Avenue
Westwood, California 90025

"A mail-order and networking company serving the new seeker and scholar as well." Herbs, jewelry, gifts, tools, and books from Abracadabra to Zen. Catalog: $5.00.

Pyramid Books and the New Age Collection
P.O. Box 48
35 Congress Street
Salem, Massachusetts 01970
(508) 744-6261 (Monday through Saturday, 10 A.M. to 5 P.M. Eastern Standard Time)

For a current catalog, send $1.00.

Quintessential Oils
847 Thirty-fifth Street
Richmond, California 94805

Write for a free sixty-four-page catalog featuring aromatherapy, massage, and herbal products, as well as candles, incense, books, supplies, and other items.

Ritual Creations
P.O. Box 6394
Norfolk, Virginia 23508
(804) 440-8341

Pagan ritual wear and adornments. Call or write for more information or to request a catalaog.

Rosewynd's Simples
453 Proctor Road
Manchester, New Hampshire 03109

Oils and incense for ritual and magickal use. Also has handcrafted wood amulets, runes, bath salts, wands, and other magickal items as they become available. Nearly everything in the catalog is made by Rosewynd or other Witches personally known to her.

Please include a large self-addressed stamped envelope when requesting a catalog.

Runa-Raven
P.O. Box 557
Smithville, Texas 78957

Runic and magickal books, Norse and Germanic jewelry (including a wide selection of Thor's hammers), compact discs, audio- and video-tapes, rune-staves, and other magickal tools. Catalog: $1.00.

Runes and Bindrunes
P.O. Box 364
Dania, Florida 33004

Handcrafted sterling silver charms, earrings, pendants, pins, and custom designs. Send a self-addressed stamped envelope to receive a free catalog.

Sacred Rose
P.O. Box 331389
Fort Worth, Texas 76163

Magickal jewelry, sacred oils, spiritual stones, and powerful talismans. Free catalog.

The Sage Garden
P.O. Box 144
Payette, Idaho 83661
(208) 454-2026

Herbs, common and hard-to-find essential oils, spell kits, amulets, talismans, garb, statuary, runes, unique anointing oils, filler-free incense, bath and beauty items, and jewelry. Publisher of WPPA member publication *Artemesia's Magick!* Other services include Tarot readings and custom orders. Free catalog with large self-addressed stamped envelope with three first-class stamps.

Salem West
1209 N. High Street
Columbus, Ohio 43201
(614) 421-7557

The "home of the Real Witches' Ball" has created a "religious supply catalog" for the Wiccan/Neopagan community. Books, herbs, candles, incense, oils, spell kits, jewelry, talismans, rital items, Tarot, and divination supplies. Free catalog.

Serpentine Music Productions

P.O. Box 2564

Sebastopol, California 95473

(707) 823-7425; fax: (707) 823-6444

Hard-to-find Pagan music. Inquire about its volume discount program for religious groups. Catalog: $1.00.

Seven Sisters of New Orleans

12265 Foothill Boulevard, no. 17

Sylmar, California 91342

(818) 834-8383

The "leading manufacturer of spiritual oils, incense, and bath and wash products." Also carries candles, perfumes, books, crystal balls, herbs, mojo bags, prayer cards, spell kits, statues, Tarot cards, and Voodoo dolls. All orders are shipped within twenty-four hours. A free gift is sent with each order. (The value of the gift increases as the amount of your order increases.) Catalog: $2.00.

Sew Mote It Be

P.O. Box 781

Bellingham, Washington 98227

Offers custom-made, handcrafted "spell coats." Each coat is available for $75.00 (includes shipping and handling). To order one for happiness, love, energy, or prosperity, send a photo of yourself, your color choice, size, and the spells you wish to have stitched into your reversible, unisex coat.

Shadow Enterprises

P.O. Box 18094

Columbus, Ohio 43218

(614) 262-1175

Offers a unique collection of one-of-a-kind items, fine metaphysical supplies, ritual tools, and jewelry; new, used and rare books; collectibles, book search service, and much more. For more information, send $1.00.

Shadow's Grove

P.O. Box 177

Cedar Creek, Texas 78612

Gemstone wands, Goddess goblets, calendars, incense, herbs, cauldrons, oils, handcrafted tree spirit brooms, prayer staffs, and more. Catalog: $5.00 (refundable with your first order).

Shell's Mystical Oils

P.O. Box 691646

Stockton, California 95269

Carries over three hundred different herbs, some of which are very hard to find. Also occult oils, incense, tinctures, candles, altar covers, stones, charms, bags, sprinkling powders, made-to-order full-length ritual robes and capes, and much more. Catalog: $2.00.

Sidda

P.O. Box 186

Blue River, Oregon 97413

Obsidian athames, ceremonial blades, antler or obsidian herb knives, and obsidian mirrors. Send $1.00 for a brochure.

Solomon Seal Occult Service Co.

9 E. Main Street

Kutztown, Pennsylvania 19530

(610) 433-3610

Occult books and supplies. Catalog: $2.00.

The Source

P.O. Box 484

Warrington, Pennsylvania 18976

Send $3.00 for a two hundred-page psychic directory and New Age product catalog (refundable with your first order).

Southworth Enterprises

P.O. Box 440624

Aurora, Colorado 80044

(303) 888-5667

Celtic jewelry catalog: $3.00 (refundable with your first order).

Technicians of the Sacred
1317 N. San Fernando Way, Suite 310
Burbank, California 91504

Books, music, oils, and ritual supplies related to Neo-African systems, Voudoun, and ritual magick. Catalog: $5.00.

Touch Stone
1601-A Page Street
San Francisco, California 94117
(415) 621-2782

Candles, crystals, ritual oils, altar goods, books, incense, and other occult items. Catalog: $2.00.

The Unicorn Forge
105 Crescent Street
Mazomanie, Wisconsin 53560

Knives and swords, all manner of metalwork, positive path *only*. Write for prices, giving specifics, including sketches with dimensions, if known. All edged tools are forged. All pieces warranted against defects in materials and workmanship and cleansed prior to shipping to give the owner the purest receptacle for charging his or her needs.

Whispered Prayers
932 W. Eighth Avenue, Suite D
Chico, California 95926
Web site: www.whisperedprayers.com
(916) 894-2927

Magickal teas, bath salts, spell kits, books, tumbled stones, herbs, oils, and more. Free mail-order catalog. Wholesale packet also available. No minimum order required.

White Light Pentacles/Sacred Spirit Products
P.O. Box 8163
Salem, Massachusetts 01971
(800) MASTERY
(978) 745-8668
(978) 741-2355

This company is dedicated to the propagation of the Wiccan arts and magickal sciences. It is the distributor of thousands of authentic spiritual tools, talismans, jewelry, and supplies, plus many other offerings for the celebration of life. Cast a mighty spell in your home or office! Catalog: $3.00.

Widening Horizons

21713-B N.E. One Hundred Forty-First Street
Woodinville, Washington 98072
(206) 869-9810; fax: (206) 869-1821

A complete line of numerology software. Call or write for a free catalog and samples.

Willow Keep

P.O. Box 664
Wilton, New Hampshire 03086
(603) 672-0229

Herbs, pathworking tapes, Pagan T-shirts, incense, natural wands, dolls, altar statues, bronze pentacles, and more. Also workshops and open rituals. Catalog: $1.00 (refundable with your first order).

Witch Works

P.O. Box 1839
Royal Oak, Michigan 48068

Send a self-addressed stamped envelope to receive a free brochure on "empowered herbal oils with moon-cultivated herbs, gemstone aligned."

Witchery Company

P.O. Box 4067
Middletown, Rhode Island 02842

"A collection of hard-to-find quality items sure to be of interest to the serious practitioner." Catalog: $2.00.

Woman of Wands

P.O. Box 330
South Lee, Massachusetts 01260
Phone/fax: (413) 243-4036

Specializing in Goddess religion, women's health, and Wicca. Catalog: $3.00 (credited on your first order).

World Tree Publications
  P.O. Box 961
  Payso, Arizona 85547

The outreach ministry of the Asatru Alliance offers a large selection of books, tapes, videos, rune sets, statues, jewelry, ritual manuals, and other items for the serious Asatruari. Free illustrated catalog.

Worldwide Curio House
  P.O. Box 17095-G
  Minneapolis, Minnesota 55417

The "world's largest Occult Mystic Arts supply house." Thousands of curios, books, herbs, oils, gifts, unique jewelry, and talismans. Items from all over the world. Three catalogs: $2.00 (220 total pages).

Wren Faire Designs
  4290 Pepper Drive
  San Diego, California 92105
  (619) 282-2889

A small catalog of jewelry designs, including custom silver crowns and handfasting rings.

Zephyr Services
  1900 Murray Avenue
  Pittsburgh, Pennsylvania 15217
  (800) 533-6666; (412) 422-6600

Write or call for a free catalog of New Age software.

10

Psychic and Paranormal Organizations

The world of psychic powers and paranormal phenomena is a mysterious and truly fascinating place to explore. Many Wiccans, Pagans, and other magickal people around the world are in tune with their psychic sides or are working to cultivate their powers of clairvoyance, and most have experienced the paranormal in one way or another.

It is important to mention here that not everyone who is connected with the Craft is psychic, and being a psychic is certainly not a requirement for being a Wiccan, Pagan, Witch, or Magician. However, for those individuals who do take an interest in things of a psychic nature, the following collection of listings (arranged alphabetically) has been assembled.

This section of the book is also a good one to consult if you have ever considered participating in psychic research programs or if your interests and experiences run the gamut of such things as Bigfoot, lake monsters, ghosts, haunted houses, or anything classified as "the unexplained."

Academy of Psychic Arts and Sciences
100 Turtle Creek Village, Suite 363
P.O. Box 191129
Dallas, Texas 75219

American Society for Psychical Research
5 W. Seventy-third Street
New York, New York 10023
(212) 799-5050

The purpose and scope of the society is to investigate all forms of paranormal and psychic phenomena; to collect, classify, study, and publish such reports; and to maintain a library on psychic research and other related subjects. It publishes a journal and newsletter. Write for membership and subscription information.

Arizona Bigfoot Center
P.O. Box 412
Paulden, Arizona 86334
Contact: Lyle Vann

Association for Research and Enlightenment
P.O. Box 595
Virginia Beach, Virginia 23451

An organization dedicated to perpetuating the work of Edgar Cayce (the "Sleeping Prophet"). Sponsors psychic research, publishes a bimonthly magazine, and offers classes, lectures, and workshops.

Bigfoot Central
P.O. Box 147
Bothell, Washington 98041

Bigfoot Information Project
114 Rosewood Drive
Greenbelt, Maryland 20770
Contact: Mark Opsasnick

Bigfoot Investigation Center
4180 Cat Lake Road
Mayville, Michigan 48744
Contact: Art Kapa

Borderland Sciences Research Foundation
P.O. Box 429
Garberville, California 95440

Central Premonitions Registry
P.O. Box 482
Times Square Station
New York, New York 10036

Ghost Research Society
Dale Kaczmarek, president
P.O. Box 205
Oak Lawn, Illinois 60454

Haunt Hunters
2188 Sycamore Hill Court
Chesterfield, Missouri 63017

International Fortean Society
P.O. Box 367
Arlington, Virginia 22210

International Society for the Study of Ghosts and Apparitions
Jeanne D. Youngson, president
29 Washington Square West PHN
New York, New York 10011

International Society of Cryptozoology
P.O. Box 43070
Tucson, Arizona 85733

Lake Champlain Phenomena Investigation
P.O. Box 2134
Wilton, New York 12866

Michigan/Canadian Bigfoot Information Center
c/o Wayne W. King
Caro, Michigan 48723
(616) 673-2715

New Age Metaphysical Research Association
1201 Lake Air
Waco, Texas 76710

New York Fortean Society
John Keel, president
P.O. Box 22024
New York, New York 10025

North American Bigfoot Information Center
1923 Glenwood Drive
Twinsburg, Ohio 44087

Parapsychology Foundation
228 E. Seventy-first Street
New York, New York 10021

Pennsylvania Association for Study of the Unexplained
6 Oak Hill Avenue
Greensburg, Pennsylvania 15601
Contact: Stan Gordon

Psychic Connection International
13067 Calais Street
New Orleans, Louisiana 70129

An organization for individuals interested in psychic as well as spiritual services. Offers a free psychic referral service.

The Psychic Society
P.O. Box 331058
Fort Worth, Texas 76163

An organization "dedicated to the research of psychic phenomena and to learning the mysteries of life." Write for its free newsletter and a membership application.

The Society for Psychical Research
49 Marloes Road
London W8 6LA
England
(071) 937-8984

Founded in 1882, its "purpose is to examine without prejudice or prepossession, and in a scientific spirit, those faculties of man, real or supposed, which appear to be inexplicable on any generally recognized hypothesis." It publishes a quarterly journal (one-year subscription: $36.00/£20) that focuses on all forms of paranormal phenomena. Address all membership inquiries to the secretary at the above address.

Strange Research
P.O. Box 2246
Rockville, Maryland 20852
Contact: Mark Chorvinsky

11

Resources for Gay and Lesbian Pagans

A growing number of gays and lesbians are turning their backs on many of the patriarchal and homophobic mainstream religions and embracing the Earth-centered paths of Neopagan spirituality. They are hearing the call of the Goddess (and the Horned God) and are finding spiritual fulfillment, magickal empowerment, and acceptance within the world of the Craft.

The Goddess loves all, regardless of our sexual orientation. She does not make judgment calls, nor does She invoke punishment upon any of Her children—whether straight, gay, lesbian, bisexual, or transgendered—because of his or her sexuality. In Her words, from the *Charge of the Goddess*: "All acts of love and pleasure are my rituals."

This section is not included for the purpose of separating between heterosexual and homosexual Pagans. Rather, it is intended as a helpful resource guide to gay-lesbian covens, support groups, networking groups, and various organizations devoted to helping gays and lesbians connect on a spiritual, as well as a magickal, level. This section also brings to light the wonderful diversity that exists within the Wiccan/Neo-Pagan community. And diversity, like the Goddess Herself, should always be celebrated!

Festive Circles Update
c/o GLPC
P.O. Box 26442
Oklahoma City, Oklahoma 73126

A newsletter published by the Gay and Lesbian Pagan Coalition. Sample copy: $3.00. Please make all checks and money orders payable to Inner City Publications.

Gay and Lesbian Pagan Coalition (GLPC)
P.O. Box 26442
Oklahoma City, Oklahoma 73126
Contact: Desmond Stone

An international referral network for gay and lesbian Pagans (including bisexual, transgendered, and transsexual persons). Founded in 1990, GLPC publishes the *Festive Circles Update* newsletter.

Gay Metaphysical Spiritual Association
P.O. Box 5592
Santa Monica, California 90405

An organization devoted to spiritual and personal growth.

Gay Metaphysicians
P.O. Box 770973
Lakewood, Ohio 44107

Hoblink
Box 22
4–7 Dorset Street
Brighton
East Sussex BL2 1WA
England

"A British organization specifically for gay and bisexual Neopagans."

Lady Mandragora/Gerina Dunwich
P.O. Box 4263
Chatsworth, California 91313

Wiccan and Pagan marriages and handfastings performed, regardless of gender or sexual orientation, by a Wiccan High Priestess who is a legally ordained Minister of the Universal Life Church. All spiritual paths and Wiccan traditions served. Send a self-addressed stamped envelope for more information.

Pantheos

Joe Lawrence Lembo, editor
P.O. Box 9543
Santa Fe, New Mexico 87504

A quarterly nationwide personal networking newsletter for gay and bisexual Pagan men. One-year subscription: $15.00; Canadian subscription: $16.00

Queer Pagans

P.O. Box 1618
Canal Street Station
New York, New York 10013

A newsletter published by The Coven of the Middle Piller. Free in the New York City Metro area. Subscribers outside of New York are asked to send a donation.

The Radical Faeries

(718) 625-4505

An eclectic group that hosts many unique events focusing on "queer spirituality" and Earth-nature awareness. Also publishes the *Faeriegram*, a community project of the New York Radical Faeries.

Rainbow Wind

c/o Sarah Glenn
P.O. Box 8275
Lexington, Kentucky 40533

A "Queer Pagan Network" serving Kentucky and surrounding states. Member of ERAL (Earth Religion Assistance List) and WARD (Witches Against Religious Discrimination).

Sappho Lesbian WitchCamp

c/o Sappho
Box 21510
1850 Commercial Drive
Vancouver, British Columbia V5N 4A0
Canada

Spirit Journeys

P.O. Box 3046
Asheville, North Carolina 28802
(704) 258-8880; fax: (704) 281-0334

Sponsors events for gay and bisexual men that encourage self-discovery and passion for life. Offers workshops, retreats, and journeys, many of which incorporate a mystical or cultural theme and include meditation, ceremony, wandering sacred sites, and exchanges with indigenous people.

Touching Body and Spirit

Sunfire, editor
Victoria Valentine, Associate Editor
P.O. Box 957
Huntington, New York 11743

A gay male publication "committed to bringing you information that will help you make the right choices concerning the spiritual direction of your life." Published quarterly by the TBS Network, the journal contains reviews of books and tapes, articles on workshops, interviews, and a listing of workshops and ongoing groups "dedicated to the spiritual development of gay men." Sample copy: $3.00; one-year subscription: $10.00. Membership in the TBS Network, including a subscription and a listing of all network members (published annually and updated quarterly) is $20.00 yearly. Write for a free membership application.

The Trident

Abrasax Publications
P.O. Box 1219
Corpus Christi, Texas 78403

A newsletter of the Servants of the Star and Snake, covering Tantric sexuality and the occult from a bisexual and gay perspective. Write for more information.

12

Festivals, Gatherings, and Workshops

Pagan gatherings and festivals compare to no other event. They are magickal happenings that unite the Wiccan and Pagan communities, provide education and enlightenment through workshops and lectures, and allow many Witches to come out of their proverbial broom closets and be themselves. A Pagan gathering or festival is also an ideal place for Pagans to connect with others of a like mind, as well as for non-Pagans to learn about Neopagan spirituality and the ways of the Craft. And it is not uncommon for one to be filled with music, dancing, drumming circles, arts and crafts, celebrities, psychic readers, teachers, vendors, magick, diversity, and colorful characters.

Gatherings and festivals are held at many locations throughout the world and at various times throughout the year. However, a good number of them are held on dates that coincide with the solstices, equinoxes, and Sabbats of the Wheel of the Year. Their locations often change and new events spring up constantly. Some are open only to women, and some only to men. But most are open to all, regardless of gender, race, age, sexuality, or spiritual tradition.

For locations, directions, dates, prices, and other details, call or write to the person or organization that sponsors the event or is listed as a contact.

Alabama

Bear Tribe   3750-A Airport Boulevard, no. 223, Mobile, Alabama 36608; (334) 471-1373

Arizona

High Desert Mid-Summer Gathering   Sponsored by The Sacred Grove, 16845 N. Twenty-ninth Avenue, no. 1346, Phoenix, Arizona 85023; (602) 433-7951

Stirring Forth of Spring Festival   Sponsored by the Mooncircle Pagan Network, P.O. Box 12104, Tucson, Arizona 85732; (602) 881-1186

Arkansas

Ozark Pagan Council   P.O. Box 605, Springdale, Arkansas 72764

California

Ancient Ways Festival   Sponsored by Ancient Ways, 4075 Telegraph Avenue, Oakland, California 94609; (510) 653-3244

Church of All Worlds   P.O. Box 488, Laytonville, California 95454; (707) 984-7062

Harvest Moon Celebration   Sponsored by the Educational Society for Pagans, P.O. Box 18211, Encino, California 91316

International Goddess Festival: Goddess 2000 and **Hungarian Hot Springs Goddess Tour**   Sponsored by The Women's Spirituality Forum, P.O. Box 11363, Piedmont, California 94611; (510) 444-7724

Merry Meet   Sponsored by Covenant of the Goddess, P.O. Box 1226, Berkeley, California 94701

Ravenwood (and others)   Sponsored by Freya's Folk, 537 Jones Street, no. 165, San Francisco, California 94102

Colorado

Earth Tribe Universal   Sponsored by the Al-Mali Institute, 3000 E. Colfax, no. 355, Denver, Colorado 80203; (303) 754-2994

Sabbat Gatherings   Sponsored by The Web, P.O. Box 1871, Boulder, Colorado 80306; (303) 939-8832

Connecticut

CraftWise Pagan Gathering   Sponsored by CraftWise, P.O. Box 457, Botsford, Connecticut 06404; (203) 874-5832

Florida

Church of Iron Oak   P.O. Box 060672, Palm Bay, Florida 32903

LifeSpring Gathering   Sponsored by Steve Dugas, 2190 Traymore Road, Jacksonville, Florida 32207

Magickal Mabon Weekend   Sponsored by PAN, P.O. Box 290684, Temple Terrace, Florida 33687

Georgia

DragonPhyre   Sponsored by Phoenix Enterprises, 2800 W. Highway 5, Bowdon, Georgia 30108

Spiral   Sponsored by The Wyrd Sisters, P.O. Box 658, Dahlonega, Georgia 30533

Illinois

Eleusis   P.O. Box 257996, Chicago, Illinois 60625

Pagan Fest Chicago   Sponsored by the Pagan Interfaith Embassy, 3257 W. Eastwood, Chicago, Illinois 60625

Pan Pagan Festival   Sponsored by the Midwest Pagan Council, P.O. Box 160, Western Springs, Illinois 60558

Spring and Fall Pagan Gatherings   Sponsored by the Circle of Danu (and other local groups), 1310 W. Lunt Avenue, no. 507, Chicago, Illinois 60626

Indiana

Elf-Fest and **Wild Magick Gathering**   Sponsored by the Elf Lore Family (ELF), P.O. Box 1082, Bloomington, Indiana 47402 (812) 275-0923

Halloween Ball and **Thunder Fest**   Sponsored by the Lion's Nest, R.R. no. 18, Box 78, Bedford, Indiana 47421

Spirit Gathering   Sponsored by Spirit Weaver's Nest, P.O. Box 2867, Toledo, Ohio 43606; (419) 531-9785

Kansas

Heartland Spirit Festival   Sponsored by the Heartland Spiritual Alliance, P.O. Box 3407, Kansas City, Kansas 66103; (816) 561-6111

Maryland

Free Spirit Festival   Sponsored by the Free Spirit Alliance, P.O. Box 5358, Laurel, Maryland 20726; (301) 604-6049

In Gaia's Lap (An annual women's gathering)   P.O. Box 65237, Baltimore, Maryland 21209; (888) 740-4242

Massachusetts

Annual Women's Herbal Conference   Sponsored by Blazing Star Herbal School and Sage, P.O. Box 6, Shelburne Falls, Massachusetts 01370; (413) 625-6875

Hearthfire, Rites of Spring, Suntide Celebration, and **Twilight Covening**   Sponsored by EarthSpirit, P.O. Box 723, Williamsburg, Massachusetts 01096; (413) 238-4240

Rowe Camp   Kings Highway Road, Rowe, Massachusetts 01367; (413) 339-4954

Minnesota

Merry Meet   P.O. Box 13158, Minneapolis, Minnesota 55415

Mississippi

Gulf Coast Womyn's Festival and **Spirit Fest**   Sponsored by Henson Productions, P.O. Box 12, Ovett, Mississippi; (601) 344-2005

Missouri

Laid-Back Labor Day Fest   Sponsored by Earth Rising, Inc., P.O. Box 10442, Kansas City, Missouri; (816) 561-6111

Pagan Picnic   Sponsored by CAST, P.O. Box 2564, St. Louis, Missouri 63114; (314) 772-1274

Traditional Annual Yule Ritual and Bash   Sponsored by Greenleaf, P.O. Box 924, Springfield, Missouri 65802

New Hampshire

Old Hampshire Fair   Sponsored by Town and Gown Neopagan Focus Group, c/o Unitarian Universalist Fellowship, 20 Madbury Road, Durham, New Hampshire 03824; (603) 868-5050

New Jersey

The Goddess Is Alive!   Sponsored by Moon Dancers, c/o Peregrine, 7 Stevens Road, no. 62, Wallington, New Jersey 07057

Womyngathering: The Festival of Womyn's Spirituality   P.O. Box 559, Franklinville, New Jersey 08322; (609) 694-2037

New Mexico

Feast of the Gods and **Open Summer Sessions**   Sponsored by Our Lady of the Shining Staar, P.O. Box 520, Church Rock, New Mexico 87311; (505) 488-5364

Mabon Mountain Mysteries   Sponsored by the Cimarron Local Council of the Covenant of the Goddess, P.O. Box 1107, Los Alamos, New Mexico 87544; (505) 662-5333

Wiminfest   P.O. Box 80204, Albuquerque, New Mexico 87198; (800) 499-5688

New York

Sirius Rising, Heartsong, and others   Sponsored by Brushwood Folklore Center, 8881 Bailey Hill Road, Sherman, New York 14781; (716) 761-6750

Starwood   Sponsored by ACE, 1643 Lee Road, no. 9, Cleveland Heights, Ohio 44118; (800) 446-4962

Wise Woman Center   P.O. Box 64, Woodstock, New York 12498; (914) 246-8081

North Carolina

Serpentstone   P.O. Box 368, Chandler, North Carolina 28715

Ohio

Goddess Gathering   Sponsored by The Temple of Wicca (and other groups), P.O. Box 2281, Lancaster, Ohio 43130

Green Dome Temple   P.O. Box 14059, Cincinnati, Ohio 45250

International Pagan Spirit Gathering   Sponsored by Circle Sanctuary, P.O. Box 219, Mt. Horeb, Wisconsin 53572; (608) 924-2216 (weekdays 1–4 P.M. Central Standard Time)

Lumen's Gate   Sponsored by N'Chi, P.O. Box 19566, Cincinnati, Ohio 45219; (513) 791-0344

OTO National Conference   Sponsored by Black Sun Oasis, P.O. Box 4866, Akron, Ohio 44310

Pagan Community Council of Ohio Gatherings   Sponsored by PCCO, P.O. Box 82089, Columbus, Ohio 43202; (614) 261-1022

The Real Witches' Ball   Sponsored by Salem West, 1209 N. High Street, Columbus, Ohio 43201; (614) 421-7557

Witchstock   Sponsored by Harvest Moon Haven, 215 High Street, Fairport Harbor, Ohio 44077

Oregon

Earth and Sky Gathering   Sponsored by Aerious, 93640 Deadwood Creek Road, Deadwood, Oregon 97430; (503) 964-5341

National Rainbow Gathering of the Tribes   P.O. Box 5577, Eugene, Oregon 97405

Northwest Fall Equinox Festival   Sponsored by The Nine Houses of Gaia, Inc., P.O. Box 14415, Portland, Oregon 97214; (503) 239-8877

Pennsylvania

Drum and Splash   Sponsored by the Church of the Four
Quarters, R.D. no. 1, 62-C Silvermills Road, Artemis, Pennsylvania
17211

Foxwood Mayfest Pagan Music Festival (Artemis,
Pennsylvania)   Sponsored by White Dove, 108 Alabama Avenue,
Beckley, West Virginia 25801

Sisterspace   542-A S. Forty-Eighth Street, Philadelphia,
Pennsylvania 19143

South Carolina

Witchstock   (Anderson, South Carolina) Sponsored by Serpentstone,
P.O. Box 368, Chandler, North Carolina 28715

Tennessee

Highlands of Tennessee Samhain Gathering   Sponsored by Avalon
Isle, P.O. Box 6006, Athens, Georgia 30604

Nashville Panathenaia   Sponsored by the Church of All Worlds, P.O.
Box 488, Laytonville, California 95454; (707) 925-6499

Texas

Council of the Magickal Arts   P.O. Box 33274, Austin, Texas 78764

Solstice Celebration and **Pan Thelemic Festival**   Sponsored by
Scarlet Woman Oasis OTO, P.O. Box 3203, Austin, Texas 78764;
(512) 443-7382

Vermont

Trillium   360 Toad Road, Charlotte, Vermont 05445

Virginia

Autumn Dance   c/o Rick Johnson, 5007-C Victory Boulevard, no. 165, Yorktown, Virginia 23693; (804) 874-5732

Ecumenicon and **Sacred Space Conference**   Sponsored by the Ecumenicon Foundation, 5400 Eisenhower Avenue, Alexandria, Virginia 22304; (703) 823-7560 (ask for Ecumenicon).

Washington

Hecate's Sickle (and others)   Sponsored by the Aquarian Tabernacle Church, P.O. Box 409, Index, Washington 98256

Wisconsin

Circle Sanctuary Gatherings   Sponsored by Circle Sanctuary, P.O. Box 219, Mt. Horeb, Wisconsin 53572; (608) 924-2216

Earth Conclave   P.O. Box 14377, Madison, Wisconsin 53714; (608) 244-4488

Gathering of Priestesses and **Witches Gathering for Hallows**   Sponsored by RCG, Box 6677, Madison Wisconsin 53716; (608) 257-5858

Canada

Wic-Can Fest   P.O. Box 125, 940 Danforth Avenue, Toronto, Ontario M1L 1B1

Witchcamp   Sponsored by B.C. Witchcamp News, P.O. Box 21510, 1850 Commercial Drive, Vancouver, British Columbia V5N 4A0; (604) 253-7189

Womynspirit Festival   Sponsored by the Womynspirit Collective, 62 Hayes Avenue, Guelph, Ontario N1E 5V8; (519) 763-3959

Other Countries

Annual Ritual of the Circle of the Dragon   Sponsored by Circle of the Dragon, B.P. 68, 33034 Bordeaux Cedex, France; 56-94-73-99

Big Green Gathering   P.O. Box 123, Salisbury SP2 0YA, United Kingdom; 01747-870-667

Each Sabbat   Sponsored by Arkana, Georgstrasse 4, 22041 Hamburg, Germany; (040) 687623

European Rainbow Gathering Greece   Contact: Julietta-Pangiota Sinoy, 8 Parapamisou Street, 175-72 Zografou, Athens-Hellas, Greece

The Fellowship of Isis Seasonal Festivals   Sponsored by The Fellowship of Isis, Clonegal Castle, Clonegal, Enniscorthy, South Ireland

Glastonbury Goddess Conference   2–4 High Street, Glastonbury BA6 9DU, United Kingdom

Pagan Rituals and Celebrations   Sponsored by Baelder, 60 Elmhurst Road, Reading, Berkshire RG1 5HY, England

Polmaddy Summer Solstice Bash   Sponsored by Thistledown, P.O. Box 7453, Kirks DG7 3SJ, Scotland

Talking Stick Festival   Sponsored by Talking Stick, P.O. Box 3719, London SW17 8XT, England; (081) 767-3473

13

The Left-Hand Path

First and foremost, it is very important to note that the practice of Wicca is as distinct from the Left-Hand Path (Satanism, sorcery, Crowley, etc.) as it is from Christianity. In fact, the tailfeathers of most Wiccans become greatly ruffled when any connection between the two is even hinted at.

However, the few things that Wicca and the Left-Hand Path *do* have in common are that both are plagued by gruesome misconceptions (created and perpetuated largely by the propaganda of conservative Christian groups), and neither is currently accepted by the majority of mainstream society.

Perhaps one of the most misunderstood and feared traditions of the Left-Hand Path (even by most Wiccans and Pagans) is that of Satanism. This religion is far from being the baby-killing, devil-worshipping cult that its detractors claim it is. A Satanist's concept of Satan is not the same one that has been defined by Christianity, and modern Satanism is a term that more accurately refers to a tradition that affirms as good the natural desires and impulses that have long been denounced as "evil" by those of the Christian faiths. True Satanists (such as those who are members of San Francisco's Church of Satan and follow the teachings of Anton LaVey's *Satanic Bible*) do not perform human sacrifices nor do they eat the flesh of newborn babies to acquire power or appease the devil. In fact, most Satanists do not even believe in the devil.

Notwithstanding, there is a handful of disturbed and dangerous individuals and groups throughout the world who label themselves Satanists or followers of the Left-Hand Path, and many unknowing and misguided persons (young people in particular) routinely fall victim to them.

This is perhaps the main reason why I have elected to include this section, as there need to be more resources for education and guidance. I also strongly feel that if an individual feels drawn to the Left-Hand Path, it is only fair that he or she be permitted that freedom of choice. And by making the proper resources available to them, I hope that seekers of this religious-magickal path will move in the right direction and safely connect with others of a like mind.

In addition to the resources presented in this section, Left-Hand Path books and ritual supplies can be obtained at many of the stores listed in chapter 8: "Magickal and Metaphysical Shops."

Organizations and Resources

Abyss Distribution

48 Chester Road
Chester, Massachusetts 01011
(413) 623-2155; fax: (413) 623-2156
E-mail address: Abyss Dist@aol.com.

This New Age/Pagan/occult mail-order company offers an excellent Left-Hand Path catalog supplement (upon request) of books and grimoires, including a wide selection of works by and about Aleister Crowley. Free catalog.

The Black Order of Pan-Europa

P.O. Box 774
Clarkton, Missouri 63837

The Church of Epiphany

4533 MacArthur Boulevard, Suite 339
Newport Beach, California 92660

Church of Luciferian Light
P.O. Box 7207
Tampa, Florida 33673

The Church of Satan
P.O. Box 210666
San Francisco, California 94121

The Church of Tiamat Grotto
60 Newtown Road, Suite 51
Danbury, Connecticut 06810

The Embassy of Lucifer
P.O. Box 1229
Terrace, British Columbia V8G 5P7
Canada

Infernacula
P.O. Box 792-666
San Antonio, Texas 78279
Fax: (210) 348-8666

A combination catalog and magazine of diabolical arts and craft works. Posters, banners, altar cloths, candle holders, medallions, statues, and more. Price: $3.50 plus an age of consent form; $4.50 outside the United States.

International Guild of Occult Sciences
255 El Cielo Road, Suite 565
Palm Springs, California 92262

Complete information and catalog: $3.00

Left-Hand Path Study Group
c/o Ronald Vroman, no. 235815
KCF, Kincheloe, Michigan 49788

The Leviathan Grotto
P.O. Box 5297
Santa Cruz, California 95063
Contact: Rev. Michael Charles Boe

Lucifer's Den
P.O. Box 402161
Hesperia, California 92340

(760) 606-0288

Web Site: www.lucifersden.net

Grotto of free thought. Contact: Brian Nalls, administrator.

Maledicta

Fax: (304) 346-6209

E-mail address: info@maledicta.com

Specialists in Left-Hand Path and Satanic merchandise.

Netherworld

701 N. Macquesten Parkway, no. 122-S

Mount Vernon, New York 10552

Baphomet pentagram pendants cast in pewter or sterling silver. Write for more information.

Pan-European Fraternity of Knowledge

60 Elmhurst Road

Reading

Berkshire RG1 5HY

England

Temple of the Vampire

P.O. Box 3582

Lacey, Washington 98509

Vampire Information Exchange

P.O. Box 290328

Brooklyn, New York 11229

Founded in 1978, this organization distributes information on vampires and vampirism in both fact and fiction. It publishes the *VIE Newsletter* five or six times per year.

Periodicals

The Abyss

P.O. Box 774

Clarkton, Missouri 63837

Editor: Max Frith.

Sample copy: $4.00; outside of the United States: $6.00.

The Ambassador
P.O. Box 1229
Terrace, British Columbia V8G 5P7
Published weekly. Sample copy: $4.00 (Canadian funds).

Battle of Bewitchment
P.O. Box 5069
451 05 Uddevalla
Sweden
Sample copy: $6.00 (U.S. funds). Make checks payable to Robert Hoog.

The Black Flame
P.O. Box 499
Radio City Station
New York, New York 10101
International forum of the Church of Satan. Double-issue price: $6.00 ($8.00 outside of the United States); one-year subscription (two double issues): $12.00; foreign subscriptions: $16.00.

The Black Pun-kin
P.O. Box 32017
1386 Richmond R.D.
Ottawa, Ontario K2B 1A1
Canada
A publication upholding the principles and philosophy of Anton Szandor LaVey's Church of Satan. Price: $7.00 (Canada and United States); overseas: $10.00. Make all checks and money orders payable to Robert A. Lang.

The Cloven Hoof
P.O. Box 210666
San Francisco, California 94121
The official bulletin and tribunal of the Church of Satan, the original voice of contemporary Satanism. Single issue: $5.00 (foreign: $7.00); four-issue subscription: $35.00 (foreign: $40.00).

Dark Rising
P.O. Box 8392
Tampa, Florida 33674

The official forum of the Black Order of the Shaitan Warrior. Sample copy: $3.00 (cash or money orders payable to Brad W. Reinert, no personal checks accepted).

Devilcosm
DWR
P.O. Box 173
Madison, Indiana 47250
Editor: Eric W. Thompson

A magazine of Satanic, Iconoclastic, and Occult Music. Sample copy: $3.00 (foreign: $4.00); four-issue subscription: $12.00 (foreign: $16.00).

The Devil's Tavern
c/o Douglas Richards, editor
P.O. Box 16474
Pensacola, Florida 32507

The international forum of the Infernal Garrison. Sample copy: $6.00.

Diabolica
c/o Azazel
P.O. Box 53
Allen Park, Michigan 48101

An independent forum of Satanic thought. Sample copy: $6.00 (foreign: $7.00); one-year subscription: $11.00 (foreign: $13.00). Make all checks (U.S. funds) payable to Azazel.

Endemoniada
Lucifera
611 W. One Hundred Fifty-Second Street, no. 1-D
New York, New York 10031

A black metal music magazine for Satanic females. Sample copy: $3.00 (cash or money order, payable to Elena Leon).

Esoterra
Chad Hensley, editor
630 S. Carollton Avenue, no. 110
New Orleans, Louisiana 70118

The journal of extreme culture. Sample copy: $6.25.

The Nammtar Journal
  60 Newtown Road, Suite 51
  Danbury, Connecticut 06810

  A publication from the Church of Tiamat Grotto. Sample copy: $5.00.

Not Like Most
  Purging Talon Publishing
  P.O. Box 8131
  Burlington, Vermont 05402

  A publication of Satanism in action. Sample copy: $2.00 (foreign: $3.00).

The Public Satanist
  P.O. Box 201835
  Bloomington, Minnesota 55420

  A publication of Satan's Playground Grotto. Sample copy: $5.00 (check or money payable to Brett Randall). Satanic poetry, interviews, and more.

The Raging Sea: The Voice of Reason
  c/o The Leviathan Grotto
  P.O. Box 5297
  Santa Cruz, California 95063

  Sample copy: $3.95.

The Raven
  Grotto ODM
  P.O. Box 163
  Stratford, Connecticut 06497

  Sample copy: $4.00; four-issue subscription: $15.00.

Ravens' Chat
  c/o J. P. Tabone
  B. P. 236
  31004 Toulouse Cedex
  France

  Sample copy: $5.00.

Satanic Parenting
IZM Enterprises
P.O. Box 353
Maple Park, Illinois 60151

Editor: Lydia Gage. "Sharing ideas for the Infernal Empire." Sample copy: $2.00; four-issue subscription: $6.00.

Scapegoat Magazine
Goat's Head Press
P.O. Box 36121
Los Angeles, California 90036

Sample copy: $5.00 (foreign: $6.00); three-issue subscription: $15.00 (foreign: $18.00).

14

Pagan Potpourri

This section contains a little of this and a little of that, but all the entries are important to the Pagan, Wiccan, and New Age community, serving it in one way or another. You will find listings for many talented craftspeople and artists, psychic readers and counselors, computer bulletin boards, spiritual retreat centers, museums, and other persons, places, and things that could not be listed in any of the previous sections of this book.

California

Faerie Dance Tours
204½ Broadway
Costa Mesa, California 92627
(714) 548-5268; fax: (714) 642-3861

Power Places Tours and Conferences
24532 Del Prado
Dana Point, California 92629
(800) 234-TOUR; (714) 487-3450; fax: (714) 487-3456

The "leader in spirit-centered journeys and conferences" offers "profound journeys with a like-minded group of international spiritual pilgrims" to various places around the world "that have proven throughout millennia to open the mind, expand awareness, and accelerate spiritual evolution."

Sacred Women's Journeys
P.O. Box 5544
Berkeley, California 94705
(510) 525-4847

Offers group tours and cruises to exotic places, chanting, and Goddess rituals. For spiritual-minded women.

Colorado

American Tarot Association
P.O. Box 17164
Boulder, Colorado 80308

Benefits of membership include: bimonthly newsletter, correspondence courses, individualized instruction, and listing in the Registry. Write for complete details.

Colorado Women's Center for the Performing and Visual Arts
P.O. Box 142
Fairplay, Colorado 80440
(719) 836-2177

A Pagan center providing cultural and spiritual retreats for women.

Florida

Pagan's Way
P.O. Box 5442
Hollywood, Florida 33083
(305) 925-1620; (305) 925-8403

A Pagan computer network.

Louisiana

Maison de la Luna Noir
726 Third Street
New Orleans, Louisiana 70130

A guestroom for Pagans, Sorcerers, Voodooists, etc. Current price: $15.00 per night.

New Orleans Voodoo Museum
724 Dumaine Street
New Orleans, Louisiana 70130
(504) 523-7685; (504) 522-5223

Open seven days a week, 10 A.M. to 6 P.M. General admission: $5.25.

Maine

Venus Adventures
P.O. Box 167
Peaks Island, Maine 04108
(207) 766-5655

Goddess tours (small groups) for fun, education, and inspiration. Call or write for additional information and tour destinations and prices.

Massachusetts

Rajj
P.O. Box 204
Monument Beach, Massachusetts 02553

Dream empowerment through Rajj. Inspirational channeling in response to individual dreams. Rajj, channeled, is close to the dream-realm, giving dynamic responses, sharing valuable insights, and revealing dream's natural creative power. Send dream, questions, and check ($25.00 per dream) to Rajj.

Rebecca Nurse Homestead
149 Pine Street
Danvers, Massachusetts 01923
(508) 774-8799

The historic homestead of Rebecca Nurse (who was hanged as a Witch in 1692 on Salem's Gallows Hill). Guided tours and a twenty-five-minute slide show on the historic "Witch hysteria of 1692." Adult admission: $3.50; children under sixteen: $1.50. Open approximately June through late October. Hours: 1:00 P.M. to 4:30 P.M. Closed Mondays.

Salem Wax Museum of Witches and Seafarers

288 Derby Street
Salem, Massachusetts 01970
(508) 740-2929

Hours: September through May (10 A.M. to 5 P.M.); June through August (10 A.M. to 7 P.M.). Adult admission: $4.00; seniors: $3.50; children: $2.50.

Salem Witch Museum

192 Washington Square
Salem, Massachusetts 01970
(508) 744-1692

Offers a complete look at the Salem Witch Trials of 1692. Open daily, year round. Hours: September through June (10 A.M. to 5 P.M.); July through August (10 A.M. to 7 P.M.). Adult admission: $4.00; seniors: $3.50; children six to fourteen years old: $2.50. Group rates available.

Witch Dungeon Museum

16 Lynde Street
Salem, Massachusetts 01970
(508) 741-3570

A presentation of a Witch trial adapted from the 1692 historical transcripts, reenacted by professional actors. Open daily from 10 A.M. to 5 P.M. Adult admission: $4.00; seniors: $3.50; children: $2.50.

Witch House

310½ Essex Street
Salem, Massachusetts 01970
(508) 744-0180

The restored home (circa 1642) of Jonathan Corwin, one of the Salem Witch Trials' infamous judges. Preliminary examinations of women and men accused of the crime of Witchcraft took place in this building. Open from March 15 through June 30, and Labor Day through December 1. House: 10:00 A.M. to 4:30 P.M. Adult admission: $5.00; children five to sixteen years old: $1.50.

Minnesota

International Druid Archival Deposit
Carleton Archives (re: Druids)
Carleton College
Northfield, Minnesota 55057
(507) 663-4270

Directors: Eric Hilleman and Michael Scharding, college archivists. Founded in 1963 and open to visitors, Monday through Friday, 9 A.M. to 5 P.M.

Missouri

Diana's Grove
P.O. Box 159
Salem, Missouri 65560
(314) 689-2400

A retreat center on 102 wooded acres with a hot tub, swimming hole, and trails. Holds Pagan gatherings. Open to visitors by appointment only.

Gaea Retreat Center
P.O. Box 10442
Kansas City, Missouri 64171
(816) 561-6111

Located on 168 acres, this is an interfaith network center owned by Earth Rising, Inc. and open to all life-affirming traditions. Includes a dining hall, open-air pavilion, nine cabins, and a large circle area. By reservation only. Call or write for rental rates.

Montana

Wild Womyn Wilderness Treks
185 Red Dog Trail
Darby, Montana 59829
(406) 821-3763

"Celebrating womynhood and exploring the magic of nature," since 1984. Group size is limited. Call or write for additional information.

New Mexico

La Caldera de Hekate
3212 Rio Grande N.W.
Albuquerque, New Mexico 87107
(505) 344-8484

An urban sanctuary dedicated to work in the areas of death and dying. Includes a Kiva and outdoor circle area. Holds regular ceremonial events. By appointment only.

New York

The Amalthea Center
1790 Route 22
Keeseville, New York 12944
(518) 834-5331

An educational center dedicated to creative studies that empower the Self. It offers courses and individual sessions in various modes of creative expression, as well as holistic studies and therapies. Services provided include: piano and art lessons, meditation classes, private readings and soul recovery work promoted through stress management and empowerment coaching, energy field balancing, and hypnotherapy. Courses and workshops are offered throughout the year. Please call for topic information, dates, and times.

High Valley: A Place to Be
R.R. 2, Box 243
Sunset Trail
Clinton Corners, New York 12414
(914) 266-3621

A nonprofit retreat center staffed by practicing Pagans. Located on two hundred acres of sacred grove and open 365 days a year for all who wish to be connected to the Earth.

Kathleen's Bijoux
c/o Kathleen Kmen
HCR-1, Box 184
Malone, New York 12953
(518) 481-6705

Nestled in the most northern Adirondacks, near Titus Mountain, Kathleen's Bijoux offers custom jewelry at affordable prices. Handmade paper creations and unique Pagan-oriented jewelry that incorporates the Goddess and Native American spirituality. Other possibilities include wood, bone, crystal, and more. *Bijoux* is French for gems or jewels, as well as that which is precious.

Rev. Maria Solomon
52 Libby Avenue
Hicksville, New York 11801
(516) 433-9118

Well-known author, TV and radio personality, and internationally known Hungarian psychic offers accurate, insightful readings through ancient methods, covering business, health, love, money, spirituality, and other topics via mail and telephone.

Pennsylvania

Katwood Sanctuary
c/o Changes Unlimited
34 E. State Street
Quarryville, Pennsylvania 17566
(804) 372-2810

A Pagan nature center on forty acres of field and forest, with sacred sites, organic gardens, a petting zoo, camping, bonfires, circles, and more. Accepts donations. By appointment only.

Texas

The Brewers' Witch BBS
8880 Bellaire B-2, no. 139
Houston, Texas 77036
(713) 272-7346 (message); (713) 272-7350

A computer network serving the Pagan community of southern Texas.

Witchcraft Museum
107 E. Avenue E
Copperas Cove, Texas 76522

Vermont

Laurelin Retreat
R.R. 1, Box 239
Christian Hill Road
Bethal, Vermont 05032
(802) 234-9670

A spiritual retreat center providing sweat lodges, vision quests, weekend workshops, and annual Church of Sacred Earth Summer Revels. By appointment only.

Virginia

Electronic Coven
222 W. Twenty-first Street, no. F-145
Norfolk, Virginia 23517
(804) 625-5192

(Formerly Write Place BBS.) A Pagan-oriented computer network. Member of the national Pagan Information Net (PIN). Twenty-four hours.

West Virginia

Mountain Vision, Inc.
P.O. Box 890
1290 Richwood Avenue
Morgantown, West Virginia 26505
(304) 296-3008; fax: (304) 296-3311

A meeting place for Pagan spiritual groups. Provides a social center, workshop, seminar, conference center, and metaphysical book-lending library.

Nationwide

The Goddess Hotline
(900) 737-GODS

Consultations, soul readings, and mentoring by Z. Budapest. The best times to call are Tuesday through Friday, between 5 P.M. and 8 P.M. Pacific Standard Time. $3.99 per minute (the first minute is free). Twenty minutes maximum. You must be over eighteen to call.

United Kingdom (Scotland)

Dalriada BBS
2 Brathwic Place
Brodic, Isle of Arran KA 278 BN
Scotland
Phone: (40) 0770-302532

Celtic heritage society, Rime Net, and Paganlink conference.

15

Who's Who in the Magickal Community

In this section you will find the biographical profiles of some of the women and men (past and present) who, through their diverse talents and hard work, have contributed greatly to the NeoPagan movement and helped shape it into what it is today. These Wiccans and Pagans, who are all magickal and beautiful in their own ways, deserve recognition for all the positive things they have done (and continue to do).

Unfortunately, some of these great individuals are no longer with us. Their passings were a great loss to the worldwide magickal community. However, although they may be gone, their achievements and contributions to the Craft are to be commended and surely will never be forgotten.

"An it harm none, love,
and do what thou wilt."

Blessed Be!

Cairril Adaire

Graphic designer and "Anarcho-Celtic" solitary Witch. Born: December 23, 1967. Founder and national coordinator for the Pagan Educational Network (PEN), founded in 1993 and dedicated to educating others about Paganism and building community. Publisher of *Water*, PEN's quarterly newsletter. Board member of the Wiccan Community Fund. Member of Environmental Defense Fund, Greenpeace, American Civil Liberties Union, Southern Poverty Law Center, Bloomington Feminist Chorus, and Institute for First Amendment Studies. Interests include: singing, music, his/herstory, politics and current events, feminism, writing, folklore, Celtic culture, civil rights and freedom issues, travel, Discordianism, science, anthropology, personal growth, and rites of passage. Mailing address: P.O. Box 1364, Bloomington, Indiana, 47402.

Vicky Adams

Vicky's interest in the occult was sparked by the Hammer horror classics, the television series *Dark Shadows*, and the World Book Encyclopedias that she read as a child. Later, as a teen, although information about magick was scarce in Sydney, she actively sought out and found what little she could and quickly devoured it. As she became older, Vicky became well-known in the Sydney, Australia occult scene as well as a highly admired graphic designer. Recognized by several groups and people in her area as one of the leading faces in the occult, Vicky's thirst for knowledge led her to Los Angeles where she wandered in upon the occult shop Panpipes. There she found an unlimited source of knowledge and support. Vicky quickly became familiar to the Los Angeles occult scene where she is admired for her knowledge. Vicky is currently still residing at Panpipes as the senior practitioner. Vicky has been featured in both media and print as both an occultist as well as a graphic designer and is one of the few occultists recognized as a consultant for the television and movie industry. In 2000, Vicky helped coproduce the first annual Pagan Day Festival and is currently helping coproduce the next fest. She is co-owner of Unearthly Delights and Mousebytes Design. She is currently coauthoring a book on Haitian and Caribbean voodoo. Mailing address: Panpipes Magickal Marketplace,

1641 Cahuenga Boulevard, Hollywood, California 90028; (323) 462-7078; Web site: www.panpipes.com

Margot Adler

Born: April 16, 1946, in Little Rock, Arkansas. She is a well-known and highly respected Pagan, journalist, and lecturer. Education and degrees: B.A., University of California; M.S., Columbia University, Graduate School of Journalism; Nieman Fellow, Harvard University. Author of the popular book *Drawing Down the Moon* (1979, revised edition 1986).

Victor Anderson

Cofounder of the Faery Tradition of Wicca, he was born in New Mexico and initiated into the Craft at the age of nine. Author of *Thorns of the Blood Rose,* a book of Witchcraft-oriented poetry.

Clyde Anthony

Magickal-Wiccan name: Rajj. Poet, writer, and dancer. Born: February 16, 1934. Career includes professional dance and theater in San Francisco and New York City. Appeared on the March 1964 cover of *Dance Magazine*. His interests and talents range from trance-dancing to channeled poetry to dream-mediumship. Mailing address: P.O. Box 204, Monument Beach, Massachusetts 02553.

Rev. Paul V. Beyerl

Wiccan priest, author, and educator. Born: September 2, 1945, with a Virgo rising. Founder of the Rowan Tree Church, the Mystery School (teaching the Tradition of Lothlorien), *The Unicorn* newsletter (published since 1977), the Hermit's Grove, and the Hermit's Lantern. Well-known throughout the Neopagan and Wiccan world, Beyerl's columns and articles have appeared in many publications. A guest speaker at many of the early Pagan gatherings, he has conducted seminars and workshops throughout the United States, and since 1986 has appeared annually as guest presenter at the Harvest Moon Celebration in Los Angeles. In addition to recognition as an herbalist and astrologer, Beyerl is known for his presentations on aspects of ritual, death and dying, ethics, alchemy, initiation, meditation, and visualization techniques, and for his performances of ritual that incorporate the skills of theater and music. Trained in classical music and the founder of the Unicorn Ensemble of Minneapolis (a chamber quartet), he is now retired from a ten-year career as a professional flutist. Author of *The Holy Books of the Devas* (1980, revised and expanded in 1993), *The Master Book of Herbalism* (1984), *A Wiccan Bardo: Initiation and Self-Transformation* (1989), *Painless Astrology* (1993), and *A Wiccan Reader* (1994). Mailing address: P.O. Box 0691, Kirkland, Washington 98083.

Isaac Bonewits

Druid priest, magician, and activist. Born: October 1, 1949, in Royal Oak, Michigan. Founder of the Aquarian Anti-Defamation League, Schismatic Druids of North America, and a Druidic fellowship known as Ar nDraiocht Fein. Established the *Druid Chronicler* in 1978 (later renamed *Pentalpha Journal*), and served as editor of *Gnostica* for one and one-half years. He holds a bachelor of arts in magic from the University of California at Berkeley, and is the author of *Real Magic* (1971) and *The Druid Chronicles (Evolved)*.

Goldie Brown

Astrologer and herbalist. Born: April 28, 1951, with a Gemini rising. Coven member, solitary practitioner of the Old Religion (Witchcraft), and Traditionalist. Member of Tuatha de Danaan (Elder), Pittsburgh Pagan Alliance (coordinator and scribe), Fellowship of Isis, and Witches' Anti-Defamation League. Special talents, hobbies, and interests include astrology, herbs, runes, writing, publishing, music, sewing, gardening, ecology, and nature. Publisher of *Wyrd: Poetry Quarterly;* previously published *Rose Runes,* a Craft journal (1978–1981), and the *Owlet,* a Witches' newsletter (1975–1979). Mailing address: P.O. Box 624, Monroeville, Pennsylvania 15146.

Raymond Buckland

Born: August 31, 1934. Founder of the Seax-Wica tradition of Witchcraft. Educated at King's College School in London and holds a doctorate in anthropology from Brantridge Forest College in Sussex, England. Initiated into the Craft by Lady Olwen, the late Gerald Gardner's High Priestess. Established the first Museum of Witchcraft and Magic in the United States, and the Seax-Wica Seminary in the state of Virginia. Author of numerous books, including: *A Pocket Guide to the Supernatural* (1969), *Witchcraft Ancient and Modern* (1970), *Practical Candleburning Rituals* (1970), *Mu Revealed* (1970, under the pseudonym Tony Earll), *Witchcraft From the Inside* (1971), *The Tree: The Complete Book on Saxon Witchcraft* (1974), *Here Is the Occult* (1974), *Amazing Secrets of the Psychic World* (1975), *Anatomy of the Occult* (1977), *The Magic of Chant-O-Matics* (1978), *Practical Color Magick* (1983), *Buckland's Complete Book of Witchcraft* (1986), *Ray Buckland's Magic Cauldron* (1995), and *Wicca for Life* (2001).

Z. Budapest

Born: January 30, 1940, in Budapest. Founder and leader of the main branch of Feminist Dianic Wicca, also lecturer and presenter of workshops. Served as High Priestess of the Susan B. Anthony Coven (established in 1971 on the Winter Solstice) and the Laughing Goddess Coven. She directs the Women's Spirituality Forum in Oakland, California and works on a Goddess-oriented cable television program called *Thirteenth Heaven*. Author of *The Holy Book of Women's Mysteries* (two volumes). Mailing address: P.O. Box 11363, Oakland, California 94611.

Pauline and Dan Campanelli

Solitary Wiccan artists and authors. Interests include researching Mediterranean and Old European magick and Witchcraft, the origins of current holiday traditions, and the practice of Witchcraft. Authors of: *Wheel of the Year: Living the Magickal Life* (1989), *Ancient Ways: Reclaiming Pagan Traditions* (1991), *Circles, Groves and Sanctuaries* (1992), *Rites of Passage: The Pagan Wheel of Life* (1994), *Halloween Collectables* (1995), and *Romantic Valentines* (1996). Their paintings are reproduced by the New York Graphic Society and distributed worldwide. A book, *The Art of Pauline and Dan Campanelli* (New York Graphic Society, 1995), features their paintings and lifestyle.

Mailing address: c/o Llewellyn Worldwide, P.O. Box 64383, St. Paul, Minnesota 55164.

Phil Catalano

Parapsychologist and engineering manager. Born: February 12, 1947. Solitary practitioner (Wiccan, Shamanic, Celtic). Holds a bachelor of science degree in parapsychology and is a member of IANS (International Association for New Science) and BOTA (Builders of the Adytum). Student with Occult Mystery School. Interests include UFOs, paranormal phenomena, sacred gemstones, magick, and metaphysics. Mailing address: P.O. Box 621165, Littleton, Colorado 80162.

Susann Cobb

Wiccan name: Peri Wyrrd. Born: January 7, 1963, with a Gemini rising. For more than ten years she has been involved in the book publishing community in the areas of sales and marketing; worked for leading metaphysical and health book publishers (Harper San Francisco and Inner Traditions). She is a member of ESC (Earth-Spirit Community), Earth Drum Council, and Moonfire Women's Spirituality Circles. Interests include Pagan gatherings, community outreach and education, and drumming as transformation. Mailing address: R.R. 1, Box 55, Rochester, Vermont 05767.

Arnold Crowther

English Witch, professional stage magician, founding member of the Puppet Guild, and a leading spokesperson for the Craft. Born: October 7, 1909. Died: May 1, 1974. Author of *Let's Put on a Show* (1964), *Linda and the Lollipop Man* (1973), *Yorkshire Customs* (1974), and *Hex Certificate* (published in the late 1970s). Coauthor of *The Secrets of Ancient Witchcraft* (1974) and *The Witches Speak* (1976).

Patricia Crowther

English Witch, professional singer, magician, and puppeteer, and a leading spokesperson for the Craft through her books and lectures and the media. Author of *Witchcraft in Yorkshire, Witch Blood!, Lid Off the Cauldron,* and numerous articles that have appeared in such periodicals as *Prediction, Gnostica,* and *New Dimensions.* She is the coauthor of *The Secrets of Ancient Witchcraft* (1974) and *The Witches Speak* (1976). With her husband Arnold, she produced *A Spell of Witchcraft*—the first radio series about the Craft to air in Great Britain.

Scott Cunningham

Born: June 27, 1956, in Royal Oak, Michigan. Died: March 28, 1993. Cunningham was a prolific Wiccan writer and a practitioner of the Craft since 1971. He offered many lectures, taught groups across the country, and made occasional media appearances in an effort to dispel the misconceptions about Witchcraft and to educate the public about Wicca as a contemporary religion. Author of *Magical Herbalism* (1982), *Earth Power: Techniques of Natural Magic* (1983), *Cunningham's Encyclopedia of Magical Herbs* (1985), *The Magic of Incense, Oils and Brews* (1987), *The Magical Household* (1987, with David Harrington), *Cunningham's Encyclopedia of Crystal, Gem and Metal Magic* (1987), *The Truth About Witchcraft Today* (1988), and *Wicca: A Guide for the Solitary Practitioner* (1988). In addition to his books about Wicca and magick, he had twenty-one published novels between 1980 and 1987.

Jymie Darling

Jymie's interest in the occult started in grade school when she was asked to research a paper on the subject at the school's library. Myths about witches and witchcraft raised her curiosity, which was further fueled at her Catholic high school when she was told that all religions were correct. Jymie's mother reinforced that idea, and so began her quest for knowledge about the ancient theologies. Jymie joined the air force in 1988 as a munitions system specialist and was first stationed in Las Vegas, Nevada. There she searched out the local occult stores and libraries where she studied and asked questions. After her tour there, Jymie was sent to England, where she read all she could on local myths and legends. She went to the sites of these legends and soon found the few underground occult stores, where she became a frequent visitor, asking questions and devouring books.

Jymie came back to Los Angeles, California after six years in the air force. There she began her Web design business and eventually found Panpipes Magickal Marketplace in Hollywood. She became their Webmaster as well as their manager. In 2000, Jymie coproduced the first annual Pagan Day Fest and invited all theologies to attend. It was an instant success.

Jymie is recognized by the media as a leading representative of the occult community and has been featured internationally. She also does script consultations for both the television and movie industries. Today, she is busy with her businesses, Unearthly Delights and Mousebytes Design. Jymie is currently still manager of Panpipes, and also teaches the courses offered there. She is writing her first book, a formal introduction to the occult systems of magick and is preparing for the second annual Pagan Day Fest. Mailing address: Panpipes Magickal Marketplace, 1641 Cahuenga Boulevard, Hollywood, California 90028; (323) 462-7078; Web site: www.panpipes.com

George Hiram Derby

Born in New Orleans, Louisiana to a thirty-third-degree Master Mason and practicing ceremonial magician father and a well-known tarot-reading mother, George was heavily involved in the world of magick from the day of his birth (which he never gives, as he doesn't like his astrological information known). Dedicated to his father's ceremonial tradition Circle Hiram the Mage (an older Cabalistic/Masonic practice) on his twelfth birthday, he was the last initiated member and later became the sole survivor of the order. At fourteen, with the assistance of his parents, George was taken under the reluctant tutelage of Aunt Ida, a highly respected Root Woman in the West Bank New Orleans suburb community of Algiers, where he spent the next four years learning Mojo (the magickal aspects of Voodoo). As an eager student of occultism, he went on to study the older religions, magickal doctrines, and secret orders of the Cabalistic, Egyptian, Greco-Roman, African, Afro-Caribbean, Teutonic, Goetic, and Hermetic systems and the modern neopagan religion commonly referred to as Wicca. In his late teens, George began teaching courses in eclectic occultism at bookstores and lodges throughout the United States, and over the years, as his reputation as a Master Occultist grew; he took his lectures, seminars, and workshops around the world. George became a student of anthropology and comparative religions and eventually earned a Master's in anthropology from Georgetown University. While still a student, he began teaching courses in ancient religions, witchcraft, and magic at two-year colleges to (as he says) "be able to buy beans and bacon." In the late 1950s, George assisted the Master Occultist and metaphysician Donald R. Blyth in forming a small group of free-thinking occultists called the Brotherhood, some of whom later became the earliest member of the Brotherhood of the Ram, from which eventually evolved the Ram Occult Center and later yet became Panpipes Magickal Marketplace. In more recent years, George has taken over the day-to-day operation of Panpipes Magickal Marketplace as its executive director and master practitioner, where he continues to oversee the training of interns, apprentices, and students. George is the founder and prelate of the Church of Theophysics and heads its international diocese. George's long-awaited work *An Exegesis of Theophysics*, which contains his twenty-first-century scientific and biochemical interpretations of many traditional theological and occult philosophies, is at long last finished, but he has made the decision to release it only posthumously. He is also coauthoring a series of spellcraft books, which are expected to be released over the next two years. Mailing address: Panpipes Magickal Marketplace, 1641 Cahuenga Boulevard, Hollywood, California 90028; (323) 462-7078; Web site: www.panpipes.com

Gerina Dunwich

Born: December 27, 1959. Tradition: Bast-Wicca, pre-Gardnerian Traditional Witchcraft, and hoodoo; student of many occult arts, including the Tarot and other methods of divination, spirit-channeling, wortcunning, and past-life regression. Career: book author, editor, and publisher of *Golden Isis* since 1980, professional astrologer, and antique shop proprietor. Founder of the Pagan Poets Society, Wheel of Wisdom School, and Coven Mandragora. Member of The Author's Guild, The Authors League of America, and the Fellowship of Isis. She is also a member of the American Biographical Institute Board of Advisors and is listed in a number of reference works, such as *Who's Who in the East, Who's Who of American Women, Personalities of America,* and *Crossroads: Who's Who of the Magickal Community.* Author of *Candlelight Spells*

(1988), *The Magick of Candleburning* (1989), *The Concise Lexicon of the Occult* (1990), *Circle of Shadows* (1990), *Wicca Craft* (1991), *The Secrets of Love Magick* (1992), *The Wicca Spellbook* (1994), *The Wicca Book of Days* (1995), *The Wicca Garden* (1996), *The Wicca Source Book* (1996, revised 1998), *Everyday Wicca* (1997), *A Wiccan's Guide to Prophecy & Divination* (1997), *Wicca A to Z* (1998), *Magick Potions* (1998), *Your Magickal Cat* (2000), *The Pagan Book of Halloween* (2000), and *Exploring Spellcraft* (2001). In addition, her poetry and articles have been published in many journals, and she has been interviewed on numerous radio talk shows across the United States and Canada. Appeared as a guest speaker at the 1996 Craft Wise Pagan gathering in Waterbury, Connecticut, the 1997 Real Witches' Ball in Columbus, Ohio, and at the 2000 Pagan Day Festival in Westwood, California. Mailing address: P.O. Box 4263, Chatsworth, California 91313.

Reed Morgan Dunwich

Writer, poet, and publisher of the *Silver Pentagram,* a Witchcraft journal. Born: February 2, 1948. A member of the Craft since 1965, he formed the Northern Star Coven in 1968 and continues to serve as its High Priest. He holds bachelor of science degrees in psychology and computer science from the University of Pittsburgh and is a member of the Wiccan/Pagan Press Alliance, the Order of the Crystal Moon, the Pagan Poets Society, the Mathematical Association of America, and the Challenger Center for Space Science Education (founding member). Reed's poetry and articles have appeared in many Craft journals, including *Mystic Magick; Georgian Monthly; Converging Paths; Midnight Drive;* and *Golden Isis.* Interests and talents include astronomy, geology, math, and physics, reading books about the Craft, communicating intuitively with the Goddess, poetry, and dancing to rock music. Mailing address: P.O. Box 9776, Pittsburgh, Pennsylvania 15229.

Janet Farrar

Born: June 24, 1950, in London, England. Initiated into the Craft in 1970 by Alexander Sanders. With her husband Stewart, coauthor of many Witchcraft books: *Eight Sabbats for Witches* (1981), *The*

Witches' Way (1984), *The Witches' Goddess* (1987), *Life and Times of a Modern Witch* (1987), and *The Witches' God* (1989).

Stewart Farrar

Born: June 28, 1916, in Highams Park, Essex, England. Died: February 7, 2000. Educated at City of London School and University College, London. Served as president of the London University Journalism Union and was the editor of *London Union* magazine. Initiated into the Craft by Alexander Sanders. Coauthor of *Eight Sabbats for Witches* (1981), *The Witches' Way* (1984), *The Witches' Goddess* (1987), *Life and Times of a Modern Witch* (1987), and *The Witches' God* (1989). In addition to books on Witchcraft, Farrar is also the author of numerous occult novels and several detective novels.

Ed Fitch

Wiccan High Priest and key founder of the organization Pagan Way. Initiated into the Gardnerian tradition of the Craft by Raymond Buckland and his then-wife Rosemary. Published the *Crystal Well*, a magazine of Neo-Romantic Paganism. Interests and hobbies include Odinism, dance magick, and geomancy. Author of *The Grimoire of the Shadows, The Outer Court Book of Shadows,* and *Magical Rites From the Crystal Well* (1984).

Selena Fox

Well-known and respected founder and High Priestess of Circle Sanctuary, published author, and Pagan religious freedom activist. Born: October 20, 1949, in Arlington, Virginia. Attended the College of William and Mary and holds a bachelor of science degree in psychology. Selena is the founder of the Wiccan Shamanism Path of the Wiccan Religion. She also teaches, frequently speaks at lectures, and presents many workshops. In addition, she is a legally recognized Wiccan minister and a leading spokesperson on the Craft to the media. Some of her interests and hobbies include herbcraft, dreamcraft, healing, Goddess lore, Shamanism, chant-making, and singing. Mailing address: Box 219, Mt. Horeb, Wisconsin 53572.

Carolyn Frances

Poet, artist, composer, dancer. Born: April 19, 1942. Graduate of the Boston Museum School of Art, Modern and Mid-East Dancing. Composer of electronically-enhanced voice-sound works using channeled poetry and sounds of the environment. Mailing address: P.O. Box 204, Monument Beach, Massachusetts 02553.

Gavin Frost

Born in 1930 in Staffordshire, England. Graduated from London University with a bachelor of science degree in mathematics, and then a doctorate in physics and math. He also holds a doctor of divinity degree from the Church of Wicca. Cofounder of the Church and School of Wicca (1965) and author of more than a dozen books, including *The Witch's Bible* (1975), which he coauthored with his wife Yvonne.

Yvonne Frost

Born in Los Angeles, California, in 1931. Graduated from Fullerton Junior College in 1962 with an associate of arts degree in secretarial skills. Also holds a doctor of divinity degree from the Church of Wicca. Cofounder of the Church and School of Wicca (1965) and author of more than a dozen books, including *The Witch's Bible* (1975), which she coauthored with her husband Gavin.

Gerald B. Gardner

Founder of what came to be known as the Gardnerian Tradition which, in modern Witchcraft, is the dominant tradition. Born: June 13, 1884, in England. Died: February 12, 1964. Gardner is best remembered as the individual chiefly responsible for the Witchcraft revival in the modern West. The descendant of a Scottish Witch who was burned at the stake in 1610, Gardner was initiated into the Craft in 1939 by a woman called Old Dorothy Clutterbuck, the High Priestess of a New Forest coven. He was made an honorary member of the Ordo Templi Orientis by Aleister Crowley, and made numerous media appearances, enjoying the public spotlight in the 1950s and early 1960s. Author of several novels and the following nonfiction Craft books: *Witchcraft Today* (1954) and *The Meaning of Witchcraft* (1959).

Ellen Evert Hopman

Magickal name: Willow. Born: July 31, 1952, with a Capricorn rising. She is a master herbalist and lay homeopath who holds a master of education degree in mental health counseling. In addition, she teaches, holds workshops, and works as a counselor and a tour guide to sacred sites of Europe. She is a Bard of the Gorsedd of Caer Abiri in Avebury, England; vice president of Keltria, the International Druid Fellowship; and a professional member of the American Herbalists Guild. Other memberships include the Nature Conservancy, Author's Guild, Druid Clan of Dana, Order of Bards, Ovates and Druids, Order of the White Oak, Maple Dragon Clan of Vermont, and North East Herb Association. Author of *People of the Earth—The New Pagans Speak Out; Tree Medicine, Tree Magic; A Druid's Herbal for the Sacred Earth Year;* and the video *Gifts of the Healing Earth.* Mailing address: P.O. Box 219, Amherst, Massachusetts 01004.

Jade

Born: July 2, 1950 with a Gemini rising. Creator of the Women's Theological Institute, Cella Training Program (the first institute offering an in-depth training course for women wishing to be ordained priestesses.) Author of *To Know: A Guide to Women's Magic and Spirituality.* Cofounder of the Reformed Congregation of the Goddess—the first legally incorporated tax-exempt religion serving the women's spiritual community. Cofounder and coordinator of *Of a Like Mind,* the largest women's newspaper and network exploring Goddess spirituality for women. Copublisher of *Solitary: By Choice or by Chance,* a journal for those who practice the Craft alone. Vocal recording artist with Triple Crescent, a Goddess-oriented musical group. Jade has spoken and sung widely about women's spirituality and Dianic Wicca. She is an outstanding presenter and public speaker with an extensive knowledge of Feminist Witchcraft. Mailing address: P.O. Box 6677, Madison, Wisconsin, 53716.

Rik Johnson

Born: August 24, 1952. Gardnerian Wiccan and High Priest of the Desert Henge Coven (formed April 1982, one of the oldest covens in the state of Arizona). First and Second Degree Gardnerian, Third Degree Traditional (done by an Alexandrian but not an Alexandrian Elevation; seeking Third Degree Gardnerian.) Occupations: clerk in legal system, also Arizona National Guard civil engineer. Won civil rights victory by forcing the Air Force to list his religion as Wicca. Performs legalized handfastings in Arizona and teaches the oldest public class on Wicca in that state. Consulted by police in "occult" crimes. Lectured at the University of Arizona. Helped the police academy form a class on how a police officer should deal with Witches. Facilitated the Tucson area Wiccan Network (1995) and performed numerous public rituals for the TAWN Fall Fest. Published in numerous newsletters. Enjoys collecting Craft-related material such as term papers, news articles, videos, and music. Constantly seeking material on Wicca to be used for public classes and currently working on a Wiccan songbook, a Wiccan humor book, a technical manual on magick, and a book entitled *Theology of Witchcraft.* Mailing address: P.O. Box 40451, Tucson, Arizona 85717.

Anodea Judith

Founder and director of Lifeways, charter member of Forever Forests, president of Church of All Worlds. Born: December 1, 1952. Educated at Clark University, the California College of Arts and Crafts in Oakland, California, and John F. Kennedy University. The sister of comedian Martin Mull, Judith is an artist and songwriter, and helps others through her work as a professional therapist. Interests include Witchcraft and magick, psychic development, ecology, bioenergetic therapy, chakras, theater, and art. Author of *Wheels of Life: A User's Guide to the Chakras* (1987) and accompanying tape.

G. M. Kelly

Writer and novelist, editor of *The Newaeon Newsletter* (established in 1977). Born: March 23, 1951, with a Pisces rising and Moon in Libra. Magickal name: Frater Keallach 93/676. "No special 'talents,' psychic or otherwise, certainly not very good at making money appear—blast my ethics and integrity!" Interests include Tarot, I Ching, Thelema, Aleister Crowley, Magic/k (both ceremonial and "tantric"), the Old West, Native Americans, the American Civil War, and numerous other things. Author of *Grimm Justice: A Mythological Western; Sins of the Flesh;* and various short stories published under pseudonyms. "However, my most impressive accomplishment to date is that I have survived almost forty-five years now in a hostile social and economic environment and even more impressive, my sense of humor is intact." Mailing address: P.O. Box 19210, Pittsburgh, Pennsylvania 15213.

Sirona Knight

Born: Samhain, November 2, 1955, 3:43 P.M., in San Jose, California. Sirona Knight lives in the Sierra foothills of Northern California with her family—her husband, Michael, and their son Skylor, five beagles, and a family of Siamese cats. Her ancestors include James Smithson, founder of the Smithsonian Institute, and she comes from a long line of Daughters of the Revolution. Practicing magick for over sixteen years, Sirona is a Third Degree Craft Master and High Priestess of the Celtic Druid Tradition. She is the creator and coauthor of the popular and award-winning Shapeshifter Tarot deck and has written a number of books on Celtic spirituality, including *Celtic Traditions, The Pocket Guide to Celtic Spirituality, Greenfire* and *Moonflower.* She has also written books about Wicca and magick, including *The Witch and Wizard Training Guide, The Wiccan Spell Kit,* and *The Wiccan Web.* As a longtime contributing editor for Magical Blend magazine, she has interviews many magickal notables. She has a master's degree in stress management and is a hypnotherapist and past life regression counselor. Sirona lectures and teaches monthly workshops, makes radio and television appearances, and maintains strong Internet visibility: www.sironaknight.com; bluesky@dcsi.net

Lady Sheba

Famous Witch Queen and psychic. Born in the mountains of Kentucky (birthdate unknown) to a family whose religious and magickal link to the Craft spanned seven generations. She was introduced to the Old Religion by her grandmother and initiated as a Witch in the 1930s. Founder and High Priestess of the American Order of the Brotherhood of Wicca. Author of *The Magick Grimoire* and *The Book of Shadows* (1971).

Sybil Leek

Born: February 22, 1917, in Stoke-on-Trent, England. Died: October 26, 1982, in Melbourne, Florida. Miss Leek moved to the United States in the early 1960s and achieved fame and success as a modern Witch, astrologer, and occult author. Her psychic predictions of the Kennedy assassinations and the election of Richard M. Nixon as president of the United States are documented. Edited and published her own astrological journal and wrote an internationally syndicated column. Author of over sixty books, including the best-selling *Diary of a Witch* (1968), *Sybil Leek's Book of Curses, ESP: The Magic Within You, My Life in Astrology, Numerology: The Magic of Numbers, Moon Signs, Herbs: Medicine and Mysticism, Reincarnation: The Second Chance, The Sybil Leek Book of Fortune Telling, Phrenology, Telepathy: The Respectable Phenomenon, The Story of Faith Healing, Sybil Leek's Astrological Guide to Successful Everyday Living, Tomorrow's Headlines Today, The Tree that Conquered the World, Astrological Guide to Presidential Candidates, Sybil Leek's Book of the Curious and the Occult, Sybil Leek's Book of Herbs, Astrology and Love, Astrological Guide to Financial Success, How to Be Your Own Astrologer, The Assassination Chain, Zodiac of Love, The Night Voyagers: You and Your Dreams, Telepatia,* and *Star Speak: Your Body Language from the Stars.*

Dr. Leo Louis Martello

Magickal name: Nemesis. Witch, graphologist, lecturer, book author, and activist for both civil and gay rights. Born in Dudley, Massachusetts under the sign of Libra. Died: June, 2000. Martello was publicly prominent in the modern Witchcraft movement since the 1960s. Educated at Assumption College in Worcester, Massachusetts, the Institute for Psychotherapy in New York City, and Hunter College in New York City. He held a doctor of divinity degree from the National

Congress of Spiritual Consultants, was an ordained minister (Spiritual Independents, nonsectarian), and served as pastor of the Temple of Spiritual Guidance from 1955 to 1960. Founder and director of the American Hypnotism Academy in New York (1950–1954); treasurer of the American Graphological Society (1955–1957). Sponsored a public "Witch-In" in New York City's Central Park on Halloween/Samhain in 1970. Founder and director of the Witches Anti-Defamation League. Interests included: treasure-hunting, handwriting analysis, and dreams. Author of numerous magazine articles and books, including: *Witchcraft: The Old Religion; Black Magic, Satanism and Voodoo; Understanding the Tarot; It's Written in the Cards; What It Means to Be a Witch; Weird Ways of Witchcraft; It's Written in the Stars; Curses in Verses; Witches' Liberation and Practical Guide to Witch Covens; Your Pen Personality;* and *The Hidden World of Hypnotism.* He also wrote the introductions for the following books: *Secrets of Ancient Witchcraft and Witches' Tarot* (Crowther); *The Witches Speak* (Crowther); *Witch Blood!* (Crowther); and *The Meaning of Witchcraft* (Gardner).

Leila Moon

Solitary Witch and spiritual specialist. Born: June 15, 1966, with an Aries rising. Writes horoscopes for the Craft periodical *Spinning in the Light.* Interests and talents include psychic Tarot-channeling, palmistry, crystal healing, candle magick, and aromatherapy. "Initiated by the Golden Dawn and completing initiation for Vodon. As we gain and develop in our priesthood of spiritual knowledge, we pass on to those who are in need of spiritual help." Mailing address: 1725 E. Charleston Street, Las Vegas, Nevada 89104.

Karin Muller

Licensed minister, licensed practical nurse, desktop publisher, ceremonialist-Shaman. Born: December 26, 1964, with a Libra rising. Solitary Wiccan (apprentice to Feri). Founder and director of the Full Circle Center for Spiritual and Community Development. Coordinator and leader of several large Pagan rituals annually in her local area. Publishes the quarterly *Anamnesia,* serving the Pagan community of western Massachusetts and beyond. Bachelor of arts in women, spirituality, and power from Mount Holyoke College, where her thesis work examined the feminist Witchcraft movement in the Pioneer Valley. Talents and interests include some Shamanic healing, public ritual, women's spirituality, and empowerment. Mailing address: 37 Clark Road, Cummington, Massachusetts 01026.

John Opsopaus

Magickal name: Apolonius Sophistes. Solitary practitioner of the Hellenic Tradition. Occupation: computer scientist. Member of Church of All Worlds, Ar nDraiocht Fein and OTO Published articles include "Hellenic Neopaganism," "Neoclassical Sacrifice," "Rotation of the Elements," a Hellenic version of the Lesser Banishing Ritual, and various hymns to goddesses and gods. Maintains several Worldwide Web sites devoted to Hellenic Neopaganism and the occult, including the Pythagorean Tarot. Runs the Omphalos networking service for Neopagans following Greek and Roman traditions. Interests and talents include divination (Tarot, I Ching, dice oracles, alphabet oracles), ancient numerology, ancient music, mythology, ritual construction, alchemy, and archetypal psychology. Mailing address: U.T. Box 16220, Knoxville, Tennessee 37996.

Jeffrey Parish

Jeffrey Parish is the owner of Le Sorciere, a "new generation" Witchcraft/metaphysical store in the Hillcrest area of San Diego. He has been an eclectic solitary Witch for thirteen years. He recently made the decision to learn and teach in a group, and is enthusiastically working in a newly formed coven. Jeffrey is a transplant from Denver, Colorado, where he was born and raised in the Lutheran religion. Like many Witches, he felt he was different from an early age. However, he had no name for the things he felt, but knew them to be right. When he discovered the Craft in his early twenties, he knew he had come home. As a Craft practitioner, Jeffrey practices a very unique blend of Wicca, Catholicism, Voodoo, and Santeria. His personal philosophy is to equally embrace all religions and traditions of the world due to his belief that there are many paths to the top of the mountain, and that *all* paths lead to God/dess. Upon his discovery of the Craft, Jeffrey dreamed of opening a store with an emphasis on Witchcraft. In July of 1999 the dream was realized, and Le Sorciere opened its doors to the Craft community of San Diego. It is Jeffrey's personal mission to educate people about Witchcraft and how it fits perfectly with other religions and traditions. He also donates as much of his time and abilities to the Craft community as he can. His strong belief in networking and community are his main focus for the future. He has now begun to publish *New Generation News*, a magickal newsletter affiliated with his store. A book is also in the works. Jeffrey is always happiest when magick is in the air. He is defiantly a Witch with a mission. Mailing address: Le Sorciere, 1281 University Avenue, San Diego, California 92103.

Pete Pathfinder

Born under the sign of Aries. Founder of both the Aquarian Tabernacle Church and the Center for Non-Traditional Religion. Cofounder and publisher of the journal *Panegyria*. In 1985 he served as public information officer for the Covenant of the Goddess. Originated the Dial-A-Pagan telephone information service (206-LA-PAGAN). Mailing address: P.O. Box 409, Index, Washington 98256.

Lee Prosser

Solitary practitioner of Shamanism and Vedanta. Occupation: researcher. Born: December 31, 1944. Founder of the Oneness Center for Spiritual Living, legally recognized Interfaith minister, and member of the Pagan Poets Society. Education: prelaw at California State University at Northridge: undergraduate degrees in English and sociology, master's degree in social science. Numerous publications since 1963. "To share knowledge that will aid a person on the personal path to self-knowledge and self-discovery is one of the best gifts you can give that person. Self-knowledge is the key to enlightenment." Interested in Shamanic covens, Hindu magick, Hindu mythology, and all aspects of the Hindu goddess Durga. Author of *Desert Woman Visions: 100 Poems* (1987), and *Running From the Hunter* (1996). "I have held a lifelong interest in Wicca, Vedanta, and Shamanism. Additionally have done research in early Christianity and early Pagan religions. One of my beliefs is found in the *Rig Veda:* Truth is One. Sages call it by various names." Mailing address: P.O. Box 1586, Claremore, Oklahoma 74018.

Silver Ravenwolf

Born: September 11, 1956, with a Gemini rising. Clan Head of The Temple of the Morrighan Triskele (Black Forest Tradition, founded in 1991). Director of International Wiccan/Pagan Press Alliance; Director of Witches Anti-Discrimination League. Interests include criminal magick and divination. Major contributor to *The Magickal Almanac* (1994, 1995, 1996, and 1997) and author of *To Ride a Silver Broomstick; Hexcraft: Pennsylvania Dutch Magick; Beneath a Mountain Moon; To Stir a Magick Cauldron;* and *Angels, Companions in Magick.* Mailing address: P.O. Box 1392, Mechanicsburg, Pennsylvania 17055.

Deirdre Sargent

Born: October 14 (Scorpio rising). Solitary Wiccan and member of Wolf's Head Coven (formed in 1993). First officer, Educational Society for Pagans; Elder at Large, Covenant of the Goddess, National Board. Coeditor of *Pagan Digest;* articles published in *Pagan Digest, Pallas Society News, Unicorn, Maypole,* and other publications. Provides classes and lectures to both the Pagan and cowan communities on a wide variety of metaphysical and scholarly subjects. Occupations: MIS systems analyst and actor (stage, Shakespearean). Interests include religious studies with emphasis on the early saints of the Christian church and their links to Paganism, the Templar Knights, the Masonic connection to modern Witchcraft, and the phenomenon of human sacrifice past and present in Mesoamerica.

Steve Savedow

Born July 19, 1961, in Daytona Beach, Florida at 6:40 P.M. Owner of Serpents Occult Books, author of *The Magician's Workbook, Goetic Evocation,* and the translator of the first English edition of *Sepher Rezial: The Book of the Angel Rezia.* Former professions include: musician/drummer in Southern rock band for thirteen years in Daytona Beach; firefighter/E.M.T.; veterinary assistant; and automotive, motorcycle, and marine mechanic. His first magickal experience occurred at the age of five. While suffering from a rare bone disease and being immobile in a full body cast for fourteen months, he began experiencing "mystical dreams" in which he went to "school" and learned about such subjects as mythology, the powers of nature, how to talk with elemental spirits, and so on. As a result, he learned to become lucid in dreams at a very young age. He was initiated into a small Witch coven at the age of thirteen in Cassadega, Florida and studied Witchcraft during his teen years. He began serious study of ritual magick and qabalah at the age of nineteen, and extensively practiced the arts of ritual magick, specially Solomonic magick and Goetia, during the years 1983 through 1993. He studied and practiced the arts of Enochian magick during the years 1991 to 1996. He was initiated into the O.T.O. in 1989 (and was expelled from the order in 1992). Steve opened Serpents Occult Bookstore in 1989, which is still prospering as a mail order/Internet business today. Mailing address: P.O. Box 290644, Port Orange, Florida 32129. E-mail: stevesavedow@aol.com

Herman Slater

Magickal name: Govannan. Wiccan High Priest and public advocate for the Craft. Initiated into the New York Coven of Welsh Traditional Witches in 1972. Proprietor of the Warlock Shop in New York City (which later changed its business name to the Magickal Childe.) Slater hosted a weekly cable television show called *The Magickal Mystery Tour*, which aired in Manhattan in 1987. Author of *A Book of Pagan Rituals*, *The Magickal Formulary*, and *The Magickal Formulary II*. Date of death: July 9, 1992.

Rev. Maria Solomon

Professional psychic, ordained minister, occultist, hypnotherapist, writer, lecturer, teacher, parapsychologist, and Shaman. Born: August 11, 1950. Founder of the Sylvan Society; member of the New York–New Jersey Psychic Guild, Floating Healing Meditation Circle, Hungarian Writers Guild, NAFE, Long Island Dowsing Association, and AAH. Honorable member of the Tuscarora Indian Tribe. Interests and talents include rune casting, Tarot trance, spiritual work, past lives, healing, candles, herbs, oils, spellcraft, Kirlian photography, biorhythms, astral projection, numerology, graphology, palmistry, psychometry, crystals and stones, Hatha Yoga, Tai Chi, and Qi Gong. "My father is a psychic. Both my grandparents on my mother's side were spiritualist trance mediums. My grandfather also did automatic writing. My mother has a feel for herbs. My favorite colors are yellow, pink, and orange." Author of *Psychic Vibrations of Crystals, Gems, and Stones; New Age Formulary;* and *Maria Solomon's Money Empowerment.* Numerous articles published in *Nightingale News, Ghost Trackers, ULC News, Innerlight, Gnostic Times, UFO Universe, The Alternative, Psychic Fair Network News,* and *Psychic Press.* Guest appearances on radio, television, cable, and satellite TV. Conducted psychic fairs and ran a nationwide metaphysical catalog. Goals: "To assist people internationally and teach them how to attain higher awareness of their true selves." Mailing address: 52 Libby Avenue, Hicksville, New York 11801.

Rainbow Star

Musician and member of Rainbow Link Coven (established in 1985). Traditions: Druid, Greek, Roman, and Faery. Born under the sign of Libra with a Leo rising. Member of Ar nDraiocht Fein. Interests include herbalism, Tarot, and music. Goals: "Heal the Earth, heal all waters, heal the air, heal all spirits, create joy!" Mailing address: P.O. Box 1218, Greenville, Mississippi 38702.

Starhawk

Feminist Witch, book author, and peace activist. Born in 1951. Initiated into the Faery Tradition. Founder of the Compost and Honeysuckle covens and Reclaiming (a feminist collective based in San Francisco). She teaches at several colleges in the Bay Area and travels throughout the United States and abroad giving lectures and workshops. Author of *The Spiral Dance: A Rebirth of the Ancient Religion of the Great Goddess* (1979), *Dreaming in the Dark* (1982), and *Truth or Dare: Encounters of Power, Authority, and Mystery* (1987).

Tarostar

Born under the sign of Aries. Education: University of Las Vegas; Kent State University, Ohio; Defense Language Institute, Monterey, California. Numerous articles published in *Georgian Newsletter* (Bakersfield, California). Lectures on Tarot, demonology, and the Craft. Author of *The Sacred Pentagram; The Witch's Formulary and Spellbook;* and *The Witch's Spellcraft.*

Lady Tareena

Born: January 23, 1947. Accountant and editor. Member of Guardians of Light and Life (formed in 1990), Clan of the Spider—Universal Life Church. Talents and interests include: psychic channeling, Tarot, and astral journeys. She is a Priestess of Isis as well as an honorary Zulu Sangomo, and has many other honorary titles within the world's cultures. She has studied many religious cultures from all corners of the Earth, and holds six different business degrees. Through all of her studies the thing that mattered most has been her ability and desire to help others learn and understand the intricacies of life and spirit. Mailing address: Spinning in the Light, 850 S. Rancho Drive, no. 2-355, Las Vegas, Nevada 89106.

Tony Taylor

Computer network specialist and Keltrian Druid. Born: July 27, 1950, with a Leo rising. Member of the Caer Duir grove (established in 1988), Henge of Keltria, Ar nDraiocht Fein, and The Order of Bards, Ovates, and Druids (OBOD). Cofounder of The Henge of Keltria; editor-in-chief of *Keltria: Journal of Druidism and Celtic Magick.* Mailing address: c/o Henge of Keltria, P.O. Box 48369, Minneapolis, Minnesota 55448.

Patricia Telesco

Magickal name: LoreSinger. Professional writer and administrative assistant, part-time herbalist. Born: February 21, 1960. Solitary (eclectic and Kitchen Witchery) and member of Tempio della Stregheria. Coordinator of Metaphysical Artists for Gaia, a networking cooperative of writers, illustrators, and craftspeople with a quarterly newsletter, *Abracadabra.* Coordinated the *Magi* newsletter for four years; trustee for the Universal Federation of Pagans. Taped a segment for the show *Home Matters* (Discovery Channel, September 1993). Member of the Society for Creative Anachronism. Has given numerous lectures and workshops across the country. Numerous articles published and author of *A Victorian Grimoire* (1992), *The Urban Pagan* (1993), *A Victorian Flower Oracle* (1994), *Kitchen Witch's Cookbook* (1994), *A Witch's Brew* (1995), *Folklore, Fantasy,*

Fiction (1995), *Folkways* (1995), *The Herbal Arts* (1998), *The Wiccan Web* (with Sirona Knight, 2001), *A Floral Grimoire* (2001), and *Labyrinth Walking* (2001). Contributor to *The Magical Almanac* (1994 editor, 1995, 1996, and 1997) and the *Llewellyn Moon Sign Book* (1994, 1995, 1996). Interests include: animal card, rune, flower, and oracle readings, cookery magick, carving wands, brewing ritual wines, and good fellowship. Also interested in magickal teachings for children. Goals: "To find more mainstream publishers with whom I can work to educate the public on magickal and New Age traditions." Mailing address: 2377 Kensington Avenue, Amherst, New York 14226.

Michael Thorn

Registered nurse and leader of the Kathexis Coven (established 1982, Gardnerian.) Member and former president of Covenant of the Goddess. Interests include gay spirituality and ceremonial magick. Author of *Wiccan Resources: A Guide to the Witchcraft Community.* Mailing address: P.O. Box 408, Shirley, New York 11967.

Doreen Valiente

Born: January 4, 1922. Died: September 1, 1999. English High Priestess of the Craft, poet, and a woman considered by many to have been one of the most influential Witches of modern times. Author of numerous articles and the following books: *Natural Magic* (1975), *An ABC of Witchcraft Past and Present* (1973), and *Witchcraft for Tomorrow* (1978). She lived in Sussex, England.

Apophis Samhain Valkyrie

Writer and Wiccan minister. Born: September 27, 1969. "I am the founder of the Occulterian Life Church located in the Athens-Wausau, Wisconsin, area. I have been involved in Nature Spirituality all of my life." Author of *Wicca Unchained* and *Bats, Cats and Broomsticks: A Guide to Wiccan Tolerance and Understanding* (church published). "My interests include the forming of a newsletter-journal where correspondence from a variety of churches and organizations (Wiccan-Pagan) can be dispersed, discussed, and known. The Pagan community needs a more formal communicational networking among various groups to where others of the Pagan audience may know 'what's what' in their community." Mailing address: P.O. Box K, Athens, Wisconsin 54411.

Susun S. Weed

Born: February 8, 1946 with an Aquarius rising. Magickal/Wiccan name: Lady Iona. Green Witch, author, educator. She is the founder of the Wise Woman Center in Woodstock, New York, editor-in-chief of Ash Tree Publishing, and the creator of the Amazon Tarot Deck. Author of *Wise Woman Herbal for the Childbearing Years* (1987), *Healing Wise* (1990), *Menopausal Years the Wise Woman Way* (1993), *Breast Cancer? Breast Health! The Wise Woman Way* (1996). Interests and talents include herbal medicine, Tarot, color and sound healing, Shamanic journeys, talking with plants, animal totems, earth attunement, and energy healing. Susun describes herself as a "gardener, goatherd, cheesemaker, sock knitter, and friend of the fairies." Mailing address: P.O. Box 64, Woodstock, New York 12498

Marion Weinstein

Book author, entertainer, and media spokesperson for the modern Witchcraft movement. Graduated from Barnard College with a bachelor's degree in English literature. Studied film at Columbia University and worked in Los Angeles as a commercial artist and animator. She also studied acting, dance, and voice. Hosted a radio program in New York City called *Marion's Cauldron,* which aired regularly on radio station WBAI-FM (1969–1983). Formed Earth Magic Productions in 1979, which launched a quarterly newsletter in 1988 called the *Earth Magic Times.* Author of *Positive Magic* (1978), *Earth Magic: A Dianic Book of Shadows* (1979), *Racewalking* (1986), and *Remember the Goddess* (1989).

Carl Llewellyn Weschcke

Magickal name: Gnosticus. Book publisher, president of Llewellyn Worldwide, and early publisher of Wiccan books. Born: September 10, 1930, with a Pisces rising. Solitary practitioner of Wicca (Celtic Tradition). Member of the ACLU, NAACP, and AFA. Interests include Witchcraft, Shamanism, Tantra, ceremonial magick,

Qabalah, and meditation. Mailing address: P.O. Box 64383, St. Paul, Minnesota 55164.

Morning Glory Zell

Born: May 27, 1947. She did her first vision quest in 1968. Studied Wicca, Celtic Shamanism, and Goddess history. Ordained as a Priestess in the Church of All Worlds in 1974; founded the Ecosophical Research Association in 1977. Helped develop a sacred wilderness retreat and the Living Unicorn project. Traveled, lectured, and taught college courses with her husband Oberon on Neo-Paganism, the Gaia Hypothesis, and Goddess reemergence. She is a Goddess historian, lore mistress, and Priestess of Potnia Theron. Took formal training with Joanna Macy and John Seed as a presenter for the Council of All Beings in 1990. Published two short stories from her "Tales of the Verdeveldt" cycle in Marion Zimmer Bradley's *Sword and Sorceress* anthologies; currently working on a book to be titled *A Gospel of Gaia*. Morning Glory is also the manufacturer, business manager, and proprietor of Mythic Images, which produces museum-quality replicas of ancient goddesses and gods sculpted with Oberon. Mailing address: P.O. Box 982, Ukiah, California 95482.

Oberon Zell

Born: November 30, 1942, with an Aquarius rising. Publisher of *Green Egg* magazine, sculptor for Mythic Images, and Priest of the Church of All Worlds. Talents: ritualist, workshop presenter, mediator and counselor, artist (especially sculpture and graphics), writer, theologian, magician. Hobbies: paper masks, plastic models, scuba diving, sex, reading, and movies. Interested in cosmology, dinosaurs, archaeology, science fiction (especially *Star Trek* and *Babylon 5* on TV), ancient history, sex, nature, Gaia, goddesses, cryptozoology, and Shamanism. Founded the Church of All Worlds in 1962. Incorporated in 1968, it became the first Neo-Pagan church to obtain full federal recognition in the United States. As the first to apply the terms *Pagan* and *Neo-Pagan* to the newly emerging nature religions of the 1960s and through his publication of *Green Egg* (1968–1975; 1988–present), Oberon was instrumental in the coalescence of the Neo-Pagan movement. In 1970 Oberon formulated and published the theology of deep ecology, which has become known scientifically as the Gaia Thesis. With his soul mate Morning Glory, he founded the Ecosophical Research Association, whose projects have included raising unicorns, chasing mermaids, visiting ancient sacred sites, and exploring the underworld. Oberon is currently working on a book to be titled *The Gospel of Gaea*. Voted Favorite Pagan Writer in 1992; given the Silver Broomstick Award in 1994; *Green Egg* winner of the WPPA Gold Award in 1992, 1994, and 1995, and WPPA Bronze Award in 1993. Featured in many books, especially *Drawing Down the Moon; The Pagan Path; Encyclopedia of Witches and Witchcraft; Witchcraft: The Old Religion; People of the Earth: The New Pagans Speak Out,* and others. Mailing address: P.O. Box 982, Ukiah, California 95482.

16

Recommended Reading

Books About Wicca, Goddess Religion, Earth Spirituality, and Contemporary Paganism

Adler, Margot. *Drawing Down the Moon: Witches, Druids, Goddess-Worshippers, and Other Pagans in America Today.* Boston: Beacon Press, 1986. An excellent source on contemporary Paganism from Feminist Wicca to Men's Spirituality. Contains a resource guide to Pagan gatherings and festivals, periodicals, and organizations.

Andrews, Ted. *Animal-Speak: The Spiritual and Magical Powers of Creatures Great and Small.* St. Paul: Llewellyn, 1993. From dreams to earthly sightings, this comprehensive book details many meanings of birds, animals, insects, and reptiles.

Buckland, Raymond. *Buckland's Complete Book of Witchcraft.* St. Paul: Llewellyn, 1986. This is an excellent Witchcraft book for beginners.

Budapest, ZsuZsanna. *The Holy Book of Women's Mysteries.* Oakland, California: Wingbow Press, 1989. Perfect for the Goddess in every woman; healing, blessings, celebrations, divination, and much more.

Campanelli, Dan, and Pauline Campanelli. *Circles, Groves, and Sanctuaries.* St. Paul: Llewellyn, 1992. Focuses on the sacred spaces of today's Pagans. Illustrated with over 115 inspiring photographs.

Campanelli, Pauline. *Wheel of the Year: Living the Magickal Life.* St. Paul: Llewellyn, 1993. Seasonal rituals and charms for the Sabbats and the long weeks between them. Coven Mandragora and I have performed a few of the rituals in this fine book and have found them to be very beautiful and most enjoyable.

Crowther, Arnold, and Patricia Crowther. *The Secrets of Ancient Witchcraft.* New York: Citadel Press, 1974. A great book for both the novice and the seasoned Witch. Traces many modern religious customs back to their prehistoric Pagan origins. Offers Sabbat ceremonies (which are ideal in their present form for solitary practitioners or easily adapted for coven use) and explains the meanings of the Witches Tarot (which was created by Arnold Crowther for use in the circle and based upon Witchcraft symbolism).

Eisler, Riane. *The Chalice and the Blade.* New York: Harper and Row, 1987. If you are not already angered by and working to reverse thousands of years of patriarchal ravaging, then strap yourself in for the ultimate shift in perspective. Your life may never be the same after reading this.

Farrar, Janet, and Stewart Farrar. *The Witches' Goddess: The Feminine Principle of Divinity.* Custer, Washington: Phoenix Publishing, 1987. This book offers an excellent overview of the Goddess as She was worshiped in ancient times throughout Western Europe and the Near East. Rituals to invoke Celtic and Mediterranean goddesses as well as a comprehensive list of goddesses from nearly every culture around the world are also included.

Fitzgerald, Waverly. *School of the Seasons: Aligning With the Rhythms of the Earth.* Seattle: Priestess of Swords Press, 1993. A wonderful book that serves as an introduction to the correspondence course, *School of the Seasons.* Offers powerful suggestions for honoring our cycles.

Guiley, Rosemary Ellen. *The Encyclopedia of Witches and Witchcraft.* New York: Facts on File, 1989. A must for every Witch's personal library! Highly informative and well illustrated. Covers both ancient Witchcraft and contemporary Wicca. Also contains interesting profiles and photos of numerous and well-known modern Witches.

Guiley, Rosemary Ellen. *Harper's Encyclopedia of Mystical and Paranormal Experience.* San Francisco: Harper San Francisco, 1991. More than five hundred cross-related entries. An excellent educational source for Witches, Shamans, students of the occult arts, and all who are interested in the New Age. Lavishly illustrated.

Harris, Maria. *Dance of the Spirit.* New York: Bantam Books, 1989. The seven steps of women's spirituality are presented in a way that will appeal to women of all persuasions.

Hopman, Ellen Evert, and Lawrence Bond. *People of the Earth: The New Pagans Speak Out.* Rochester, Vermont: Destiny Books, 1996. A fascinating collection of interviews with a variety of contemporary Pagan leaders and teachers. Also contains photographs and a resource section.

Morwyn. *Secrets of a Witch's Coven.* West Chester, Pennsylvania: Whitford Press, 1988. Very informative and an ideal book for the novice Witch. Presents the modern Craft in a positive light.

O'Gaea, Ashleen. *The Family Wicca Book.* St. Paul: Llewellyn. Highly recommended for Wiccans and Witches who are raising (or planning to raise) their children in the Craft. Addresses the needs and experiences of the Wiccan family.

Sjoo, Monica, and Barbara Mor. *The Great Cosmic Mother: Rediscovering the Religion of the Earth.* San Francisco: Harper and Row, 1987. Traces the history and worship of the Great Goddess from a modern feminist perspective. Discusses Her various symbols and sacred images, moon and blood mysteries, the persecution of Witches, and the recent economic exploitation of global militarism, among other things. Informative and very thought-provoking.

Starhawk. *The Spiral Dance.* San Francisco: Harper and Row, 1979. One of the first (and best) textbooks on Goddess spirituality, offering meditations, rituals, and spells. Highly recommended for all who seek the path of the Goddess.

Books About Herbs and Wortcunning

Beyerl, Paul. *The Master Book of Herbalism.* Custer, Washington: Phoenix Publishing, 1984. An excellent and very informative book for all who are interested in the healing and ritual use of herbs.

Cunningham, Scott. *Cunningham's Encyclopedia of Magical Herbs.* St. Paul: Llewellyn, 1985. An illustrated collection of over four hundred magickal herbs from A to Z. In my opinion, this is one of the finest herbal reference books on the market today. It is fully indexed and cross-indexed by name, common names, use, and rulership.

Hylton, William H., ed. *The Rodale Herb Book.* Emmaus, Pennsylvania: Rodale Press, 1974. Although this is not officially a "Witchcraft book," throughout its pages you will find numerous references to Witches and their connections to various plants. This book mainly focuses on the medicinal use of herbs; however, it also offers recipes and instructions for making herbal potpourri, plant dyes, and more.

Books About Magick and the Divinatory Arts

Almond, Jocelyn, and Keith Seddon. *Understanding Tarot.* London: Aquarian Press, 1991.

Fitch, Ed, and Janine Renee. *Magical Rites From the Crystal Well.* St. Paul: Llewellyn, 1984.

Greer, Mary K. *The Essence of Magic: Tarot, Ritual, and Aromatherapy.* Van Nuys, California: Newcastle Publishing Company, 1993. A wonderful introduction to scent and evoking the powers represented by the Major Arcana. This book also includes Tarot spreads and some numerology with regard to personal destiny.

Hope, Murry. *Practical Greek Magic.* London: Aquarian Press, 1985. An excellent description of the theory of Greek magick and its practical application.

Konraad, Sandor. *Classic Tarot Spreads.* West Chester, Pennsylvania: Whitford Press, 1985. Recommended for both the novice and experienced card reader. Includes twenty-two classic spreads.

Noble, Vicki. *Motherpeace: A Way to the Goddess Through Myth, Art, and Tarot.* New York: HarperCollins, 1983. Accompaniment to the Motherpeace Tarot Cards, this book offers a feminist perspective and feminine-empowering version of the Tarot.

Slater, Herman. *A Book of Pagan Rituals.* York Beach, Maine: Samuel Weiser, 1978.

Stein, Diane. *The Women's Book of Healing.* St. Paul: Llewellyn, 1987. Explore ways of using gemstones, chakras, and the laying on of hands, as well as other ways of curing disease.

Telesco, Patricia. *Spinning Spells, Weaving Wonders.* Freedom, California: The Crossing Press, 1996. Arranged alphabetically by topic, over three hundred spells for nearly every positive purpose imaginable are contained in this book. Also included are appendixes for magickal associations, Pagan deities, and handcrafting various items for use in spellcraft.

Books About Astrology

Llewellyn's Moon Sign Book and Lunar Planning Guide. Published annually by Llewellyn Publications (St. Paul), this is a great book for helping to determine the astrologically ideal dates for almost any activity (such as gardening, fishing, buying or selling, legal or business matters, or gambling). Weather and earthquake forecasts, predictions of world events, and monthly horoscopes are also included in this reliable reference source. Llewellyn also publishes the annual *Sun Sign Book,* which offers detailed personal horoscopes for all twelve signs; the *Daily Planetary Guide* (an annual astrology datebook); and a full-color astrological calendar containing a fifteen-month retrograde table, monthly horoscopes, a lunar planting guide, and much more. Highly recommended for the professional astrologer as well as the novice stargazer, and anyone interested in the mystical science of the stars.

Sakoian, Frances, and Louis S. Acker. *The Astrologer's Handbook.* New York: Harper and Row, 1989. One of the most comprehensive astrology books ever published. Includes complete instructions for interpreting any natal chart and easy-to-follow directions for casting your own charts.